APHAEA ASTARTE ATHENESIC ATHARA ANNA

AL-UZZA ALLATU AEGEA ANTEA ANDRASTE

ARMA ATROPOS ATL ARTEMIS AGROTERA

ATAENSIC ANATH ALTHEA ARIANHOD AMAZON

ANNU ASSINIBOIN ASHERATH AAH APHRODITE

APHRODISIAC ATARGATIS ASHTORETH ANNIS

AL-ILAT ARDVI-SURA-ANAHITA AUCHIMALGEN BELILI

BRITOMARTIS BRIGENTIS BRITOMART BRIZO

BRIGIT BLODEUWEDD BINAH BRIDE CALLISTE

CARDEA CIRCE CYBELE CORONIS CERES

CERRIDWEN CANDRAS CITATLI CALLIOPE CABAR

CHANGING-WOMAN CYNTHIA CHANG-O DANU

DIANA DICTYNNA DIVIANA DELIA DERKETO

DEMETER DAPHOINE DAPHNE DEDE DORIS

DEBORAH NOTRE DAME THE DIVINE EA EPONA

ELYTHIA ETOINE ENODIA EUROPA EUAN

EURYNOME FLEACHTA FREYA FRIGG GE

GAUS GODA HATHOR HERODIANA HILDE

HOLDE HELD HEL HENG-UGO HINA HECATE

HEARTHA HERA HELEN-DENDRITUS HELEN-SELENE

HELEN HUR ISIS INDUS IEMANJA IO

ISHTAR INA IRINI IXCHEL JOTMA

JUNO-LUCETIA JUNO JUNE KALLISTO KUBABA

KYBEBE   KHENSU   KALI-DURGA   KUAN-YIN   KRA

KILILI   LEUCIPPE   LUCINE   LAPHRIA   LUNA

LUNUS   LATONA   LUGIDUS   LUGAD   SAINT LUAN

LEVANAH   LILITH   LILY   MOLUA   MOLING

MORGANA   MONA   MERT   MERSEKERT   MYRTEA

MA-TSU-P'O   MENE   MANAT   MAWU   MELUSINE

MUSEOS   MUSE   MOON   MAAT   MAJA   MARINA

MYRRHINE   MAIR   MARY   MYRRH   MARION

MERRY   MAGNA MATER   MARY-GYPSY   THE MEASURER

MAY-BRIDE   THE-GREAT-MOTHER   NUAH   NEITH

NANA   NET   NINDA   NKOSUANO   NISENE   NIPAI-GICUX

OPS   OLWEN   OUPIS   OSTARA   PE

PANAGIA-ARKOUDIOTISSA   PARASHAKTI   PHOSPHOROS

PROTHIRIA   PASIPHAE   PERSEPHONE   PHOEBE

PROSERPINE   QUEEN MARIE   QUADESH   MAMA QUILLA

RIMMON   RIGANTONA   RHEA   SIN   SAMHAIN

SHING-MOO   SOMAS   SELK   SERQ   SIVA

SHARRAT-SHAME   SARASVATI   SHADDAI-EL-CHAI   SOPHIA

TIAMAT   THAMMUZ   TRIVIA   TABOR   TRIFORMIS

TECUCIZTECATL   UNKATAHE   URIKITTU   URANIA   VACH

VESTA   VIRAGO   THE VIRGIN   WHITE-SHELL-WOMAN

WHITE GODDESS   ZU-EN   ZERYNTHIA

MOON, MOON

ANNE KENT RUSH

RANDOM HOUSE / MOON BOOKS

Copyright © 1976, Anne Kent Rush
Cover design, book design Anne Kent Rush
First Printing: 25,000 paper; 1,500 Cloth; July, 1976
Typeset at Vera Allen Composition, Castro Valley, California
Text Type: Palatino
Printed and Bound under direction of Michele Koury, Random House

Co-published by: Random House
                   201 East 50th Street
                   New York, N. Y. 10022

          and: Moon Books
                   P.O. Box 9223
                   Berkeley, Ca. 94709

Moon Books is an independent women's publishing company operating out of San
Francisco, California with distribution through Random House, Inc. in New York. We are
committed to making a wide variety of feminist material available in the general market.

Distributed in the U.S. by Random House and simultaneously published in Canada by
Random House of Canada, Ltd., Toronto.

The author grants free reprint permission of her words in this text (not material written by
others) up to 150 words.

Library of Congress Cataloging in Publication Data

Rush, Anne Kent, 1945-
  Moon, moon.

  Bibliography: p.
  1. Moon (in religion, folk-lore, etc.)   2.   Folk-lore
of woman.   3.   Femininity (Psychology)   I. Title.
GR625.R87   398'.362   76-16003
ISBN 0-394-73230-8
ISBN 0-394-40767-9 pbk.

Manufactured in the U.S.A.
98765432
First Edition

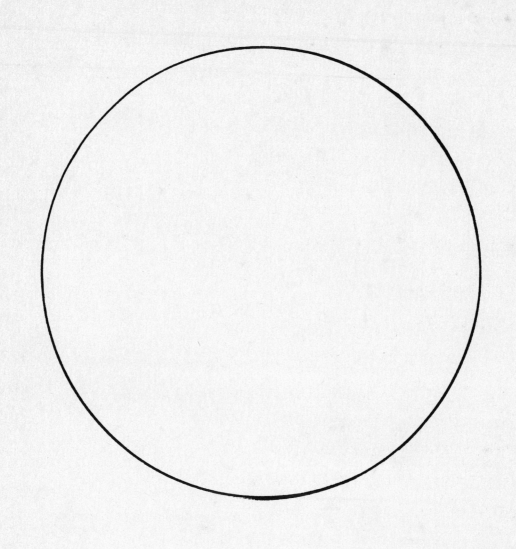

CONTENTS

NOW

THEN

CONTENTS

NOW

NOW

THE MUSE

The position of the moon in a culture is the same as the position of women in that culture; our fates are inexorably shared. Knowledge and attitudes about the moon have paralleled those about women and the female principle down through recorded time.

Awareness of the moon is part of the current cycle of re-balancing the female principle. Moon study is the study of the psychic and physical balance of power in the world and has revealed itself to be as practical and as vast as i had dreamed. This book comes out of the beginning of my explorations and reflects my desire that these areas eventually will become everyday knowledge.

An unmistakable fact emerging is that awareness of the changeover from matriarchal social structures to patriarchal systems has been eliminated from our social upbringing and from our formal educations. Why was i not exposed to more information about the moon since it obviously is a significant element in our lives? After focusing on this area i can only conclude that there has been a methodical suppression of this material, by obliterated or rewritten history and by selective teaching.

The major layer of this process began long ago at a time in recorded history, around 1,500 B.C. when the critical occupation of almost every culture was the struggle between matriarchal and patriarchal social systems. It continued through the witch hunts of Northern Europe. This struggle was synonymous with the battle between the worship of the moon and the worship of the sun. Today the suppression of these issues has been largely successful, so that it is difficult for us to even conceive of their existence.

The attempt was (and is) to eliminate this knowledge completely. When this has not been possible the process has been to discredit, to distort and to co-opt. So

16

now, when exploring moon-related issues, the places to look are often into areas considered minor or groundless and into the dustier corners of religious history and academic research. It is important also to examine what is presented as Factual History and to develop the skills of "reading through" presentations of events, much as one "reads through" the picture of life in ads or more obvious propaganda. It is always central to listen to our own individual and collective female body experience.

The most accessible information in print on the moon as a psychic-political symbol is in the works of M. Esther Harding, Helen Diner, Robert Graves, Erich Neumann, Margaret Murray and James Frazer. From their different fields of study each delineates part of the story. Harding talks about the moon as religious deity; Neumann deals with the moon as a psychological symbol of matriarchal consciousness; Murray with magic and witchcraft and Graves with the moon as artistic Muse. All these views have their political foundations and implications.

> The rise of masculine power and of patriarchal society probably started when man began to accumulate personal, as over against communal, property and found that his personal strength and prowess could increase his personal possessions. This change in secular power coincided with the rise of sun worship under a male priesthood, which began to supersede the much earlier moon cults, which, however, remained in the hands of women. Sun worship was usually introduced and established by an edict of a military dictator, as happened in Babylon and Egypt, and probably in other countries as well.
>
> The results of this change in emphasis between masculine and feminine were far-reaching. Perhaps one of the most important was that the concept of what constituted religious, or spiritual values, which had been symbolized by the moon, was transferred to the sun and came under masculine control.[1]
>
> M. Esther Harding, WOMAN'S MYSTERIES

Neumann attempts to describe the reality gap inherent in a dialogue between matriarchal consciousness and patriarchal consciousness, the necessity to remain aware of this in personal communications as well as in historical interpretations and the ultimate need for balance between what he calls "the logos and eros principles" in the world.

> Moon-consciousness, as matriarchal consciousness might be called, is never divorced from the unconscious, for it is a phase, a spiritual phase of the unconscious itself . . . The comparative passivity of matriarchal consciousness is not due to any incapacity for action, but rather to an awareness of subjection to a process in which it can "do" nothing, but can only let happen . . . It is an inner possession, realized and assimilated by the personality but not easily discussed, for the inner experience behind it is scarcely capable of adequate verbal expression and can hardly be transmitted to anyone who has not undergone the same experience . . . For this reason, a plain and simple masculine consciousness finds the "knowledge" of matriarchal consciousness unverifiable, willful, and, par excellence, mystic.[2]
>
> Erich Neumann, "On The Moon and Matriarchal Consciousness"

It is heartening and enlightening to read such essays by men, as it is evidence of their recognition of what can be a common link of perception between us. Yet it is necessary to remember the persistence of that gap and, therefore, to read male expositions on the female psyche with some reserve.

> Matriarchy not only signifies the dominance of the Great Mother archetype, but, in a general way, a total psychic situation in which the unconscious (and the feminine) are dominant, and consciousness (and the masculine) have not yet reached self-reliance and independence.[3]
>
> Erich Neumann, "On The Moon and Matriarchal Consciousness"

Irene C. de Castillejo, who has written a book on similar subjects called KNOW-ING WOMAN, corrects Neumann's misperceptions. Her work reminds us of the necessity of returning ultimately to primary sources for our information on the female psyche.

> I cannot stress too strongly that matriarchal consciousness or diffuse awareness is not identical with the formless chaos of the unconscious. Its difference in quality from masculine focused consciousness with which we are all familiar, lies in its whole unbroken state which defies scientific analysis and logical deduction, and is therefore not possible to formulate in clear unambiguous terms.[4]
>
> Irene C. de Castillejo, KNOWING WOMAN

Harding and Neumann both discuss the importance of exploring attitudes toward differences in matriarchal and patriarchal consciousness. They point out that when these psychological and social elements are out of balance, one or the other becomes branded as dangerous. From the gradual military patriarchal take-over to women's position of social suppression today, patriarchal 'superiority' has become institutionalized and more easily perpetuated.

> Any development, at any stage, that strives toward patriarchal consciousness, toward the sun, looks on the moon spirit as the spirit of regression, as the terrible mother, as a witch.[5]
> Erich Neumann, "On The Moon and Matriarchal Consciousness"

The detrimental effects of social imbalance are certainly clear to us when we find our environment polluted beyond imaginable repair and our lives and thinking becoming more mechanized and violent by the day. The rise of women's consciousness and the political feminist movement is the critical shift in this process. Restoration of balance is the task of every aspect of the women's movement and involves a restoration of moon consciousness.

> Only in later periods of development, when patriarchy has fulfilled itself or gone to absurd lengths, losing its connection with Mother Earth, does individuation bring about a reversal. Then, patriarchal sun-consciousness reunites with the earlier, more fundamental phase, and matriarchal consciousness, with its central symbol, the moon, arises from the deep, imbued with the regenerating power of its primal waters, to celebrate the ancient hieros gamos of moon and sun on a new and higher plane, the plane of the human psyche.[6]
> Erich Neumann, "On The Moon and Matriarchal Consciousness"

Clues for beginning this exploration come from mythology because mythology does not rely on one-dimensional logic for its teaching, and as such it is one of the few remaining examples of recorded non-linear and non-patriarchal process. Poetry, especially ancient poetry, offers more clues.

The language of poetic myth anciently current in the Mediterranean and North-ern Europe was a magical language bound up with popular religious ceremonies in honour of the Moon-goddess, or Muse, some of them dating from the Old Stone Age, and this remains the language of true poetry—'true' in the nostalgic modern sense of 'the unimprovable original, not a synthetic substitute.' The language was tampered with in late Minoan times when invaders from Central Asia began to substitute patrilinear for matrilinear institutions and remodel or falsify the myths to justify the social changes. Then came the early Greek philosophers who were strongly opposed to magical poetry as threatening their new religion of logic, and under their influence a rational poetic language (now called the Classical) was elaborated in honour of their patron Apollo and imposed on the world as the last word in spiritual illumination: a view that has prevailed practically ever since in European schools and universities, where myths are now studied only as quaint relics of the nursery age of mankind.[7]

Robert Graves, THE WHITE GODDESS

Records of matriarchies and goddess-worshipping civilizations are available to us also through religious history. One discovers that witches were people who practiced doctrines of healing and sprituality outside the patriarchal establishment, which in Medieval Europe was most strongly The Church (and currently is The Law). One also discovers that in very ancient religions the word 'Virgin' did not mean 'non-sexual'—it meant 'un-married.' Vestal Virgins, the Virgin Diana and the Virgin Mary were orginally personifications of independent balanced female power; they have been gradually altered to become images of women which support patriarchal systems.

In tracing the process of female sexual oppression, one sees that to strengthen its political position patriarchy instituted monogamy and monotheism. Monogamy is only necessary and deified in a system in which it is of concern to know who the father is, and in which women are considered property. In a matrilinear culture such information is irrelevant, and such a cruel concept as 'illegitimacy' does not exist. Monotheism also comes under fire because it does not permit women and men to worship-respect their own essence. The phases in history in which cultures revered equally gods of both sexes (such as in early Egypt) or those in which the deities are portrayed as gynandrous/androgynous and of equal status (as in certain cycles of all religions) are the most balanced and 'civilized' ones. It is important to examine our monotheism of the logos sun, to question the values of a patriarchal family system which ostracizes some children because the father can't be named and to question a science which considers the moon as secondary to the sun, as a dead rock to be used potentially as a dumping place for nuclear wastes.

20

When beginning to re-acquaint myself with the moon, i did much reading and also integrated her movements into mine. I paid attention to the relationship of my menstrual cycles with the moon's cycles, to the changes in my friends' moods as the moon changed, to the tides and the weather. The first revelations came by allowing myself to make place for the moon in my daily living. These moments have remained the strongest and most palpable knowing. I started with the recognition that because the moon was shining on me at night and pulling on me during the day, it probably had been 'speaking' to me for a long time, and i had not been listening. I had to learn its language. I decided to begin my research at night by standing and looking out an open window.

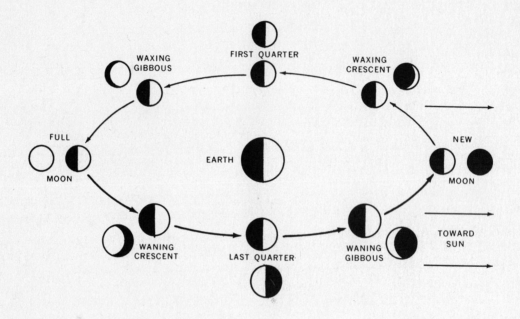

SCIENTIFIC MYSTERIES

. . . In fact, many scientists now believe that the discoveries on the moon have only helped to confuse former apparently straightforward theories about the formation of all the planets.

—From a report on the NASA-Apollo research

One of the basic claims of modern science is that you can count on it because it eliminates the subjective and the personal. Science has been almost exclusively a man's world and has become culturally our major source of information on the moon. Supposedly the first and important discoveries of the mysteries of the moon were made by men, Hipparchus, Newton, Galileo, Darwin, Laplace, and Cassidy.

Further research shows that Babylonian and Druidic priestesses were calculating the moon's movements long before NASA; and even earlier, in Paleolithic times, people also lived according to their observations of lunar cycles, recording their rituals in the cave paintings.

Many recent findings about the moon corroborate ancient "myths" to remind us that our **myths** were their **science**. Remembering its youth and its limitations, studying modern science can be interesting. Modern science is also interesting to study for illumination on the nature of patriarchal values and the changes they are now undergoing. Significantly the most striking result of the highest achievements of modern science, the space flights, has been the conclusion that something is lacking in the calculations. Science is not quite the comfort it used to be, even for scientists.

We can include scientific information in our log of moon knowledge if we remind ourselves that we must question every "fact" because it has been selected partially on the basis of its support of a one-dimensional system which excludes the human psyche and which is capable of being described on paper. It seems critical to examine the effects on our civilization of following this god and to take another look at the quality of life in ancient pre-science civilizations, which had more complex and multi-layered conceptions of reality.

This first section contains some of the scientific findings about the moon as well as the response of a lunar astronaut to his moon walk and his return to earth. Beginning the book with this scientific space event, i feel i am starting at the point where most of us are in our moon-consciousness. The effect of the phenomenon of the space flights on our modern psyches is of tremendous importance, because for all of us these events stretch our sense of the possible and alter our understanding of our position within the cosmos.

Selenography

Since 1958, more than fifty spacecraft have flown near or landed on the moon. Twelve American astronauts have walked on and sampled its terrain. Two un-manned Soviet vehicles have travelled the lunar surface and five scientific obser-vatories left by American astronauts on the moon continue to transmit environ-mental information to earth receptors. Over 30,000 photographs taken from lunar flights have captured in great detail the surface features of the moon.

What we knew before the space flights was information about the size of the moon (diameter is approximately 2158 miles) and the rhythm of its rotation. The moon turns completely around on its axis once every 27.3 days, which is also the time it takes it to travel around the earth. That its rotation on its axis (imaginary center line around which a body rotates) and its rotation around the earth are the same means that it keeps the same face, or side, always toward the earth. Thus we never saw the far side of the moon until very recently when spacecraft flew around and photographed it.

As the moon is orbiting around the earth, they are both travelling around the sun. An orbit is defined as the path of a celestial body around another. It is thought that a combination of the pull of gravity and the push of centrifugal motion keeps celestial bodies within orbit. Most planetary moons appear to be significantly smaller than the planet around which they orbit. In this respect, as far as we can see, the earth's moon is unique in that it is much closer to the size of the earth. Because of this and because the gravity of the sun is the dominant force which controls both the earth and the moon, the earth/moon system is regarded as a double planet rather than as a planet and satellite.

Because of the size of the moon sphere, about 1/4 that of earth, and its comparable lighter density, it does not have enough gravity (a term for which there is no scientific explanation) to hold an atmosphere of gases around itself. Its gravity

24

is about 1/6 that of the earth's. This means that there is no air as we know it around the moon nor are there any radiation belts which keep in surface temperature and out most passing particles. This vulnerability of the moon to collision by space particles such as meteorites is one of the theories of the cause of the moon's many craters and mountains. Another theory is that the jagged surface was formed by its own internal volcanic eruptions in the past. Data gathered from the space flights did not settle this question. Observations by simple telescopes on earth have made it clear that the moon's surface is full of extreme changes in altitude on its terrain, but until the lunar landings it was not certain what these huge craters and valleys contained.

The moon's distance from the earth, though still not known exactly, is approximately 240,000 miles. The moon's lack of atmosphere causes the temperatures to range from 215° above zero (Fahrenheit) in sunlight, to less than 270° below zero "at night." A lunar day and a lunar night are each 14 earth days long. The moon is not perfectly spherical. Its equatorial diameter, which points toward the earth, bulges slightly—an estimated one and one-third miles. The moon's gravitational influence on the earth seems to be slowing it down. Earlier the earth and moon moved faster and also are both thought to have been hot glowing masses.

Phases of the Moon

When i first tried to write down my understanding of the light phases of the moon, i thought something was askew so i mailed a copy of my explanation to my uncle, Norton Williams, an aeronautical engineer. He phoned me in great distress. I had written that the phases of the moon were due to the shape of the earth's shadow on its surface blocking out the sun's light—my whole premise was wrong. I had to start all over; i must read some basic astronomy text books, he said, and get it right!

My uncle had saved me from disaster, but since i had come to my innovative theories from reading astronomy texts, i decided i needed someone to talk it all over with. I asked my friend Pat Grosh, Doctor of Statistical Psychology in the Computer Sciences Department at the University of California, Berkeley, astronomer and pilot, for aid. She immediately understood my predicament and passed on to me the "only technique which had made her understand it." This is the technique of the apple and the orange and the flashlight.

In a dark room, line up an orange and an apple on the floor with the beam of your flashlight. The orange, between the flashlight and the apple-earth, is the moon. Rotate the orange slowly as you also move it in a circle around the apple. Watch the light patterns and see if they approximate the following explanation!

. . . As the moon revolves about the earth moving from west to east in a counter-clockwise direction, it rotates once on its axis counter-clockwise. Since its period of rotation is about equal to the time it takes to complete one revolution around the earth, the moon shows only one face to us on earth. However, because the moon moves at varying speeds in its orbit and "wobbles" at different times, it is possible to see more than 50 percent of the moon's surface. During one revolution of the moon, the sun illuminates all sides of it, but observers on earth can only see parts of one hemisphere as it is illuminated.

Because the moon shines only by reflecting sunlight, viewed from earth it appears to change shape or go through "phases." The cycle of the moon's phases is caused by the changing relative positions of the sun, moon, and earth. Only one-half of the moon is illuminated by the sun at any one time. The moon reflects about 7 percent of the light striking it. (The sun is about 400,000 times brighter than the full moon.)

The moon rises about 51 minutes later each day, because it is moving eastward during the month, so it appears at a slightly different point on the horizon. When the moon is between earth and sun, it is not visible to observers on earth because we are looking at the dark side of the moon. This is the new moon. It rises and sets with the sun. During the almost two weeks between new and full phases, the moon passes through waxing crescent phases (with the "horns" or points of the crescent pointed eastward, away from the sun); it reaches its first quarter phase, then passes through waxing gibbous phases (more than a quarter and less than full).

When the earth is between the sun and moon, the entire illuminated hemisphere of the moon is turned earthward; it is full moon. The full moon rises when the sun sets so we can see it all night. From full moon to new, the phases wane in a reverse order to the above sequence, with the eastern edge illuminated and the western part dark. It also starts rising later and later in the evening.

Eclipses

Both the earth and moon cast shadows in space away from the sun. The moon's orbit is tilted about five degrees in relation to the earth's. If both orbits were on the same plane, there would be a solar and lunar eclipse every time the moon circled the earth (each synodic period). Because the moon does not always pass exactly in front of the sun, or through the shadow of the earth at the position of full moon, the total number of eclipses can never exceed seven in any one year, and may be as few as two. As the moon passes between the earth and sun, its shadow falls on the earth. This is called a solar eclipse. A total eclipse of the sun is visible only from the area of the earth touched by the moon's dark shadow cone (umbra). The eclipse is partial in the surrounding semi-shadow called the penumbra. When the moon passes through the earth's shadow (the earth is between the sun and moon) it causes a lunar eclipse. Full moon lunar eclipses are visible from any place on earth where the moon can be seen. Bending of the sun's rays by the earth's atmosphere makes the moon visible, even during a total eclipse, as a dull red disc.

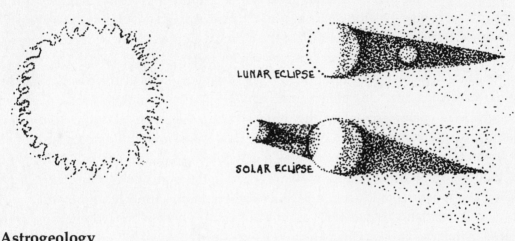

Astrogeology

Modern scientists wanted geological samples from the moon for three main areas of information: to decipher its thermal history and the evolution of its surface features; to apply that knowledge to unraveling the mystery of the early history of the earth and perhaps of other planets; to study the sun's past by studying its effects on the moon. All the information gathered from the lunar flights has been shared openly and over a thousand specialists in twenty countries are now studying the lunar specimens.

The conclusion of the scientists is that the rugged terrain was caused by both internal volcanoes and moonquakes as well as outer colliding meteorites; that the star-like sprays of lighter areas on the surface are patterns, called rays, of fine dust-like particles scattered in the impact of meteors; that the dark-appearing areas once thought to be seas and, therefore, called "marias" are deeper plains. There seems to be no water on the moon. The common land formations are craters, pits, mountains, rays, plains, cones and ravines. The surface is covered with several inches of fine greyish white dust made up of tiny spheres of volcanic glass. The basic moon rock resembles terrestrial basalt formed from solidified lava. There is a high concentration of titanium, aluminum, oxygen, silicon, zircon and rare earth elements. Only three elements were found which are not known to exist on earth. In 1971 a scientist named Hubbard and his co-workers coined the term "Kreep" to refer to the composition of common moon rocks which contain potassium, rare earth elements and phosphorous.

The estimate of the moon's age, (that is, the time since its formation) is 4.6 billion years, and phases in lunar geographical history have been labeled. Pre-Nectarian refers to elements formed at the birth of the moon showing up in deeper basins and mostly on the far side of the moon. The Nectarian age is next, deposited on top of Pre-Nectarian material, and formed until 4 billion years ago. The Imbrium age begins 4 billion years ago and includes about 2/3 of the exposed lunar materials. The ages of the formation of the majority of the craters by meteor impact are the Imbrium and Eratosthenian ages which cover 2 billion years. The rayless craters (their rays have now disappeared) are thought to have been formed during the Eratosthenian age. One billion years ago was the beginning of the Copernicus age which is characterized by the highest and, therefore, thought to be the youngest strata of bright-rayed craters. Materials found imbedded in the surface of the moon thought to be parts of foreign meteors are called "mascons." The core of the moon is thought to be still molten. Because there are no atmospheric gases circling the moon to conduct sound waves, there is no sound on the moon.

The only land formations on the earth similar to the lunar formations were created by meteor impact. The oldest rock ever found (over 4 billion years old) was found on the Apollo 15 mission and christened the "Genesis rock." Scientists are interested in the very old rocks because the record of the beginnings of the earth's formation are lost due to erosion and recombination of materials on the earth's surface. The surface of the moon is relatively unchanged because there is no atmosphere or water to erode it, so that early formations remain. Amateur astronomers around the world have formed "Operation Moonblink" which includes observations of visible color changes on the moon's surface thought by some to be gaseous crater eruptions which indicate the moon is still active. Otherwise scientists conclude that the moon's formative activity has ceased. It is called a dead planet.

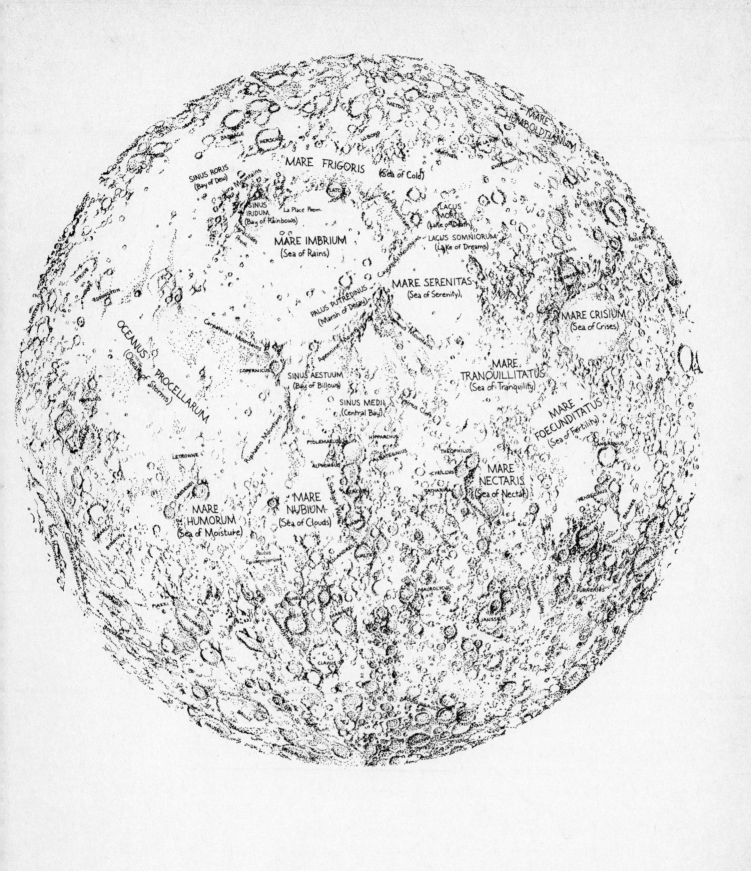

SPACE FLIGHTS

The major mode in our modern world of relating to the moon has been to examine it through scientific methods. Focus on the moon in the sixties was political with the "space race" between the U.S. and the USSR to out-do each other technologically. When President Kennedy made the commitment in 1961 to put an American on the moon "before this decade is out" the space race was stepped up and the Apollo missions commandered by NASA in Houston, Texas, took on a celebrity atmosphere. Sure enough, July 20, 1969, the U.S. kept its promise, making it the first earth nation to have men walk on another planet. The first astronauts on the moon were Neil Armstrong, Edwin Aldrin and Michael Collins. They left a steel plaque which reads, "We came in peace for all mankind."

At the time of the space flights, i certainly did feel they landed for "mankind." The political use of the flights and the aspect of claiming yet another piece of the cosmos for "mankind" through technology annoyed me. I kept thinking that if i went to the moon, i wouldn't have done it that way. I certainly wouldn't have tried to signify that i had any territorial power over the planet. Hopefully i would not have tried to transfer my earth consciousness to this foreign place; i would have tried to learn the ways of this new environment by living there for awhile and by sensing the new ecology. But more likely than any of that, i wouldn't have gone there at all. I certainly wouldn't have spent money to build rockets, considering money was supposedly short for more immediate things such as food and living basics on earth. If i had decided to focus on the moon, i would have tried to allow it to enter my life in practical ways here, to learn to live on earth by the cycles it suggests in its movements.

I knew i was not alone in my attitude. The government of Bali wanted to break off diplomatic relations with the U.S. because in Balinese culture walking on the moon is a serious violation of its sanctity. Poets of ancient mythologies made statements condemning the moon flights as an attack on our collective spiritual health. And then there were many peoples who would not even believe that it had happened at all! Certain groups in Kenya on Lamu have a belief that if anyone went to the moon, world floods would result. Since these did not occur, they concluded that it was a hoax. It seems that many Americans still hold similar views, as a poll of the U.S. showed that 15 percent of all Americans think it was a television manipulation staged in Arizona. But the other 92 percent of us believe that men did land on the moon, walk and drive around, and then return by space ship to tell us something about that planet.

It seemed very significant that the lunar flights had taken place in a marked era of renaissance of women's consciousness, connected to the movement toward psychic balance. It represented to me the need and attempts of men to connect with the moon, and they were doing it in the scientific way they were familiar with, analyzing it and claiming it.

However, some of the results of the moon flights were unexpected and fascinating and seem to illustrate that, rather than being claimed by its visitors, the moon claimed them. Every astronaut was irrevocably altered by his experience. Although officially the men were not supposed to talk about their emotional experiences on the moon flights, the news soon came out that most of them had had what would be categorized on earth as "spiritual awakenings," and they now held different views and perspectives on NASA, science and the priorities in their lives. This interested me a lot, even reassured me that if scientists insisted on tampering with lunar ecology, they would at least in turn be changed and enlightened by the experience.

Since any kind of knowledge of the moon has been nearly eliminated from our lives in the 20th century, i decided that for many people, these lunar space flights were the basic if not sole content of their moon consciousness. I wanted to see what relation these scientific events had to the knowledge of ancient moon cults and how this affected people engaged in reestablishing a relationship to the moon.

I decided to try to talk with one of the astronauts who had walked on the moon. I wanted to hear about it firsthand, and certainly they could tell me something important about what it felt like to be alive on a planet most peoples of the earth had mythologized as the land of souls waiting for rebirth.

I had read in the newspaper that one astronaut had become a psychological consultant in Los Angeles. Several had gone into various forms of business. I knew that The Noetics Institute in Palo Alto, California, was founded by ex-lunar astronaut, Edgar Mitchell as a research center into psychic phenomena and special states of consciousness. I called and got the addresses of four lunar astronauts from them and wrote to them describing my project. One of them answered. It was Jim Irwin. He had retired from the Air Force in 1972 and started an evangelical organization called High Flight Foundation in Colorado Springs, Colorado. (Later other astronauts Alfred Worden and William Pogue also joined the foundation.) Jim agreed to an interview and i arranged to fly there on a Sunday night, with an appointment early Monday morning.

When i left California Sunday afternoon, the sun was very hot and the weather was fine. That evening when i arrived in Colorado Springs it was dark and snowy. Louise Matthews, an advisory trustee of the High Flight Foundation, had arranged to meet me at the airport, but had to go to her bowling league instead. So the Executive Vice President, Rocky Forshey, met my plane. From the time i landed until i was taken to my return flight, i was graciously attended and informed about the purposes and facilities of High Flight. It became clear that this was a way of life to the employees, not "just a job."

On my way to the hotel, Rocky explained all about High Flight. It was started by Colonel Irwin in response to his lunar flight. He wanted to provide a vehicle for other astronauts to speak about their spiritual experiences and to put the ideas to use on earth. High Flight has sponsored five retreats for returned POW's and their families, and for families of MIA's during 1973. There is a space museum in construction at the center now and plans to build a larger High Flight Lodge to house retreats "that would apply the spiritual dimension to scientific, military, business and public service fields." Their address is 4050 American Drive, Colorado Springs, Colorado 80907.

Driving from the airport swirls of snow were waving across the road in a black night and i was impressed by the flatness of the landscape which moved into mountains in the distance. The snow currents were dragging clumps of tumbleweed across the road and in the bleakness of the night i felt as though i were moving closer to the moon. Rocky was willing to talk about the spiritual element of the lunar flights which was a relief as i had heard that the experience of all the astronauts had been intense and some of them were hesitant to discuss this aspect because the media tended to portray them as a little "weird." I went to bed that night tired and interested.

At the Foundation the next day, i was introduced to most of the eight-person staff and shown beautiful films of the lunar landing and walks. The films made the experience more palpable to me, as the color and motion conveyed a lot more than black and white TV had. Mainly i got insight into the lunar space flight experience by talking with Jim Irwin. He gave me lots of his time, took me to an Irish restaurant in his pick-up truck and seemed to speak very openly about many aspects of his experiences and his work.

The following pages are excerpts from some of the taped talks and from his book on the moon mission of Apollo 15. I have eliminated much of the back and forth questions and joined the text together more. I came away with a very new feeling for the whole experience of visiting another planet, and gratified that this man's general attitude seemed to corroborate my sense of the moon as a spiritual force in the universe. I talked a little with Jim about my research into mythologies of the moon, and he seemed pleased to find someone else with a "moon fetish." I'm glad he had such a spectacular experience on the moon and i'm also glad that, since space flights are a pretty expensive and troublesome way to enlightenment, he and his staff are hard at work trying to put together his concept of a way to communicate these areas on earth.

o   o   o

From TO RULE THE NIGHT: The Discovery Voyage of Astronaut Jim Irwin by James B. Irwin with William A. Emerson, Jr. (Copyright © 1973 by James B. Irwin and William A. Emerson, Jr. Reprinted by permission of A.J. Holman Co., Division of J.B. Lippincott Co.):

I was born in Pittsburgh, Penn., on March 17, 1930. My family was Irish, and that's St. Patrick's Day! My mother and father lived in the South Hills section of Pittsburgh. My father was a steamfitter in the Carnegie Museum, and some of my earliest memories are of touring this place looking at dinosaurs and other unbelievable things. He was a homebody and a military type. I think he would have loved the Air Force. The atmosphere at home did not encourage dating and Dad instilled the fear of the opposite sex in us when we were very young. "All those girls are out for your money. They're gold-diggers. And they'll give you infectious diseases." But this meant that I really started studying when I was in the 6th and 7th grades and I worked harder than I might have otherwise. My mother was the affectionate one. My mother and I have always been close. . . . I always wanted to go to the moon and would tell people so. But they didn't seem to take me seriously!

I went to the Naval Academy, the University of Michigan and then was accepted into the Air Force. It was there I learned to love flying. The solitude of flying was and is complete joy for me. Then I was almost completely wiped out in a terrible air accident. When I'd recovered sufficiently, they told me I was grounded from flying for at least a year. In 1966 I made a last effort to join the space program. I wanted the obvious advantages that the program offered. There was a lot of additional income. And there was the chance to do some great flying. The possibility of becoming famous seemed remote, but it didn't discourage me. It wasn't commonly known that they were picking guys to go to the moon. I just thought that I might get to go into orbit. Finally the announcements were made and I was selected. This was the highest honor I could imagine. . . .

There wasn't any preparation for the spiritual impact, or the psychological impact. They trained us pretty much as robots, to report the things that we saw, and to bring back the right rocks. I never dreamed that I would be involved in spiritual things.

Preparing for the flight I was kind of flippant; I felt almost like a kid. Very easy about it, very light. A test pilot has to develop that kind of attitude. You don't want to dwell on the seriousness of the situation. . . .

The day of the flight is complicated. You have to be dressed. For three hours before the flight you have to prebreathe to get rid of the excess nitrogen in your blood stream, because you're breathing 100% oxygen inside the spacesuit and you need to clear your bloodstream so you don't get the bends when you start to ascend. Then we were driven out in a van to the launch pad. We were put in position in our seats, on our backs with our legs up. We had three hours to wait for ignition. When they closed that metal hatch, it sounded like a dungeon door. At last we heard the word ignition, and we felt all that tremendous power being released beneath us on the pad. When we cleared the tower it was almost the happiest moment of my life to realize that after all those years it was now my turn. At last I was leaving the earth. The muffled roar flows through you. You just hang there. Then you sense a little motion, a little vibration, and you start to move. Once you realize you are moving there is a complete release of tensions. You feel all that power underneath you, faster and faster. You are pressed back against the couch with fantastic weight. It's the most thrilling ride you can imagine. . . .

The blue sky got blacker and blacker. Once into earth orbit we could see blue skies below and black skies above. Right in the middle of my window was a full moon. Seeing it was a terrific omen. I knew we were going to have a great mission. . . .

From insertion into orbit, we were very busy. We couldn't take time to look at the continents below us or the beautiful sunsets and sunrises. We were moving from dark to light with a tremendous flight of speed. And this was my first experience with weightlessness. I had to accept the fact that I didn't feel completely comfortable. And living in those cramped quarters in space is pretty much like being a mother in a small apartment with three sick children on a rainy day. We had equipage for everything imaginable, but we soon discovered that the most important items aboard were adhesive tape and scissors. . . . Then there was food. Eating was not relaxing. Everything is in plastic bags, which you cut open with scissors and try to catch before it floats away in blobs into the air. I had gotten my favorite place in Florida to package some of their lobster bisque according to NASA requirements. Imagine it: three men in long underwear flying to the moon and sucking in those blobs of lobster bisque. . . .

Another effect of weightlessness is that our heads swelled. The brain was accommodating itself to a different sort of blood pressure and to pure oxygen. It took a couple of days before our bodies adjusted and the swelling started to recede. Curiously enough, the brain seems to work better in space. We all found that we worked more efficiently in space than we did on the ground. There was a great clarity of mind and something akin to clairvoyance. . . .

After we left earth orbit, we never felt that we were moving. We felt we were stationary. The earth looked as though it were moving away from us. And all of a sudden, there was the moon, coming in to us. The first time we could see the whole earth we saw it as a ball in the sky. It looked the size of a basketball. Then as we got farther and farther away, it diminished in size. Finally it shrank to the size of a marble. From the moon the earth looked just like a marble. The most beautiful marble you can imagine. The earth is uncommonly lovely. It is the only warm living object we saw in space on our flight. Approaching the moon we could not see any light on its surface. You look out and there is a dark object looming up, a big mass in the darkness of night. The sun is on the other side. At this point we were not in position to see the earth. At about 12:41 we saw a very thin crescent moon in front of us. Despite the delicacy of the shape, we got the impression that the moon is very big. We were silent as we coasted in on the moon. . . .

All of a sudden we came from darkness into daylight. We were at the moon! It hits you just like that. It is the most beautiful sight to look out and see this tremendously large

34

planet. You'd never guess that the moon would be that big, even though you have seen all the pictures. But here you are seeing it with your own eyes for the first time. It is staggering. You can barely see the curvature of it. You are coming around and moving not too fast, at medium speed, and you cross the terminator, which is that line between darkness and light.

The surface of the moon is a dark gunmetal grey. It looks like molten lead that has been shot with BB's. It doesn't look real. Since there is virtually no atmosphere on the moon to diffuse the light, there is a very distinct line between darkness and light. As the reflected sunlight gets brighter, the gray turns to brown, light tan, and almost white, directly underneath the sun. So you have constantly changing color as you go around the moon. . . .

I was knocked out by what I was seeing. It was amazing. Coming from the back side, the first large feature that we saw was Tsiolkovsky Crater, with its high central peak of light-colored material surrounded by a dark sea. The crater must have been fifty miles in diameter and probably as deep as the Grand Canyon.

The back side of the moon is distinctly different from the front; it has no basins, none of the flat surfaces that you see on the front of the moon with basins, like Mare Serenitatis and Mare Imbrium. Flying over the front you see craters of every size and description . . .

I was fascinated by the majesty of the lurain. The face of the moon is beautiful in a stark, awesome, barren way. I kept telling myself, "Jim this is really a simulation. You are not really landing on the moon." If I had believed I was landing on the moon, I would have been so excited I don't know if I could have made it. It was really hard not to look out. Everything in the landing worked perfectly, but it was the hardest landing I have ever been in. The impact was tremendous, everything pitching and rolling, but we made it. We landed right on the rim of a small crater. Then we heard our contact say,

"OKAY, HOUSTON. The Falcon is on the plain at Hadley."

The excitement was overwhelming, but now I could let myself believe it. Dave and I were on the surface of the moon. We looked out across a beautiful valley with high mountains on three sides of us and the deep gorge of Hadley Rille a mile to the west. The great Apennines were gold and brown in the early morning sunshine. It was like some beautiful valley in the mountains of Colorado, high above the timberline.

There was the excitement of exploring a place where man had never been before, but the most exciting thing, what really moved me and touched my soul, was that I could feel God's presence there. In the three days of exploration, there were a couple of times when I actually looked up to see the earth—and it was a difficult maneuver in that bulky suit; you had to grab onto something to hold yourself steady and then lean back as far as you could. That beautiful, warm living object looked so fragile, so delicate, that if you touched it with a finger it would crumble and fall apart. Seeing this has to change a man, has to make a man appreciate the creation of God and the love of God. . . .

o   o   o

KR: One of the main things I was interested in when I first started doing my research on the moon was that I felt the moon to be a spiritual influence and that aspect hadn't been brought out. You certainly relate to that and integrate it in a way that most of the publicity about the lunar flights has not.

JI: Yes, true. It's been mostly scientific and very little about feelings. I guess that's why I wrote a book, to try to capture and communicate some of the feelings. I wish I had been a writer or a poet, so that I could convey more adequately the feeling of this flight. It is a great challenge to try to make people feel the same thing I felt.

KR: I think we agree on some things, and not on others. I am a spiritual person, but I don't translate it exactly as you do. Does that bother you that I have a different spiritual definition?

JI: No, because I talk with lots of people like that all the time. Many people don't even admit to having a spiritual side. But it's true that many people think of the moon as a holy place.

When we went to the Middle East we had an interesting experience. Mohammed must have been inspired when he wrote the Koran, because he predicted that man would some day leave the earth and travel through space. And when he would, that it would be a very spiritual experience, that he would feel much closer to God. For that reason, I was invited into the Moslem world, January of last year as an official guest. A great experience.

KR: Then they thought that you were the fulfillment of the prophecy!

JI: Well, they wanted to hear it firsthand. And for them to invite an American, a Christian to talk about God really transcended all differences. We really did have a wonderful time. They showed us such hospitality. I guess I shared convincing faith because they said, "If you're that close to God, why aren't you a Moslem?"

There are many Christians in the space program. And I think that a moon flight can make a Christian a better Christian. If a Buddhist were to go up, it would probably make him a better Buddhist, . . . or a Moslem. The Russians, I think, experience the same thing too, but they just can't express it. You get to a certain point in discussing spiritual matters and they just clam up. Because they realize that were they to admit feeling anything spiritually it would be a violation of the Communist Party.

KR: Can you tell me more about the flight. What was it like to walk around on the moon?

JI: When I got out of the Falcon, I remember saying, "Oh, boy, it's beautiful out here! Reminds me of Sun Valley!" Walking on the moon feels just like walking on a trampoline, the same lightness, the same bouncy feeling. And if you fall, you can just put out your hands and push back up. The surface is very soft. The only danger is the possibility of tearing your suit, and that's remote.

It's grey to brown at a distance, but you find individual rocks of all colors of the rainbow. We found black rocks, coal black. We found a white rock, green rocks, and green glass beads all welded together, fused together. They're still a mystery to scientists. Many of the rocks, we'd lift up, and we could see the variety of crystals in them, some clear, yellow, red, green, tiny crystals.

We went to the moon to learn more about the earth. Scientists think the earth and the moon were created about the same time, four to five billion years ago. The early history of the earth has been removed, but it's been preserved in fairly good form on the moon, so if we learn about the moon we'll know more about the earth.

The moon affects the tides on the surface of the earth, and it actually distorts the earth slightly in the direction of the moon. It is really obvious when you get to the moon. You can look at the distortion of the moon as a result of the earth pulling on the moon, because it is kind of pear-shaped, toward the earth. So you know, if the earth can do that to the physical moon, you can imagine what it's doing to the earth. It probably affects human beings, too.

We left scientific stations on the moon that continue to operate, sending us information, about what's occurring out in the universe, because the earth is a very isolated system. Because of the atmosphere of the radiation belts around it we really can't tell what's going on. But on the moon where there's no atmosphere, meteorites strike the surface and make big holes on the ground. Also the energy from the sun and from other sources is always passing by the moon so we can record that. The moon is perhaps even brighter now, than it was before man went there, because we've left some rather reflective objects there! We left part of the spacecraft, part of the suits, our car. We parked three cars on the moon.

o   o   o

From TO RULE THE NIGHT:

We did find a remarkable rock, a white rock that had riveted our attention. It was lifted up on a pedestal. The base was a dirty old rock covered with lots of dust that sat there by itself, almost like an outstretched hand. Sitting on top of it was a white rock almost free of dust. From four feet away I could see unique long crystals with parallel lines, forming striations. This was exactly the kind of rock we were looking for; it confirmed the suspicion that the mountains of the moon were made from rock, lighter in color and lighter in density.

If the moon were composed entirely of the sort of dense rock that had been sampled on previous missions, the moon mass would be much greater than the scientists had calculated. They knew there had to be a lighter material on the moon, and they speculated that this would be anorthosite or plagioclase.

I think it was providential that this particular rock was lifted up and displayed to us. We brought it back. Scientists will be analyzing it for years to come, but the University of New York at Stony Brook has age-dated it at 4.15 billion years, plus or minus .25 billion years. This confirms the fact that the earth and the moon were created about the same time. The oldest thing on earth discovered thus far is about 3.3 billion years old, so this little bit of ancient history is another clue to the creation of our universe. After we returned, we found that our treasure had been named the Genesis Rock. I think this discovery alone would have made our mission a success. . . .

When we were ready, we broke out the TV so Houston could catch the flag-raising scene. We picked a spot with Mt. Hadley well placed in the background, and I pushed the staff in and hit it a couple of times so it'll stay up for a few million years. Dave and I saluted the flag. It's beautiful. While we had the attention of our audience Dave and I did what we called "The Galileo Experiment." It involved Dave dropping a falcon's feather from one hand and his geology hammer from the other. They sure enough hit the ground at the same time. After the experiment, I accidently stepped on the feather. When we got back to the module, Dave was perturbed at me because he had wanted to take it back. I wonder if hundreds of years from now somebody will find a falcon's feather under a layer of dust and speculate on what strange creature flew it there!

Once I found unaccountably there were no more activities planned for me. With fifteen or twenty minutes with nothing to do, I actually had a small vacation on the moon. I started running around the Lunar Module in circles. Then I did some broad jumping. Just having a ball—you know, like a little kid. Even in the space suit, I could broad jump about ten feet, about 3 or 4 in the air. No telling how far I could have jumped if I hadn't had that suit on. It was the most relaxed time I had on the surface. . . .

When we left, Dave and I wanted a few personal souvenirs, so we took the utility lights and other loose parts off the Lunar Module. Then we jettisoned the Lunar Module so Houston could fire its engine by remote control and crash it into the surface of the moon. We forgot some things we wanted in the Lunar Module. . . .

We had both brought along many items for ourselves and for friends that would have been priceless souvenirs from the moon. There were envelopes, medallions, stamps, medals, flags, shamrocks, and coins. Dave and I had at least a hundred two-dollar bills that we were going to split after the trip. There were a number of things we left on the moon purposely. I left some medallions, flat pieces of silver with the fingerprints of Mary and our children. . . .

We gradually adjusted to the environment. The daily routine was easier, sleep was better. The mental fatigue was almost more significant than the physical. I was feeling better all the time and really hoping that the flight would be longer, because it was a good simple life. Just as we were really enjoying this life of travelling through space, it was rapidly coming to a close. So we had mixed feelings about coming back. . . .

o   o   o

KR: I imagine that returning would be very difficult. How could you feel that your normal everyday life, your mundane world, would offer any challenge?

JI: In my life, the task that I've taken on has been the most challenging, most

To Kent
my my Very
THANKS FOR BRINGING THE MOON CLOSER
Best Wishes
Jim Irwin

ASTRONAUT IRWIN SALUTES FLAG AT APOLLO 15 HADLEY-APENNINE LANDING SITE.

fruitful. It's great because people are interested in space, and interested in the moon, they're interested in talking to a guy who has been to the moon, and think he might look a little differently, or he might know something that they don't know. And I very humbly say, that I DO know something that these people don't know. Because I've had an expensive trip to the moon, a mighty expensive "vacation."

KR: Do you think that it would have been different if you had gone to another planet?

JI: I'd say that I think the effect on man's life and his relationships, that is, change is dependent on how far out he goes, while he's there. I think that the effect on man, say, when he travels to Mars is really going to be profound. Because for the round trip right now, we estimate he has to go about a year and a half. He'll travel out there, say, 35 million miles, you know, where the earth will look about the size of a marble. To see the earth shrink so that it just looks like a star, just a speck of light in space, that would be even more difficult to comprehend, to be that far away from home. The separation will be an immense degree of loneliness. It will really be a strong attraction to come back to the earth

KR: Do you have a really different feeling about the preparation now? Would you recommend an astronaut were more psychologically prepared? Is that possible? Can you prepare anybody for that?

JI: I don't think you can. I think again, it is an individual preparation. And I think that anyone that does venture out beyond the moon will be well aware of what's been documented on, say, the moon missions, and how it's affected our lives. I hope they won't be reluctant, you know, to travel out there. But they should be aware that there might be a change.

o   o   o

From TO RULE THE NIGHT:

The support we got from the crew at Houston was staggering—backup people constantly working with duplicate systems to solve all problems that we discovered or hadn't yet. We may not have been the greatest explorers on the world's stage, but we had the greatest prompters. . . .

On splashdown day we woke up and saw that we were moving towards the earth. The crescent earth looked so much like the moon that it seemed we were going the wrong direction. There was a very thin sliver of the large round ball. The earth goes through the same phases as the moon. When we left it was a full earth. When we came back it was a new earth; absolutely black like the dark of the moon, only it was the dark of the earth. . . .

On re-entry into the atmosphere, it is a beautiful sight, but the pressure of re-entry is enormous. It's a traumatic experience to go from zero G's to almost 7 G's during the entry fireball period. For about four minutes you experience this. You have seven times your weight. It's physically impossible to lift an arm up to touch a switch, or move a circuit breaker. It was amazing to me that Dave was able to talk to Mission Control while we were coming in. I couldn't take a breath. I was living on the residual oxygen in my lungs.

We were plastered against the couch. I felt I was on the verge of blacking out at 7 G's, but you could probably go to 10. We felt it so much because our bodies had become so lazy. The heart was lazy. We had lost muscle tissue; we had become flabby and weak. So, going from zero G to 7 G's felt like going from 1 or 14 on the earth as far as I was concerned.

When we hit about 60,000 feet the altimeter came off the peg and we started reading altitude. The atmosphere was slowing us down. The drogue chutes came out at 25,000 feet, and that really slowed us down, like a drag chute or speed brake in an airplane. It doesn't jerk you, it brakes you—then you start oscillating wildly underneath the drogues. Then, just before you get to 10,000 feet, the drogues are released. You can see up there; you see them go, and you feel them go. You free-fall for a few seconds, wondering whether the main chutes are going to come out. At 10,000 the main chutes come out and they slow you almost completely.

We saw the three chutes; then we saw that one had failed. It just collapsed. Well, Al saw it and I saw it, but it turned out not to be a problem. . . .

It's so good to be back to the good earth. We are sitting there eagerly anticipating the frogmen who are on the way to open the hatch. We are looking for them to appear in the window. Suddenly, Freddy the friendly frogman who has trained with us in the Gulf knocks on the window. We have been there in our underwear, and now we have our clean cover garments on—we have not worn them since we left. We feel so relaxed, so relieved that now we are back on earth.

Finally, they get the hatch open and the life jackets in there, and we put them on. Dave goes first; I go next; Al goes last. I get into the raft and, man, it's great. Beautiful. . . .

Nice and warm. The first thing I did was dip my hand in the ocean and put the water on my face. Just to feel that water—water from the earth on your face—and to breathe that air. We wanted to relax in the raft but the chopper came to pick us up. The whole thing was going too fast—I wanted to slow it down, so I could really savor it. . . .

On the flight home to earth there were times when I dreaded coming back. I had the greatest feeling in space. When we splashed down, I wanted to keep time from moving so fast. There in the soft, warm waters of the Pacific, I felt a joy at being back on earth, but I knew intuitively that this was the last calm time I was going to have. I was going to have to make speeches, to meet people, and to take part in public occasions. I had never been able to speak extemporaneously, had never been at ease on my feet. I was a quiet man; I never talked very much to anybody. I had this feeling of being in a new life, of being a new man, and I was afraid of it at the same time. Yet I didn't understand what was happening inside of me. . . .

There were a lot of congressmen there, including Olin Teague from Texas. We went down the line greeting all these people and all the Air Force and Navy brass. It was probably the warmest receiving line I had ever gone through. They had big smiles on their faces; they were really happy to see us, and we were really happy to see them.

About this time I started to feel that I didn't have the balance that I should have. It wasn't just that the ship had some motion; I wasn't as steady as I should be. Then I realized that I hadn't cleared my ears coming down. So there I was in this receiving line with my ears plugged up and uncertain about my balance.

My speech was very simple. I told them how thankful we were that we had been able to make the trip and how grateful we were to all those people back here on earth who helped us. I mentioned my Navy training and said that I had been on ships before but I had never been so happy to be on a ship as I was now. . . .

It was an astronaut-type speech. I didn't say anything about the religious experience I had had on the moon. I still hadn't gotten this together in my mind. At first I just talked about the technological voyage, not the spiritual voyage, not how I had been changed in my heart and in my spirit. . . .

Most of our time during these next days was spent in debriefing. We used the flight plan as our schedule, and we were debriefed individually on our specific assignments. I covered the Lunar Module, particularly systems problems. Occasionally, we'd break and go to the doctors for a special physical. . . .

I don't know how much permanent heart damage I suffered from the little attack I had after I left the moon, or how it related to a heart attack I had later. They already had positive evidence that the loss of potassium could have been a contributing factor. On flights since then, 16 and 17, they put an overabundant supply of potassium in the food. This solved the heart problem, but evidently it created a lot of problems in the intestinal tract.

We finally completed our debriefing. Of course we were aware that it was purely technical rather than human or psychological. Very naturally, we had withheld our individual reactions to the flight. This is not what NASA is particularly interested in, and the crews have always held back their deeply personal feelings for their own books and magazine articles. . . .

Since Apollo 15 had been advertised as the first extended scientific mission to the moon, Dave wanted to establish us as scientists. I had suggested we report our trips as pilots. Not only was I reluctant to pose as a scientist, I was becoming increasingly frustrated by being confined to the scientific message. I was much more aware of my religious or spiritual awakening, and I wanted to share this with our audiences. But I didn't want to get NASA involved, because their policy is to stay out of this area. . . .

We were guests all over the world: of the government of Belgium, of King Baudouin. We had a meeting with Golda Meir, the Prime Minister of Israel. I told her that I thought my experience with God on the moon was an answer to the prayers of millions of people who prayed for me during the voyage. Mrs. Meir turned to Mary during the course of the conversation and said, "I think this lady was as brave as you, sitting down on earth."

o   o   o

JI: We had a wonderful trip. Most of the reactions were positive. But when we came back to America we found the reactions were mixed. You know, about 15% of the American people think that we really went to Arizona, and staged the whole thing. A 25 billion dollar hoax. Well, my mother really gets up in arms when she hears that. She can't stand that people would doubt that, that her son, Jimmy, went to the moon!

KR: She doesn't doubt that?

JI: No. She believes me!

KR: Do you still feel effects of the trip?

JI: Well, I don't think I'll ever be the same. Now, whether that's a physical

42

thing or a psychological thing, I don't know. Doctors aren't that skilled at perceiving small differences.

There was the mental strain of the flight and the physical changes, because the body does change when exposed to weightlessness. The heart becomes lazy. The body throws off a lot of body fluids. The elements in the body are out of balance. The body just doesn't function the same.

KR: Did you sleep alright?

JI: I didn't sleep particularly well when I was weightless. I talk about the problem of sleeping in my book. The problem depends on where you're trying to sleep. We had three couches side by side. Al had the left one, and Dave had the right one, and I could have slept in the middle couch but that just didn't seem appropriate, three grown men sleeping together. So I elected to go onto a little chamber underneath the right couch. So I just floated down in there, and it was kind of a hammock, a sleeping bag arrangement in which I could place the lower half of my body, but the upper half was free to float around. And many times, I know the first night I would wake up and find my head cocked out in some weird angle. When I got on the surface of the moon, I slept very well. Almost as well as I do on the earth, because when you lie down, you stay there, you don't float off.

You know, when you're on the surface of the moon, you can count these flashes, or streaks, cosmic particles, energy particles that go right through the spacecraft, right through your head. And you can see them go right across your eyeball and they leave these phosphorescent streaks for a few seconds. And so in going to sleep, instead of counting sheep, you count streaks and flashes. You don't see those in earth orbit, because the Van Allen radiation belts prevent radiation particles from coming into the earth. So you just see them beyond the radiation belts like on our trip to the moon.

KR: That sounds beautiful.

JI: It's beautiful. But you see, they don't know what the long-range effect would be on, say, a crew that was going to Mars. They might end up, when they get there with their brain completely destroyed, or maybe their memory erased. Or maybe their vision gone. So that's something they'll have to plan for.

KR: Did you dream?

JI: I didn't dream or I don't recall dreaming on the moon. But I did find I was dreaming as I got closer to the earth. And my dreams were more and more what you do on the earth.

You know, I've never dreamed about the moon, which kind of surprises me. Before or after. Never dreamed about it. Have you ever dreamed about the moon?

KR: Actually, yes, I have! I did dream that I went there once. There was a moose on the moon. A very large one.

JI: You have strange dreams.

43

From TO RULE THE NIGHT:

Mary is my second wife. (My first marriage broke up because of religious differences.) Often when Mary and I are interviewed, or when we are on the same platform, somebody will say, "Well, the credit of your success really goes to the woman who has been by your side all these years." That amuses me, and it amuses her. Over the years Mary has given me support, and I love her, but many times the tensions at home almost caused me to leave the program.

There were many times when we talked openly about getting a divorce. We wouldn't fight—I'd just be silent—but these long periods of quiet would bring the children close to tears. Then the air would clear and we would come back together, and the children would get over it.

I know it was hectic for Mary at home. She had the whole burden of four kids, the house, and everything. When I was home, I was completely absorbed; I was like an automaton. I had been so programmed I was like a robot. I had to eat, drink, sleep, and dream my work—I had to be saturated. I know she understood that it had to be this way before a flight, but it didn't make it any easier. . . .

Mary is a lot closer to me now than she has been—we have both changed a great deal, and she is tremendously reinforcing to me. She was telling me earlier this year that I was going to have to learn to pace myself, to come to grips with myself. Mary is a full-fledged partner now in High Flight. She is a very strong force. She is witnessing and speaking; she even gives the invitation, and she must say the right thing, because people come forward to accept Christ.

Mary tells me that we have never really had any time alone before—that this is a new experience for us. And I see it as a new life within a new life. . . .

o   o   o

KR: Is a basic way of talking about the effect, that the experience changed your priorities, your perspectives?
JI: You know, after you've been to the moon, and you come back to the earth, you look at everything with much more appreciation, or with reverence. I'm back, but by the grace of God.

I feel now that the power of God was working in me the whole time I was on the flight. I felt His presence on the moon in the most immediate and overwhelming way. There I was, a test pilot, a nuts-and-bolts type who had gotten rather skeptical about God, and suddenly I was asking God to solve my problems on the moon. I was relying on God rather than on Houston. I went for everyone—not only the American taxpayers but the rest of the people on earth. I became less political, that is, less just an American and more a citizen of the whole earth. During this sort of flight, you are too busy to reflect on the splendor of space or on the secret awakenings that come from the inner flight that takes place at the same time. You have to try to register these experiences and examine them later. It has been sort of a slow-breaking revelation for me. The ultimate effect has been to deepen and strengthen all the religious insight I ever had. And to see, you know, everything shrink to the size of a moth ball, you realize that when you're back on the earth, no matter where you are, no matter who you're with, no matter what the circumstances, you feel at home, because you're on the earth. When you've been over a quarter of a million miles out and you come back, somehow you really feel that you belong.

We think the earth could be transformed, if somehow you could lift people up to the moon. Or even out into space and let them see. . . . We think that the bickering and the fighting and the hostility is a big waste of man's inner energy. Did I answer that question?

KR: Yes!

JI: I'm so far off, that I don't recall what the question was.

KR: Yeh! I don't either, but I'm sure you did.

REMYTHOLOGIZING THE MOON

Maggy Anthony

Maggy Anthony, a scholar of matriarchal civilizations and a writer living in Reno, Nevada, has taken some concrete steps to redefine the moon in her life. This is the story of her response to the first lunar space walk.

Just six and one half years ago, I stopped in front of the TV set with a warm jar of Gerber's strained applesauce in my hand, arrested in my movement towards one of my hungry babies. A craft straight out of Buck Rogers was settling down on the moon, and along with several million other people all over the world, I was awaiting what I had been told for several months previously was a monumental moment in the history of the world. Sure enough, it wasn't too long before the hatch opened and a figure dressed in a cumbersome white suit lumbered out and stepped out onto the moon. And promptly cut out over one half of the world's population in his historic statement: **One step for a man, a giant step for mankind.** Tears sprang to my eyes and I looked over at my children wishing they were old enough to appreciate this wonderful moment. My tears were those of happiness . . . weren't they? Suddenly I wasn't so sure. I began to be aware of a certain unease; a feeling that this event wasn't quite as marvelous as it should be, as it was touted to be.

As I walked over to the babies' chairs and started the ritual of spooning the food out of the jar, I was less there than usual. Mechanically, my hand placed the spoon into the jar, then into one of the children's mouths, then scraping the excess off the baby's chin, then back with the spoon into the jar, over and over. In my mind, I was going over the scene I had just witnessed, wondering where my uneasiness came from. First of all, I hadn't liked the clumsiness of the movements; it should have been more graceful, more glorious. It should have been done with

46

more, well, with more feeling. And there was the core of the problem. Once again, men, in their one-sided earnestness, had clumsily staked out a claim on something without regard for feelings, without using their intuition. They had worked the problems out scientifically, accomplished their physical objective, and had let the thing rest there. All the equations had been figured, all the formulae formulated; now the act was accomplished and that was that.

However, for myself, and for many more like me as I was later to find out, that was definitely not that. The formulae had not taken into consideration the human element. The mechanical, plastic American Boy astronauts that had been sent up to the moon and continued to be sent up, came back with a disease that not all the quarantines and expensive medical help in the space program could do anything about. It seemed to be a dis-ease, literally, of the soul. There was talk for awhile of the experience of loneliness in space, the trauma of going into the complete unknown, but all their psychologizing could not cover up the fact that what the astronauts seemed to be suffering from was a malaise that had been written about by people in the throes of mystical experience since the earliest days of the world. But long before this element became widely publicized, many of us began to feel that there was some sort of balance needed to offset the effects of the moon probes; that in some way we had to recover the moon for human kind. We had to recover its symbolic meaning, its mythological dimension.

In thinking about this problem, I brought it up at a session I was having with my analyst. Fortunately he was a Jungian analyst and understood my probings and ponderings over the problem. He said that since I was a teacher of mythology I had the perfect opportunity of doing something to counter all the unfeeling, scientific brouhaha that was going on. He even gave me a title: Re-Mythologizing the Moon. Enthusiastically I came up with the subtitle myself, An Antidote to the Astronauts. I left my fifty minute hour feeling considerably less confused than I had in the last four or five weeks following the moon landing.

I found a date for it that fit in with my schedule, designed a poster with a friend, had it printed and out on the streets. The whole thing flowed so smoothly that I knew that the approach was right. Once the posters were up, I began my research. It led me not only to my ordinary sources for mythology, but into worlds I had not entered before. It led me into medieval alchemy, to off-beat religious sects, but above all it led me, to my everlasting gratitude, to the matriarchal religions of the pre-Christian world.

In these religions, (I should say, "this religion" since all the Goddesses are One Goddess as the axiom goes), I found the moon-consciousness celebrated that was so much more in tune with my natural feelings than the sun-centered world of daylight. I found a whole way, an entire system whereby the moon itself governed the ways of the world. This system had a different method to measure time, had

47

different values, and related differently to the sexes and even to sex itself. I was overcome with a feeling of nostalgia for this world and system that I had never experienced. It all seemed so much more in tune with my inner feelings and values that had so little meaning in the Judeo-Christian framework in which I had been raised.

Yet when I began to put together the material I had found for the class, I began to have serious problems. I had only the vaguest material to go by and my own feelings. Having had no traditional education beyond High School, I had always felt I had to do more than a conventionally educated teacher would do. I had to research more, be more careful of the reputability of my sources and not go too far out in my own explorations so as to bring down charges of academic sloppiness and "kookiness." Then suddenly, in the midst of this dilemma, with the new-found support of a newly discovered "other way," I began to see that the very things I had thought of as disabilities were actually my greatest strengths. Since I had not "proper" academic background, I could use the very tools that such a background might well have destroyed for me; I could use my moon-consciousness to discover the ways of the moon. I could justifiably use my dreams, my fantasies, my intuitions in the realm in which these were legitimate and actually more to be trusted than any sun-consciousness. It was not until a few years later, when Robert Ornstein's book on the two hemispheres of the brain came out that I had any scientific basis for my intuition that there were two ways of perceiving reality, each as valid as the other, each needing the other for a balanced view of the world.

When the class started, to an unusually good response, the problems were there. It was hard for all of us to get beyond our expectations of what a "class" should be. The students were interested in ritual, but self-conscious about participating in one. Their analytical habits picked up in the course of their education (most were students at local colleges and universities) had made it very difficult for them to take part in any thing with feelings where the intellect had to be temporarily suspended.

I taught this class with a friend of mine, a self-confessed "moon-man." Together we tried to work out rituals that would stand up to the intellectual criticism of the class and at the same time satisfy emotional needs in the way only ritual can.

Our first ritual was one of initiation into the ways of the moon. We selected a full-moon night and conducted the ritual in a swampy area in Marin County outside San Francisco. The students were requested to wear all white, the men in white shirts and pants, the women in long white dresses or white blouses and long skirts. Once we all arrived there, in separate cars, we blindfolded the initiates and placed them in groups in the four directions. We then proceeded to perform rituals with each one in which each of the senses other than that of sight was used: we fed them "moon food," touched them with objects such as feathers, chanted to them and sounded bells. At one point during the ritual my friend and I got the giggles and we allowed it, feeling this to be part of the "lunacy." When it was all over, we parted and everyone went their separate ways. We did not want them to start analyzing the experience immediately; it needed time to gel.

After much trial and error, we found that we did not have to worry about the intellect interfering. We found that if we persisted in a ritual beyond the point where we felt a little foolish and theatrical, that the moon-consciousness took over and that the "sacred" entered. When this occurred, all action took on meaning, and judgement of the intellect which can be so life-stultifying, was suspended. The most difficult part, always, was the beginning of the ritual. At that point the emotions are still under layers of analysis and linear thinking. Then, with persistence, the right side of the brain, or what I prefer to call, as ancient Egyptians called it, the "Isis" side of the brain takes over and begins to perceive the inner reality of the acts performed. When this occurs, the point called by Jungians the "abaissement du niveau mental" or lowering of the threshold between conscious and unconscious processes, then all present are joined emotionally in such a way that an initiation of some sort always takes place.

Each class I did was comprised of a ritual and a lecture on topics having to do with the moon and its symbolism. We found that we had to do the ritual first, as the students were so eager for it that they paid little attention to the lecture material if it was presented first. In the course of six weeks, meeting once a week for two hours, we covered most of the world's moon mythologies, alchemy, tarot and astrological symbolism. Yet, recently, in talking with some of the people who took that class six years ago, I found that what they remembered had very little to do with the intellectual content of the material. What they had come away with was the feeling of the moon through the rituals and a feeling that the class was their first experience of the validity of moon consciousness.

So perhaps the only way one can "re-mythologize" the moon is through experiencing the moon through the moon hemisphere of the brain. In other words, experiencing through those very places (dreams, fantasies, creative work, ritual and intuition) that are under the domination of it and have come to be dishonored through the sun-conscious mythologies of the present day religions. In doing this we will bring to honor once more a way of relating to the world that was practised for over eight thousand years before the birth of the Christian era. In so doing, we may yet escape the future of horrors we have been brought to the brink of through thinking that one-sidedness of mind is the only way.

O may the moon and sunlight seem
One inextricable beam,
For if I triumph I must make men mad.

W. B. Yeats,
"The Tower" 1928

Leonor Fini is a French surrealist painter. One of the major themes of her work is woman as alchemist. Here she is in her ritual moon goddess costume.

LUNA THE GIVER OF VISIONS   HEL OF THE DARK

CIRCE OF DEATH   LILITH THE NIGHT PHANTOM

SOMAS THE DREAM GIVER   TIME THE GODDESS OF

INTOXICATION   CHANG-O THE FAIRY QUEEN   TRIVIA

OF SORCERY AND ENCHANTMENT   APHRODISIA THE

DIVINE

LUNACY

Lunacy, mental derangement associated with certain phases of the moon; foolish & irresponsible conduct. Lunatic, one who suffers from lunacy; wildly and giddily foolish. Lunatic fringe, the frantic and irrational members of a society or group.

I have tried to imagine why the moon, powerful and beautiful, would be attributed with causing insanity and other negative results. What were these abnormal mental states associated with certain phases of the moon? What could have been this wild and giddy conduct? And who were these irrational groups and societies? Did these terms have other meanings long ago? After reading in mythology and ancient cultural customs, i think i've come to the root of this moon madness. These words refer to activities of groups and behavior of individuals exhibited during the seasonal lunar festivals. This ceremonial behavior at one time was considered sacred in the highest order, and then, with the advent of sun-worship and patriarchal castes, the rituals were forbidden and branded madness, irresponsible. Moon worshippers were the center; then they were forced out to the fringe.

Why were lunar rituals wildly and giddily foolish, frantic, irrational and irresponsible? Why is moonstruck defined as crazed, deranged, dazed with romantic sentiment? Mooncalf, a freak, a fool. Moonshine, nonsensical talk. Moon man, a gipsy. Moonish, whimsical, fickle. Moony, resembling the moon, dreamy, absent-minded. Mooning, to wander about languidly; to exhibit infatuation. With what were these groups infatuated and of what were their minds absent? What ritual and knowledge stayed alive among the gipsies which other groups lost? And why does the moon produce romance?

It was clear to ancient agricultural peoples that crops grew seasonally in tune with the cycles of the moon, and that women's menstrual cycles and animals' mating cycles were also on a lunar rhythm. The moon was the ultimate principle of

53

fertility in the universe. The moon brought dew in the night to moisten plants after a day's drying. The moon presided over the darkness in which plants germinated. The light of the moon drew life out of seeds as they slept underground; it drew plants up with the same force with which it drew the tides, and with which it drew monthly blood from women in an earthly replica of its own cyclical growth and replenishment. The necessity of the moon and its cycles to all fertility and its regulation was indisputable.

Men's cycles and part in the process of fertility was less obvious than that of the moon or women. For centuries, the role of sperm in human procreation was not recognized. The fact that birth takes place long after the act of intercourse makes it easy to imagine why the two events were not readily associated. And not all women who had intercourse became pregnant, nor were all men fertile. Because of the undeniability of the seasons, the tides and women's twenty-eight day menstrual cycles, it seemed obvious that fertility had its source in the moon. Women were considered special communicants and liasons with the moon (priestesses). Women, the inventors of agriculture, were respected for their particular invigorating influence on plants. They became the birth givers (midwives), the healers (herbalists), the holy nurturers (cooks).

As earthly cousins and representatives of the moon, women were called upon to tap their communication with the fertility principle for the good of their community by becoming oracles and prophetesses. They were the revered religious officials in a sect because they knew the deep rhythm of the moon and how to treat her sacred earth houses and ceremonial objects. In early civilizations, when the fertility of women and the success of seasonal crops clearly delineated the survival of a community, knowing the ways and rhythms of the moon was essential, and listening to the knowledge of her priestesses, was vital. Turning away obviously would lead to death and destruction.

In such moon-principle cultures, a significant relationship was assumed between one's unconscious visions and one's conscious activities, between one's dreams and one's daily living, between one's vitality and the extent to which one lived by the cyclical principle of fertility. Because night, the special province of the moon, brought sleep and visions, dreams were revered as messages from the moon and lived out the next day as directives from the life source. The moon was thought to be the originator of all creativity, and she later became known as The Muse of the Arts.

In rituals honoring the moon, the attempt was made to please her by imitating and honoring her cycles and by enhancing and heightening the special states over which she ruled and guided. At the seasonal equinoxes, when the hours of the night and the hours of day equalized, special ceremonies were held in honor of the season's lunar cycle, in honor and recognition of the particular aspect of the fertility cycle currently at work in the world. Fall ceremonies honored the harvest. Winter ceremonies honored lighting the first hearth fires in the temple and homes, representing bringing a piece of the light of the moon (the light out of darkness) to warm one during the months of cold and gestation. Spring was, of course, a time for great festivals of rebirth to celebrate the return of fertility. The cyclical pattern of rebirth was one of the major messages shown by the moon in her periodic disappearance and return, her diminishing and her growth. She went away, but she always returned.

What people learned from the example of the lunar cycle was the basic pattern necessary for renewal. Rest, meditation, vision and gestation were as revered a part of the cycle as production. Without one, the others suffer. This is a principle of activity that our modern cultures have largely abandoned and, it seems, to great expense of individual psychological health as well as of the quality of our communal lives. Understanding of equal reverence for all parts of a cycle has been most clearly retained in the texts of Oriental religions which deal with the necessity of each person nurturing equally their elements of yin and yang.

The rites of these ancient fertility religions were joyous, mysterious and orgiastic. They were times for people to rejoice in their own instincts toward fertility and by doing so to honor and arouse this quality in the universe. They were times for bringing down the moon. Their sexuality was a sacred energy to the moon and these communal festivals replenished the fertility energy in the world. Expression of these principles is retained in some of the teachings and ceremonies of Tantra yoga, in which the participants' sexuality is sanctified by their ritual adherance to laws of cosmic balance.

In these ancient fertility rituals, visions, non sequiturs, irrationalities, dreams, whimsy, depth and breadth of emotion were valued and revered as crucial and necessary complements to the rationality of living on other days. In fact, these states were thought practical because without them the balance of life was not possible; vitality was sapped out of the individual, fertility was drained from the community, and understanding of the universe dwindled. It is here, in our modern world, that we must begin regaining our understanding of the states of lunacy.

If the moon represents and promotes the fertile principle in the world, if she heightens one's emotions, passions and visions, then exposure to the moon requires familiarity and respect for and a high degree of mastery of these states. But the modern world has become a cult of one-sidedness. Recent scientific research has shown that the two lobes of the brain control two areas of functioning in humans: the left lobe controls, in general, nerves and reactions centered on the right side of the body, that is, functions concerned with outer-directed activity such as speech and stressful, conscious activity; the right lobe of the brain controls the nerves and functioning centered on the left side of the body ruling over more inner-directed states such as meditation, fantasy, receptivity. We have become a culture which neglects its left side, neglects its meditations, its dreams, its receptivity and its passions. The phrase "the sterility of modern life" is sadly accurate and finds its source in this neglect. Sterility has become revered rather than fertility.

Fertility is too messy, too instinctual, too powerful, too uncategorizable and too uncontrollable. It unites people, makes them forget political party, racial prejudices and factory time clocks. It involves emotion, feeling and vulnerability.

The current cult of one-sidedness promotes fear of emotion, fear of feeling, fear of passion, instinct, subjectivity, irrationality, whimsy, play, love and the natural. If the moon amplifies these aspects of ourselves and if police statistics are correct that more crimes of violence and passion are committed during a full moon, then does this not indicate a culture so out of touch with its passions and uncomfortable in its emotions that people perceive themselves to be **crazy** when these feelings are heightened? These times used to be communal love festivals; they have become times of anxiety and crime. We as a culture have become violent rather than loving when our emotions are aroused. It is time we renewed and rebalanced our relationship with our passions, our unconscious and our subjective, and learned again to integrate them into our living. Perhaps then "alienation," the 'disease of the modern world,' characterized by separation from feeling and instinct, would become archaic.

Because women were the major priestesses, close communicants with the moon and the ones designated to carry out her example on earth, they became symbols of evil and heresy in the eras of intense patriarchal military struggle. Women, who in matriarchal civilizations and moon-worshipping ancient cultures were goddesses and representatives of the deity, became devils. It is no accident that woman (as Eve) is chosen to lead man (as Adam) away from prescribed Judeo-Christian knowledge. She worshipped another deity and so she was banned from the kingdom of the male god. She was no longer allowed to be a priestess. And the struggle is made current when "rational" men become hysterical at the thought of women ministers. The intensity of this fear comes from the underlying issue: the struggle between patriarchy and matriarchy for political power. To ban matriarchies as the dominant social form, you must 'discredit' women and ban their goddesses. With this ban has gone a ban on the legitimacy of half the human psyche, to say nothing of half the human race.

It is the purpose and gradual achievement of the women's movement to restore this balance in the world, to 'legitimize' the integration of action, love, deep emotion and vision. Women do not, as patronizing media would have one believe, represent emotional qualities to the exclusion of others; the female principle

56

represents their inclusion and integration with other elements. The women's movement process of re-examination is necessarily dialectical in theory and practice: it is through this process that we will come to a renewed experience and understanding of the states of lunacy.

o   o   o

I see the moon
And the moon sees me.

Artemis, goddess of the chase and of forests

Luna, Roman 1st century A.D.

Ephesian Artemis, fertility goddess of Asia Minor

THEN

The spirit-root words which all come from the original Sanscrit root <u>mati-h</u>, which means "thought, intention:"

Menos,   spirit, heart soul, courage, ardency.
menoinan,   to consider, meditate, wish
memona,   to have in mind, to intend
mainomai,   to think, to be lost in thought, to rave
mania,   madness, possession
manteia,   prophecy
menis & menos,   anger
menuo,   indicate, reveal
meno,   remain, linger
manthano,   to learn
memini,   to remember
mentiri,   to lie
men,   moon
mensis,   month
mas & ma,   to measure
matram,   measure
metis,   cleverness, wisdom
metiesthai,   to meditate, to have in mind, dream
menstruation,   cycle of the month
menopause,   cessation of menstruation
menhir,   prehistoric stone monuments found in the Britis Isles & N. France
meniscus,   a crescent-shaped body, a curved surface
menorrhagia,   an unusually heavy menstrual flow
meninges,   membranes enclosing the spinal cord and brain
mensal,   monthly
mentality,   a person's intellectual capabilities
mental,   of or pertaining to the mind

luna   lunacy   luna moth   lunar   lunate

lunar month   lunar year   semilunar bone   lunatic

lunatic asylum   lunatic fringe   lunation   luny moon

mooning   moons   moonbeam   moonblind

moonblindness   mooncalf   moon dog   mooneye

moon-faced   moonfish   moonflower   moonlight

moonlighter   moonlit   mountains of the moon

moonseed   moonshine   moonstone   moonstruck

moontype   moonwort   moony   moon dial

moon-loved   moon madness   moonraker   moonshade

moonish   wet moon   moonite   moon child

honeymoon   green cheese moon   moonrise   moonblink

moonblasted   mooncreeper   mooncurser   moondial

moonflaw   moonlet   moon guitar   moon lily

moonman   moon pillar   moon sail   moonless   moonbill

moonglade   moongod   moonie   mooniness

moonshee   moonya   moonstricken   moonshiny

sublunary   moon penny   moonlitten   moonlit

moonsick   mooncloud   moontide   moonblast

moongleam   moonblanch   moongathered

moonglittering   moonmade   moonled   moonfreezing

moonraised   moonsoaked   moontanned   moontaught

moontrodden   mooncrowned   moonarched

moonbrowed   moonset

OUPIS, THE GREEK QUEEN   CABAR, THE GREAT OF TURKEY

SHING-MOO, OUR LADY MOON OF CHINA   OTSUKISAMA,

THE ROYAL OF JAPAN   ASHERATH, JEZEBEL'S GODDESS

IN ISRAEL AND SAMARIA   QADESH, EGYPTIAN LADY OF

HEAVEN   ARDVI SURA ANAHITA OF ARMENIA, THE HIGH,

POWERFUL, IMMACULATE GODDESS OF WAR   MARY,

QUEEN OF HEAVEN   SHARRAT SHAME, QUEEN OF HEAVEN

OF BABYLONIA   MAJA, THE ALLMOTHER   MA-TSU-P'O,

TAOIST QUEEN OF HEAVEN   JOTMA, THE MIGHTY OF INDIA

KUAN YIN – BUDDHIST GODDESS OF MERCY, PROTECTRESS

OF CHILDREN   FLEACHTA OF MEATH – MOON QUEEN OF

IRELAND   MAWU, THE SUPREME BEING, AFRICA

MOON CHIEF OF KENYA   HINA, THE FIRST WOMAN –

HAWAII

THE MOTHER OF THE WORLD

She was before manifestation.
To question beyond her origin is not to understand her.
She is the moving center.
It is out of her that all has come into being.
It is in her spell that everything remains.
And back to her that everything must return.
No one is long permitted to remain what they are.

The symbol of fertility and the origin of life was the Mother Goddess. She is the oldest recorded deity, celebrated in prehistoric times in paintings depicting ceremonies of animal-masked dancers and by the "venus" statues (carvings of a pregnant woman) which are a universal phenomena in archaeological excavations of prehistoric eras.

The most common creation myth seems to be the concept that the world began as an egg, which cracked in half, usually in order to form the earth and the moon. (This corresponds to the creation hypotheses of current scientists who postulate that the earth and moon were once one planet, smaller at one end than the other; and that gradually the smaller end eroded away from the bigger end and broke loose to become our moon.) Thus the moon is mythologically synonymous with the cosmic egg, the earth, and the mother.

When you understand her history, you can understand the diversity of her symbols and personifications. She is the egg and the seed of the world. She is the mother of life and also of light. The earth is her twin sister and also her child. She is the mother of all creatures and also their bride. Her light and her magnetic force cause fertility, movement and growth. She is the fertilizer and the source.

She is darkness as well as light. Her cycles encompass all moods and all phases. She is queen of the Bright Night and of the Darkness, guide to the lost traveller and pathway to the underworld. She brings creativity and visions; she also brings sleep, darkness and death. She is the spirit of the underworld, the ruler of madness. She is the Shepherd of the Stars. She is the home of the souls of the unborn and of the dead waiting for rebirth.

She is the healer of the sick, the source of water, plants, animals and blood. She gave fire to the world to light the dark night. She can make children grow inside women and plants germinate in the earth. She returns every month after her ritual decease with renewed energy. She is the source of physical and spiritual rebirth and illumination, the Queen of dreams and of dreams come true.

She is the Goddess of Love, the fertility Queen, the spark of life in the darkness, the giver of fantasies, visions, delirium and passion. She unites opposing elements, brings light into dark and understands the necessity of death for birth.

Out of her came all things and, therefore, she is one with them and of them. She bore a son for her amusement and he became her lover. This son became the 'God of the dying year' whose winter death always culminated in a spring resurrection. She bore many children. To the female children she gave the miracle of monthly "death" and rebirth signified in their bleeding and not dying. Menstruation is a time to think of her, to honor and emulate her and to be reminded of her gift of birth.

Of her son she requires another cycle of homage. Once a year he must be sacrificed and die and be divided into parts to be reborn again in the spring. All men are representatives and servants to her fertility principle on earth. One man a year must be sacrificed to honor her source. Through his blood, the blood of a king, all men will be guaranteed fertility. He must give his sexuality over to her if he is to be reborn. Her son is Osiris, Horus, Zagreus and Jesus. Each spring he is granted rebirth. After three days' death, symbolizing the three days of darkness the moon suffers each month, her son is reborn and the world celebrates her life-giving power. At this time the cosmic egg is honored and the rabbit, a symbol of her fertility, is celebrated.

ISIS, MOTHER — SON OSIRIS
MARY, MOTHER — SON JESUS
ISHTAR, MOTHER — SON SINN
ISHTAR, MOTHER — SON TAMMUZ
ASTARTE, MOTHER — SON BAAL
ISIS, MOTHER — SON HORUS
CYBELLE, MOTHER — SON HORUS

66

ANAHITA, MOTHER — SON MITHRA
APHRODITE, MOTHER — SON ADONIS
VESTA, MOTHER — SON PALLAS
PARASHAKTI, MOTHER — SON SIVA
HERA, MOTHER — SON ZAGREUS
SELENE, MOTHER — SON PAN

Because from her all things sprang and she is part of all, her symbols and personifications are many and of both sexes, often androgynous. The earliest record of a sex attributed to the moon (after the ambiguity of the cosmic egg) is that of female—the Great Mother. As the moon was also considered the source of the fertilization of women, she was alternately personified as a male, the husband of fertile women, as Pan and Osiris, young lovers of the Great Mother. These sex changes represent her wholeness. She is complete within herself, capable of creation through balance of her inner aspects.

At first it seems that these aspects were valued equally, seen as different though essential parts of a whole system, a complete cycle, from which any loss caused damage. A true ecology. But from time to time, for political motives, one aspect or the other was more celebrated and an attempt was made to create hierarchy: the most outstanding example of such a phase in our recorded history is the era of witch burning in which worship of the moon cycles and of the goddess was outlawed by the Christian Church, and patriarchal sun worship was established by military force. Records of this time were also burned and history distorted so that information of goddess worship, which was so strong thousands were willing to die for their beliefs, is difficult to unearth. But records exist, written as well as oral. And the records are well worth studying to give us a better sense of our heritage and a better understanding of the source of the intensity of some of our current struggles.

Many feminist scholars are researching and developing theories which illuminate the history of civilization. The following chronologies are all attempts to delineate the phases her worship has gone through and her various personifications, offspring and comrades.

THE MOON GOD

Sandra Roos

Sandra Roos, who lives and teaches in California, has collected over 5,000 slides on ancient female symbolism and over 17,000 slides of women's art. Her research took her farther and farther back, finally into prehistory where "everything seemed to come together." She is working on a study which traces the shift from matriarchal to patriarchal consciousness and how this is expressed in symbolism.

Many scholars believe that the moon goddess appeared rather late in mythology and that she was preceded by a male moon god. Not only is there a great deal of factual evidence supporting this theory, but the very nature of the original goddess herself suggests it. In prehistoric times the Great Goddess was a cosmic diety. She was the vast void who gave birth to all living things, including the sun, moon and stars. According to mythology, she conceived parthenogenically and the first son she bore matured to become her lover. Having a male child was one proof of her androgyny and hence her godhood: she was not only female but male as well and could make manifest a male likeness. (A daughter was the re-creation of this androgynous self—a double—and the mythic figure Kore of the Eleusinian mysteries became a symbol of transformation, self-realization and fusion with the original mother Demeter.)

As goddess of the cosmic night, her first son-lover was probably the moon. He was the bringer of the moisture of night that made life grow (unlike the sun who was believed by many to dry up the fruits of the earth). He was the emissary of the goddess who engendered in the wombs of women the rhythms of the macrocosm enabling them to relive in microcosm the original act of creation. In ecstatic night rituals, women spoke through him and under his light to the ultimate source of all light and life, death and rebirth: the Great Goddess.

Historic man, looking for a diety in his own likeness, could no more identify with the moon god and his subservience to the goddess than he could with the bull, her sacrificial victim (moon-kings could be sacrificed as well). He chose the sun as his emblem and the goddess soon became identified exclusively with the moon, though many of her rituals continued to have cosmic significance. To historic man, however, the new moon goddess was only the polar opposite of his sun god and no longer the original unifying source of them both. The male image itself became a symbol of analytic division and separatism, while the image of the female came to suggest the unconscious, a lost world searching for the mythic images and rituals that had once been its means of articulation.

MYTH AND HISTORY

Z. Budapest, now living and working in Los Angeles, California, has compiled a chronology of the events surrounding the transformations of the goddess religions. The following is a paraphrase of her chronology:

Alexander "The Great" burned the libraries containing the sacred scrolls of the matriarchy, the maps, astrological discoveries, medicine and other learning compiled by the preceding woman-oriented culture. Tribes coming from the north into what we now call Greece found a matriarchal culture, High Priestesses and Triple Goddess temples. For 300 years these pastoral tribes were assimilated by the Hera Triple Goddess culture. It is a span of time of peace with almost no archaeological evidence of weapons. The Greeks gave up their concept of marriage in favor of the fertility magic of the priestesses. Hera adopted their male god, Dios, as her son and renamed him Zeus, after her real son Zagreus.

More tribes came in from the south side of the Danube and opposed the matriarchies. Sthenelus, leader of the Achaeans, disavowed Hera's sovereignty, claiming Zeus had no mother. However, the worship of the goddess was continued for the sake of the crops, but independent priestesses were tortured and goddess worshippers were persecuted until they swore allegiance to Zeus. Sthenelus reorganized the religion around Dios, naming him Father Zeus, Almighty Ruler and giving him Hera in marriage (an institution not formerly sacred to her). The goddess Artemis of the New Moon was relegated the title, "huntress."

The Boeotians and Athenians were outraged at the dethroning of Artemis and demanded she be included with her own name. She was, but with revised mythology stating that her mother denounced her so she turned to Zeus and was reborn from his head.

The power of Persephone, Goddess of the Underworld and Death was feared by the patriarchs for her sovereignty over destruction. A new myth was devised that said she married Zeus' brother, Hades. The Palasgians regarded this event as rape and the story handed down to us retains this interpretation. Stories of abduction and banishment to the underworld abound. Zeus then gradually became famous for his rape-exploits of women and the concept of female persecution and subjugation became sanctified. His wife was relegated the role of a frustrated hysteric.

The Egyptian patriarchs also revised their matriarchal mythology so that the story we have is that Ra, sun, deposed Hathor, his mother.

In Sumeria, where matriarchies had been most ancient and successful, Namu, Goddess of the Sea, had her sex changed to that of her male grandchild, Enil. Babylonian mythology was altered so that the god Marduk was given the province of law and order; the Goddess Tiamat was given Chaos. Then Marduk chops her up, using her body to make parts of the world.

The Christians made up a far-fetched explanation of birth in the story of Eve being formed from Adam's rib. Woman was credited with the corruption of men by leading them to other kinds of knowledge.

o   o   o

THE GODDESS IN ART

Robert Graves, in THE WHITE GODDESS compiles a history of the personifications of the Greek muse. The story of the change of poetic focus from magic to 'reason' describes the political changes taking place which marked the overthrow of matriarchy, the establishment of the police state and the subjugation of women:

At first Cerridwen is the Triple Muse, the Great Goddess of poetry and incantation. She has a son, a seasonal god, who is simultaneously her lover and her victim, the Demon of the Waxing Year.

In later myths, reflecting political shifts in power, she is courted by a rebellious star-son, the Thunder God by whom she has twins. The rebellious Thunder God takes over some of her muse powers of lawmaking and oaths. Then she becomes identified with her star-daughter and, therefore, relegated to dividing her poetic powers with her now twin-male-star-brother. Later she is multiplied into the Ninefold Muse (departmentalized inspiration), her power divided and dispersed.

This paves the way for the male twin Apollo to declare himself the Eternal Sun and the nine muses become his maids-in-waiting. To finish it off Apollo delegates their former dominions to his male cohorts.

Eventually, the Virgin Mary becomes the holder of the cauldron of inspiration, the spirit behind creation, the Dove, the holy spirit, the Grail. She is a behind-the-throne muse, necessary but robbed of her divinity and her independence.

o   o   o

70

MODERN MOON-CONSCIOUSNESS

Esther Harding, in WOMAN'S MYSTERIES, comments on the effects of this political shift and on the current movement toward reestablishing balance:

In the image of the Mother Goddess—ancient and powerful—women of olden times found the reflection of their own deepest feminine nature. Through the faithful performance of the ritual prescribed in her service those faraway women gained a relation to this very Eros. Today, the goddess is no longer worshipped. Her shrines are lost in the dust of ages while her statues line the walls of museums. But the law or power of which she was but the personification is unabated in its strength and life-giving potency. It is we who have changed. We have given our allegiance too exclusively to masculine forces. Today, however, the ancient feminine principle is reasserting its power. Forced on by the suffering and unhappiness incurred through disregard of the Eros values, men and women are turning once again towards the Moon Mother, not, however, through a religious cult, not even with a conscious knowledge of what they are doing, but through a change in psychological attitude. For that principle, which in ancient and more naive days was projected into the form of a goddess, is no longer seen in the guise of a religious tenet but is now sensed as a psychological force arising from the unconscious, having, as had the Magna Dea of old, power to mold the destinies of mankind.[8]

While over head the Moon Sits Arbitress.

—Milton, Paradise Lost, 1667

Time/Period	European and Celtic	Fertile Crescent and Africa
Prehistoric (Upper Paleolithic)	ca. 24,000 B.C., Ice Age Earliest "Venus" figurines ranging from Russia to the Pyrennees. ca. 10,000 B.C. Pre-Celtic mare goddess-Epona Epona as Giant White Horse on Chalk Downs in England.	 Venus Figurines
7,000 B.C. ~ 2,000 B.C.	Neolithic fertility goddesses Norfolk, England, found with sacrifices in Neolithic mines. Three Aspected Brigid. 7,000-6,000 Pottery figures with hybrid torso of human female buttocks and bird's body. 5,000 Bone figure of Great Goddess in Balkans. 5,000 Moon Goddess as dog in Eastern Europe.	Isis in Egypt. 3,000 Inanna in Sumeria. 2,300 Ishtar in Babylonia-Assyria. 2,100 Astarte in Israël. 2,000 Lilith - Sumer 2,000 Assyrian moontree of life. Mawu, Africa. Assyrian Moon Tree
2,000 B.C. to Christianity	Britomartis of poetry, smithcraft and healing. Lugad, moon of Ireland. Gothic "Moon" Madonna	1,800 Canaanite Lady Asherath of the Sea. 1,200 Canaanite Anath shown with Pharoah Ramses II of Egypt. 500 Chaldeans worship planet Venus as Ishtar.
Christianity to Present	Virgin Mary, the moon of our church. Black Virgin of the Gypsies Maybride of Merry England. St. Lua(n). St. Brigit.	Worship shifts to her son, husband and priests - Kaaba cleftstone. Akua' Ba - Ashanti, Africa. Pe, Pygmy Moon Goddess.

Moon Goddess

Aegean and Mediteranean	Mezo American and Oceania	Far East
Prehistoric Cretan cave worship in HeraKleion of goddess as stalagmite-later Known as Eileithyia. *Dove Goddess, Crete*	*UnKatahe, Native American*	*Lotus of the Full Moon, India*
Black Demeter in Pre-Hellenic Greece, worshipped as horse and as sow. 2,000 Selene as moon in Greece. 2,000 Aphrodite 4,000 Britomartis and DiKtynna in Crete. 3,000 Cretan SnaKe Goddess.	4,000 "Venus" figures in Mexico. Hina of Hawaii. *Polynesian Moon Goddesses* *Oceanic*	*Ch'ang-O, Goddess of the Moon, China*
1,500 Earliest Known temple of Demeter mysteries in Eleusis. 1,400 Hittite — Goddess of Arinna, Wurusemu. 1,100 Dove Goddess worship in Crete. Hera, the brave. Aphrodite of love.	900 B.C. Olmec-3 petalled flower used as motif- later became symbol of Aztec Lady of the Flowering Earth. 200 B.C. Teotihua cano Pyramid of the Moon.	Ch'ang-O, Moon of China. Lotus. Ma-Tsu-P'o, Taoist Queen of Heaven. Maja Jotma. Sarasvati of Healing. ParashaKti, India
Virgin Mary of the Bears. (SnaKe Goddess, Mediterranean)	Worship of the BlacK Virgin, Queen of the Night. Hinenui-te-po, Polynesian Mother of the Night. UnKatahe, Native American	TsuKi-Yomi, Counter of the Months, Japan.

A woman with her arms upraised is one of the basic forms of the moon symbol. In different ways this then was transformed into the animals, people and their symbols thought to be closely related to the particular powers of the moon.

o   o   o

They play a game. It is performed on an enormous parade-ground. The ground is divided into zones corresponding to the colours of the spectrum. There are a hundred and fifty violet hoops a hundred and fifty indigo hoops a hundred and fifty blue hoops a hundred and fifty green hoops a hundred and fifty yellow hoops a hundred and fifty orange hoops a hundred and fifty red hoops. The teams consist of seventy-five persons each, arranged on either side of the midline of the paradeground. Each team has equal strips of violet indigo blue green yellow orange red territory. A machine situated at the centre of the parade-ground ejects the hoops one after the other at a fast pace. They rise vertically above the heads of the players. They rotate on themselves. At the same time they describe a vast circle which continually increases, due to the momentum imparted to them by the machine. The path of their movements would be an immense spiral. The women playing must catch the hoops without leaving the colored zones allotted to them. Very soon there is an indescribable tumult of bodies jostling each other in the attempt to take hold of the same hoop or to withdraw from the confusion.

—Monique Wittig, Les Guerilleres[26]

SYMBOLS

A Symbol is a representation of something else thought to convey the essence or aspect of the other. It is different from a picture which predominantly seeks to convey outer aspects. A painting of a turtle could be intended as a nature study, or as a representation of the concept of steadiness and slowness. Greyhound dogs are usually associated with speed. A painting of a turtle and a greyhound together can become a visual story of the contrast between steadiness and speed. In this way symbols can become a language.

People develop individual symbols which have meaning only to themselves. Groups develop communal symbols of agreed meaning. The interpretation of some symbols seems to be universally shared; there are several symbols representing aspects attributed to the moon which appear to be worldwide. The colors often symbolic of the moon are black, white, silver and blue. White and silver represent her light. Blue and black represent night, germination and the original void.

Basic geometric shapes which are often symbols of the moon are the circle and the crescent. Related to these are three-dimensional forms such as the cup, the cauldron, the boat and the coffin—all containers having to do with wood and water. Another geometric shape related to the moon is the triangle. In its three-dimensional form it becomes a cone or a pillar.

Animals associated with the moon are ones associated with the qualitites of fertility and transformation (such as the rabbit and the snake). Some animals are associated with the moon because of their visual kinship, thus any crescent-horned animal is in her dominion. So are water animals such as fish and crabs, as are all nocturnal animals. Birds associated with her are doves, peacocks and swans.

I have ascribed four elements to the moon which seem to be universally symbolic of lunar qualities: blood, water, fire and stone—vitality, mutability, illumination, permanence. Plants connected with the moon are usually symbolic of her qualities, or connected to her other symbols, or are trance-inducing plants used as medicine or in the orgiastic and visionary rites: the willow, the oak, soma, mistletoe, lily, palm.

The egg is a symbol which unites almost all her aspects—the circle, the cone, birds, fertility, origin, the female. The egg of the world symbol refers to the moon and to the concept that the moon is mother and source of fertility to earth. It is also the shape of the orbit of the moon.

Knowing something about the intended meaning of these symbols, we can read the language of ancient texts and art to understand more about what other times and cultures knew and thought about the moon. In the time of the witch burnings and persecutions symbols became a relatively safe means of communicating among the initiated and of preserving knowledge and tradition. Many ancient works of art which researchers find "unexplainable" tell matriarchial or moon stories, whose symbols the patriarchs no longer recognize and are resistant to interpreting in this light. Two such instances which particularly interest me are the recent discovery of a Han Dynasty woman's tomb in China and a series of French tapestries from the fifteen hundreds called, "Woman with the Unicorn."

An article in National Geographic magazine describes the finding of a tomb containing a Chinese noblewoman from early Han Dynasty, over 2,100 years ago. She was mummified and entombed to preserve her soul and record of her life in accordance with strict Han Dynasty tradition. Her sixty-five foot high burial ground was excavated because it stood in the way of a hospital project in 1972 in Ch'ansha, capital of the Hunan Province.

The outer coffins contained fantastic treasures of silks, lacquerware, eggs, fruits, grains, wooden statuettes of attendants to help her, musical instruments and paintings, all entombed according to the "Chinese Book of Rites." The innermost casket—under twenty layers of silk—held a very un-decayed body of the noblewoman, the best preserved mummy found in China.

One hundred and thirty-eight melon seeds were found in her stomach, suggesting that her heart attack occurred right after breakfast; she was fifty years old. Found with her were herbal medicine packets of cinnamon, magnolia bark, peppercorns, all modern Chinese prescriptions for heart disease. Symbols on her casket were clouds, deer, unicorn, cranes, and horses. Her fei i, or flying garment, a robe to take her to the land of the dead, is embroidered with a woman being carried to the moon on dragon's wings. In the moon is a rabbit, a toad, and a serpent.

The official guess is that she is Lady Ch'eng, a consort of Emperor Ching (156-141 B.C. reign). Lady Ch'eng was notorious for substituting a maidservant, Lady Tang, for herself one night when the Emperor called. The maid bore a son who became a prince. The two women were lifelong friends and were buried near each other. Since the **National Geographic** article of May, 1974, archaeologists have found another woman's tomb and believe the two women were lovers.

The article originally ended by saying, **and when we open the other tomb, whose wife shall we find?** After the second excavation now it is clear that the two women were lovers and that many of the articles of pictures in the tombs have to do with their long friendship. How many other queens, women lovers and independent women's records have been found and interpreted as **somebody's wife,** because no other possibility was decipherable to the patriarchal archaeologist's eyes?

Another such find is the series of French tapestries from the early 1500's known as **La Dame de la Licorne**. They are six 12-foot by 15-foot tapestries depicting a woman accompanied by lions and unicorns. The official conjecture is that the tapestries were a wedding present to a noblewoman, Claude le Viste. Five of the tapestries are thought to represent the five senses. Now they are in the Musée de Cluny, Paris. To my eyes, the goddess is present throughout these tapestries and the subject ought to be no mystery. The first tapestry called "Á mon Seul Desir" depicts a woman in a blue and gold tent flanked by a lion, a unicorn, many goats, dogs, rabbits, birds and another woman. The lion and unicorn are holding up two banners covered with blue and silver crescent moons. Fruit trees around the tent bear oranges, figs, acorns and holly berries. Flowers and herbs cover the dark red background. The noblewoman in the center is opening a chest of jewels. If they are marriage tapestries, the woman is well attended by lunar fertility familiars. The blue tent has stylized flames embroidered on it and every fruit, flower, animal and symbol marks her as moon-blessed. "Mon Seul Desir" could be her partner or the moon herself, whose favor was required for happiness in love, and who was thought to be the real "husband" of women. There are many treasurers such as these through which older moon-conscious cultures speak to us. The symbolic language is worth learning.

The circle is a universal symbol of wholeness, without beginning or end. Thus it also represents the un-datable cycle of the universe, the original, the source and the eventual return to the source. The moon, as origin of the world, as source of life as well as destination of dead souls, is often symbolized by the circle.

The circle is a particularly female symbol, as it corresponds to the os or circular opening to the womb from which we all enter life. Roundness is considered a particularly female quality and corresponds to the circle of the full moon. The circle is also symbolic of repetitive cycles such as the lunar cycle. It is a peculiarly dual symbol combining the element of movement suggested by a circle with the fixed element of constancy.

Variations of the circle are: the dot or point as an abbreviated circle, a representation of origin and infinity; a hole (the Chinese Pi or sky symbol) represents a gateway or transition point to another state of consciousness. The circle with a hole in the center is representative of the concept of "the moving center" or the eternal yet transforming life force. Many mandalas with depicted or imaginable centers are variations of this form and are supposed to function as gateways to other planes through contemplation. A pole (the May Pole) is often used to mark and represent the mystic point of center. The center is also represented by the cross, as the place of intersection of its two lines is the center point. The number two is considered a lunar number, representing reflection, echo, integration and duality, the double.

When the Holy Grail appears it is usually depicted materializing at the center of the Round Table, surrounded by the twelve Zodiac knights, and representing the realization of the ultimate, or paradise regained. The Dalai Lama also had a round council of twelve Namshams. A frequent Chinese symbol of the ultimate being is a point of light radiating concentric circles.

The circle is a symbol of unity and oneness. A stone or gem is often said to exist at the Center. A cromlech, or sacred stone with a carved hole is a combination of these symbols. The spiral is a symbol representing the potential center. It symbolizes the breath of the spirit power, the dance; as a symbol of the relationship between multiplicity and unity, it denotes cosmic forms in motion, and the rotation of heavenly bodies. It is either contracting like a whirlpool, expanding like the nebula, or ossified like a snail shell. It is related to the lunar animals, water, healing and its relationship to ecstasy. The double spiral is the hermaphrodite or the hourglass.

The cone is supposed to be a synthesis of all other shapes and thus a symbol of wholeness. The more dimensions a shape has the less spiritual, or farther away from the elemental source it is supposed to be. Thus the cone having structure takes on a more physical and material suggestion than the circle. The cone is considered to be a particularly female symbol related to feminine anatomy. It is a kind of rounded or circular pyramid, symbolic of the earth and the great mother. Since the pyramid is a unified combination of several forms (square, triangle, point, center) it represents the ultimate. Pyramids are also linked with fire by shape. The cone is the symbol of Astarte.

The crescent stands for the aspect of change and transformation in the world and is especially linked to water as a representation of the boat and the chalice. It represents the sickle of death, as well as the cup of life. Together with the star it is the symbol of paradise.

Three-dimensional variations of the circle, the crescent and the cone, linked with moon symbology, are boats, cradles, coffins, fans, mirrors, cauldrons, coffers, chests, bowls, boxes, baskets, stones, seeds, eggs, columns, combs, spiders and spheres. Each represents a variation of the moving-stationary eternal cycle. Boats carry one on journeys across the waters of the unconscious to other realms.

Cradles are boats to earthly life and sleep. Coffins are boats to the isle of the dead. Fans are triangular (pyramid and cone) feminine forms which appear and decrease. Mirrors are related to the reflective quality of the moon's light and to water as surfaces in which to glimpse one's soul. Cauldrons are crescent containers in which to brew lunar potions. Coffers and chests usually contain treasure, or the gem said to be contained at the center of the universe.

The moon is silver without and a jewel within, cool in both aspects, inner and outer.

—Buddhist saying

Bowls are related to boats and crescents and chests as containers of liquid and life essence (milk or wine). Baskets are boats or cups one can weave from water plants. Weaving is a symbol for the creation of the world. Stones are related in form to circles (and cones) and are supposed to be the elemental form of gems which are analogous to seeds, or concentrated life essence. In this sense they contain the spark of life, fire. Seeds and eggs are related as three-dimensional-crescent-shaped life essence containers. Eggs correspond to the zero or original void source. An egg is the origin and end of all effort, the return to the source being represented by the alchemist's search for the orphic egg. The Easter egg as a symbol of immortality is synonymous with the fruit containing the seed. The egg is also synonymous with the heart as the center of the body.

Columns (combinations of stones, cones, circles and poles) are linked with the tree which is supposed to stand at the center of the world. Towers are

Beautiful magical spider

I see you as magic, But are you? No one else seems to Think you are, only I do, But That's all that matters isn't it, Oh wonderful spider.

By Po Kutchins.

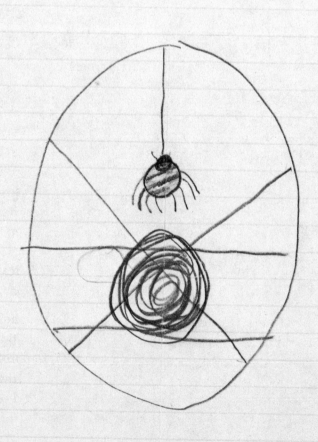

emblematic of the Virgin Mary. Combs are associated with boats, music and mermaids. They represent the transitory aspect of fertility.

Spiders in their webs, weavers like the Fates, are said to often be symbols of the moon hanging in the sky, spinning the cycles of the world; building, tearing down, and rebuilding. Spheres are combinations of many concentric circles, representative of the many orbits and layers of existence.

Cloth is another lunar symbol, purported to be the product of the moon's work. White cloth (the clouds) is produced for her people. It is also connected to the feminine symbolism of the veil, said to cover the mystery of the world. The veiled Isis represents one aspect of the moon.

INA-WHO-MAKES-WHITE-CLOTH   HINA THE MOTHER OF

THE BLACK STONE   KAABA OF MECCA   GNATOO

CLOTH MAKER OF THE FRIENDLY ISLANDS   TAPA CLOTH

MAKER OF HAWAII   CLOUD MAKER OF MANGAIA   THE

VEILED ISIS   THE SPIDER WEAVER   THE THREE FATES

THE MIRROR OF THE WORLD   MOONSTONE   THE

SILVER CHALICE   THE MERMAID COMB   FLEUR DE LIS

THE ROSE   THE KEY   THE GLOVE   THE PEARL

Another interesting correlation is that of most all of these forms with music. Most musical instruments are made in lunar forms. And music is said to symbolize godliness, life-energy, death, cyclical rhythm and yearning for the source. Most musical instruments seem to be perfect combinations of symbolic masculine and feminine shapes and, therefore, representative of androgyny, unity and sexuality.

Through singing or music blending of people's intangible spirits can be achieved. Thus musical harmony is a mystic sexual symbol representing the human possibility of the unity of our pure life energies.

The lyre in crescent form is sacred to Venus and the moon. Musical horns, made originally from crescent-shaped animal horns, are sacred to Diana.

I have named the "four elements" of the moon, water, blood, fire and stone. The moon and water are obviously connected by her gravitational regulation of the earth's tides. Blood and sea water are close in composition and both represent the elemental life fluid. Wine or juice is the symbolic ritual form of blood, drunk from a silver chalice. Stone represents the material of the moon, death, the seed of life, as well as being another form of the elemental substance of life and matter. Fire is the moon's light, generative power and illuminatory aspect. These elements figure in most ancient lunar temples and rituals.

The key, an attribute of Hecate, is related to the goddess as opener of the treasure chest, of the door to the world. Finding a key signifies the stage—after great difficulties—just prior to discovery of treasure.

All these symbols are connected to the representation of the maternal womb (often synonymous with the heart and the brain) as a chambered container of sustenance and transformation. And all these symbols are linked to the concept of the "mystery of the world" as containers of the secrets of life. Containers are wrappers for the mystical center. The Mother Goddess is the "Guardian of the Treasure."

The women say, truly is this not magnificent? The vessels are upright, the vessels have acquired legs. The sacred vessels are on the move.

—Monique Wittig

Animals related to the moon are either nocturnal or symbolize aspects of her cycle. All crescent horned animals (goats, Brahman bulls, Minoan bulls) are considered representatives of the moon. The cow is a particular combination of moon animal and female symbols of mother as milk-producer. All sea and water animals are in her domain as creatures particularly in tune with her cycles. The cow is the mother of the earth and the bull is her son. As the son, the sacrified bull represents the death of the crescent moon to bring back the full. They are sacred to Venus.

Indus bull

Brahman bull

Animals regarded as lunar are those which alternate between appearance and disappearance: amphibians, caterpillars which become butterflies, the snail which leaves its shell and returns to it, the bear which vanishes in winter and reappears in spring. Lunar objects are those which can alter their surface area (like the fan and the mirror). There is a morphological relationship between the bull, on account of its fast growing horns, and the waxing aspect of the moon, which is further evidence of the bull's symbolic function as an invigorator. The worship of the moon and horns is the worship of the creative and fecund powers of nature. They are symbols of becoming, of continuous striving toward wholeness, rather than the end result, the active process of creation.

Shells as moon symbols are a combination of the container, water and regeneration.

Frogs, toads, weasels, nightjar birds, wolves, fireflies, rats, moths, hedgehogs, bats, may beetles, pyrogota flies, owls, bedbugs, burying beetles, cockroaches and cats are all nocturnal animals. Frogs are combined water and transformation symbols as they can acclimate to air breathing or water breathing. They symbolize the connection between water and earth. Some legendary evolutionary theories held that people evolved from frogs, hence the prince can be transformed from the toad. The letter M, symbol of the legs and pubic triangle of the Great Mother, became associated with the shape of the toad.

Wax, silver and wood toad sculptures are common today as votive offerings in the churches of Bavaria, Austria, Hungary, Moravia and Yugoslavia. Toad meat was eaten to induce labor and a glandular extract of toads has been found to cause abortions. The foetus at one time was thought to be a toad which crawled into the womb. The toad is also said to have a prismatic effect on light due to a jewel in the center of its forehead. It is the symbol of peyote vision in South America.

The cat was associated by the Egyptians with the moon and was sacred to Isis and Bast. The black cat is the dark of the moon. It's capacity to see at night is associated with the concept of the moon's vision. Sphinxes are cat-variations representing the great mystery guarding the secret of life and death. Sphinxes are part lion and many mother goddesses had lion heads. Tigers are the Chinese monsters of darkness. Dragons are variations of sphinxes (as cat-snakes). The cat is related to the symbol of the mother as hunter.

Other animals representative of the hunt are the doe and the <u>deer</u> both sacred to Diana. The deer is considered miraculous because it can regenerate its horns. Other lunar symbols of <u>rebirth</u> are: the moth as the symbol of the soul looking for the light in the night; the swan as a water creature which can become an air creature and which makes music; the snake which cyclically sheds its skin. Certain <u>birds</u> are sacred to the moon because of their color, shape, or water association and because they can alternate between and connect earth, water and sky. The dove is sacred to Venus, as is the peacock. The swallow and the blue bird are sacred to Isis. Athena appears as an owl, Aphrodite as a goose (Mother Goose?).

The moon is associated with <u>sheep</u> through the allegory of her being the shepherdess of the flock of stars, her children. <u>Horses</u> and <u>dogs</u> are also associated with moon goddesses. The horse is a symbol of female independence and beauty. Dogs are guardians of women and of the gates of night or the underworld. Sheepdogs are guardians of the flock or of the children of the mother. Animals symbolic of lunar fertility are the <u>rabbit</u> and the <u>pig</u>. The ancient prescription against eating pork, kin to the prescription against eating sacred cows in India, stems from the pig's symbolic representation of the Mother Goddess. The crescent tusks of boars represent the lunar crescent.

Toes Game
Let us go to the woods, says this pig;
What to do there? says that pig;
To look for mother, says this pig;
What to do with her? says that pig;
To kiss her, to kiss her, says this pig.

Rabbits are sacred to Hecate, and in China a common folk myth is that the moon is populated by rabbits. This lunar association is the origin of the lucky rabbit's foot.

The <u>bee</u> is a symbol of complexity in its relation to the moon. There is an ancient saying, "the bee is born of the ox." The ox or bull represents earth and the bee the soul, so the symbology is that the earth produces souls. The queen of the hive is the mother symbol. Bees swarming to the hive were symbols of souls returning to the source. Bees were purported to be the builders of the temples in Delphi. Priestesses of Demeter were called Melissae, or bees. The scarab and the bee are two insects associated with the moon because they have crescent-shaped wings and antennae. Bees, moths and butterflies symbolize rebirth.

<u>Milk</u>, the complete food miraculously produced by women and female animals, was associated with the moon because of her connection with women, birth, life essence and the color white. <u>Honey</u>, as the health-giving food produced

Diana of the hunt

croissantée

by bees was considered a miraculous perfect food. The combination of milk and honey was the original ambrosia or food of the gods. The Land of Milk and Honey is paradise or return to the perfect protected source. Other foods associated with the moon are: dates, olives, bread, cakes, wine, fish and rice.

Of all the plants associated with the moon, the <u>tree</u> is most basic: the tree of life at the center of the world, the world axis, the cross, the grove, the bower. Diana's temples were in groves. The willow was sacred to Hecate, Circe and Persephone as a water tree and an herb against rheumatism. The Druids gave the forest to the sun in marriage as a symbol of the sun's opposite—dark, moist, fertile, earthly. Trees were ritually decorated to honor the Great Goddess. The May Pole is a symbolic spring flower tree; decorating the Christmas tree is a winter solstice ritual. Fruit is the egg of a tree, carrying the mysterious seed of the Great Mother. Throughout history wood has been a mother symbol and rituals involving burning wood impart fertilizing powers to the ashes. The bower is an ancient symbol of the Virgin Mary. The oak, a symbol of long life is sacred to Diana. Palm trees are often **considered the tree of life.**

Related to the tree, the <u>cross</u> is a symbol of the center or source manifest on earth (while the circle represents the source in the heavens). It combines the symbols of tree (wood); center (point where lines cross); star (squint and you'll see a cross); the crossroads (the moment of truth, the choice of which path). In these aspects the cross is the symbol of the earthly agent of the mother, her star-son, her sacrificial son, her sheep, her messenger. It is also a symbol of the union of **opposites and, therefore, of the androgyny, or gynarchy, of the moon and the source.**

The three main <u>flowers</u> associated with the goddess are: the rose, the lily and the lotus. The rose is a symbol of love and perfection and sacred to Venus and Diana. Like the lotus, its form represents the mystic center inside many layers. The rose and the lotus are forms of the mandala. **The jewel in the lotus** is the joy found at the center of one's own being through contemplation of the ultimate and adherence to her principles. The lily, being white, is a symbol of light and purity; standing in a jar of water it is a symbol of the Virgin Mary. Water is the life source and closely connected with all three plants. It is interesting that the zodiacal sign of Pisces so closely resembles the fleur-de-lis.

A few night blooming plants are: cereus, jasmine, primrose, gladeolus tristis, nymphaea, petunia axillaris, saponaria, selene noctiflora, yucca (some species). Most night blooming plants are tropical, white and redolent. They are thought to be pollinated by night-flying insects, mainly moths. Flowering plants with thorns, such as the Rose of Venus or the Holly of the Virgin, symbolize the inseparable cycle of life and death.

88

O Tannenbaum

Traditional German

TRIFORMIS OF GREECE ⊗

THE THREEFOLD MINOAN DOVE ⊗

NANA THE TRIPARTITE MOON OF ASSYRIA ⊗

PARASHAKTI THE TRIMURTI MOTHER OF INDIA ⊗

MOIKA OF DEATH   ILITHYIA OF BIRTH   CALLONE OF

BEAUTY ⊗ MA-TSU-P'O THE TAOIST QUEEN OF HEAVEN AND

HER TWO ATTENDANTS ⊗ LUNA OF HEAVEN   DIANA

OF EARTH   HECATE OF THE UNDERWORLD   OF

GREECE ⊗ DIANA   JANA   JANUS   OF ROME ⊗

HINA THE SKY QUEEN   HAUMEA THE EARTH MOTHER

PELE THE UNDERWORLD FIRE OF HAWAII ⊗ HILDE

THE SKY   HOLDA MOTHER EARTH   HEL OF DEATH

OF NORTHERN EUROPE ⊗ CELTIC BRIGIT OF POETRY, OF

HEALING, OF SMITHCRAFT ⊗ THE TRIPLE MUSE OF POETRY,

MUSIC AND THE ARTS ⊗ THE THREE FATES

COSMOLOGIES

Astrology, alchemy, palmistry, tarot and magic are related ancient systems for describing the order of the universe and our relationship to it. Most of their teachings are passed down to us in symbolic language which became secret because the practice of them was for a time outlawed by the Christian church. Symbolic language was used also because a symbol is attributed with more power than verbal description, as a closer representation of universal essences which are beyond words.

In each of these systems, the moon is a prominent symbol. The word zodiac (meaning circle of animals) refers to the apparent path of moon, sun and stars along a band of particular constellations during a full year. In astrology, the moon represents the personality, the physical body, matter, the mother and the cycle of earthly life. It is an indicator of psychic ability and is thought to be the special ruler of babies and women. Her influence operates mainly at night and in a monthly cycle. Her influence on men is in the realm of dreams, magic, madness and love. Over women, she holds a close and mysterious regulating power manifest in our menstrual cycles. She is thought to be the consort to the sun, equal in power. She is patroness of birth, death, sex and imagination, and in her shining image one can perceive the reflection of one's self. The fourth sign of the zodiac, Cancer, is said to be under special influence of the moon, as the mediator between the concrete and the formless.

Sue Handley, an astrologer who works through the San Francisco Metaphysical Center on Sutter Street, has written the following explanation of the meaning of the moon in an astrological birth chart. She read my chart and told me that since my moon was in Pisces in the ninth House, it indicated a possible ability to write, deal with publishing, and lots of travel! And that because i have Cancer Rising, i am "moon rules." (My sun is in Leo.)

The Moon in Astrology

Sue Handley

The moon in astrology is the personality, that part of a person which extends into the material world. Like water, it is the flowing part, ruling all kinds of changing things, the growing part of the personality that others come into contact and must deal with.

If the moon falls in one of the water signs (Cancer, Scorpio and Pisces) you will find a very emotional person, someone volatile who is given to "watery" things, intuition, psychic ability, music, the sea. These are people that need to live close to water, by a stream, a river bank, or if possible, by the ocean. They are very often sailors, people who love to swim, get involved in water sports, or have a career related to some form of liquid. The moon is what we call 'dignified' in Cancer, and it operates best. People with moon in Cancer are very loving, giving, outgoing, emotional, affectionate.

If the moon happens to fall in one of the air signs, (Gemini, Libra, Aquarius) you have a more intellectual person, who really enjoys playing games, loves communicating, loves to argue for argument's sake, loves to deal with writing, poetry, theatre, teaching. Intellectual communication will be extremely important to those people.

If the moon is in an earth sign (Taurus, Virgo or Capricorn) you will find someone who is practical. The earth in astrology deals with essential things, taste, touch, smell, feel, anything you can see, measure, weigh, classify. You find people with the moon in these signs into classification. Often they are artists.

Moon in Taurus people love to create beauty and to surround themselves with beauty. If the moon is in Virgo, very often they are teachers or nurses, or in any of the medical professions—anything making people feel more comfortable, or equipping people for a better life so that they can have things. In Capricorn, they are most often business-oriented, although people with moon in Capricorn are a special breed apart because that's the position **opposite** its strongest position. People with moon in Capricorn have warm emotions, but seem to be trapped in. They are afraid of rejection. They fear to be rejected by lovers and, therefore, they often break up relationships they would like to keep.

People with the moon in a fire sign (Aries, Leo or Saggitarius) are very energetic, active, self-starters. They will probably be very sportsminded, or at least love to travel. They are always starting things but not always particularly good at finishing. The exception is the moon in Leo, which gives a stick-to-it asset that the other fire signs do not have. They're going, moving; they do not like to be bored; they do not want to sit down. They like activity all the time.

The moon in a chart also relates to the person's mate, very often describing the mate of a person, whether it be male or female. Someone whose moon is in Aries, for example, will be very much attracted to Aries or the opposite sign, Libra people. Gemini marry or are attracted to Gemini or Saggitarius people. Moon in Virgo attracts Virgo and Pisces, etc. around the chart.

To be "afflicted" in a chart means to have negative angles receiving rays from negative planets, or from a positive planet coming in a negative way, such as an opposition or square position, that will bring difficulties to the mate of the person. It will also bring moods and depressions and frustrations, discouragements. When the moon is afflicted it is not so much a concrete as an emotional obstruction, a feeling of not being able to function properly. A classic example would be when Saturn is going through a sign conjuncting, opposing, or squaring a person's moon, the person would run into a long series of anxiety attacks, probably lasting about 18 months or more.

If the moon is receiving positive rays either from a positive planet or from beneficial angles, even from the so-called negative planets, the person will find their intuition and judgement greatly enhanced. They will find themselves dealing with women and children in a more successful way than usual. The moon in a chart has to do with women and children, and if it is in good aspect to the sun, or in good aspect to the planets of the chart, the individual will get along well with women and children. If it is afflicted, they will have difficulty with women and children. For example, Saturn opposing the moon in a natal chart would indicate that women will "let you down from the beginning." It could mean the loss of a mother at an early age, which is, of course, the classic let down. Whereas if the moon is in good aspect to Jupiter, the mother will always be a help and a benefit.

The moon also represents the mother, and the way you get along with your mother will largely tell you how you will get along with your mate. It is also interesting to note how often people marry or at least become involved with people born on their mother's birthday. If you ask around, you will find it is a frequent occurrence for the first love! You can then really tell how things will be in that relationship by remembering how things went between themselves and their mother, although, of course, it can be worked out better when on an adult level.

The position of the moon puts a great deal of energy in the particular house where it is found in the chart. Each house, or segment of the chart, rules a specific area of your life, and wherever you find the moon, you will find a great deal of activity. If it falls in the first house, the activity will be something that has to do with personal expression. If it is in the second house, there will be activity and careers involving money, gambling, taking chances, fluctuating income. A third house moon would likely be someone involved in commerce or teaching. Fourth house would be someone who would spend a great deal of time at home, maybe work at home. Fifth house, the person would be very much involved with children and young people, or with the arts. Sixth house would likely be a nurse, a medical person, a teacher, or someone in public service. Seventh house moon has to do with mates and partners, and the person would get along best with women; communication with love and affection will center around women. Eighth house will have a great deal of intuitive, psychic ability, possibly ability to communicate with people on the other side of the astral plane. Ninth house people would be likely to spend a good part of their time in foreign countries, doing a lot of foreign travel and/or involvement with universities and publishing. Tenth house people will be oriented toward women or young people. Eleventh house people will have mostly women for friends, as apart from business partners and mates, etc. Twelfth house people would be in touch with occult things, psychic phenomena and involved with large institutions. The moon will also indicate the number of children. Actually, if you read one of the so-called sun sign books, you will find they are more accurate if read from the standpoint of where the moon is. Our sun sign represents such a deep part that we often keep it hidden, but everybody sees our moon. It represents the part of us which is out front and shining, and that we express through.

When the Moon is in your sign, you are at your Lunar Cycle high at your best physically, emotionally and mentally. In the opposite sign, you are at your low. Plan to do important things at your high point, and routine matters on your low. Aries is opposite Libra. Taurus is opposite Scorpio. Gemini is opposite Sagittarius. Cancer is opposite Capricorn. Leo is opposite Aquarius. Virgo is opposite Pisces.

Of course, there are all kinds of variations with a chart. You have to look at the angles of every other planet to the moon, the position within the house and the degrees. This is a general cast, but I think you can get a good idea that the moon, since it is the closest heavenly body to the earth, is the most important indicator in an astrological chart.

☆   ☆   ☆

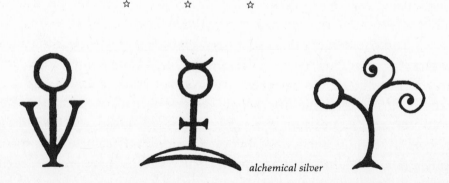

alchemical silver

Alchemy

Alchemy is related to astrology in its symbolism and its vision of the zodiacal world order. At its core is a philosophy of chemistry which parallels the transformation of certain elements into gold with the transformation of the human soul into an enlightened state. Therefore, the instructive occupation or Great Work of an alchemist is the continuous process of trying to change, by adherence in practice to strict cosmological laws, base metal into gold. The elements must be combined in a certain order to create the spiritual Philosopher's Stone, usually in the shape of an egg. Silver, representing the moon is among the stone's ingredients and represents the volatile or mutable principle and multiplicity. The meaning of the symbol of the hermaphrodite, often used in alchemy as a symbol of the ultimately evolved person, is explained in an old French text as, **That which failed to become two in one flesh, will succeed in becoming two in one spirit.**

Tarot

The tarot was one of the books of knowledge in the matriarchal libraries of Alexandria which Alexander the "Great" burned down. Afterwards, ancient scientists and scholars devised another set. What we have today are mutations of the old ones, but they are clues to ancient matriarchal knowledge. The pattern in which the tarot cards is laid out is intended to facsimilate the tree of life, the symbol of the goddess at the center of the world. It is important, as in all altered systems, to apply interpretations to the symbols clear of current sexist attitudes, to alter them to your intuition. The moon card represents voluntary slow change. It has to do with developing a new personality. It is a card of positive evolution (unless surrounded with sword cards, representing hidden enemies). The picture on the moon card, the eighteenth enigma, usually shows a crab in the mud, dogs barking at the moon in which is a woman, two castles in front of mountains and woods and inverted drops of water being drawn from the earth to the moon. It is said to teach the strengths and dangers of the world of appearances and imagination. Older moon cards hold the image of a harpist singing in the moonlight to a young woman letting down her hair. The second enigma of the tarot is the card of The Great Priestess, a representation of Isis as the goddess of night. She is seated on a throne between two columns joined by a veil. She leans against a sphinx and wears a crescent crown. She signifies on the negative side, intolerance, and on the positive, moral clarity and the wisdom of women.

Palmistry

In Palmistry a portion of a person's hand is named 'the Mount of the Moon.' It is the section of the palm marked off for indications of one's receptive, inner life and is said to relate to the aspects of sensuality and creativity. The size (relative to the size of the hand), shape, ridge patterns and linear formations in this area signify qualities of these aspects. The formations on the mount of the moon indicate the degree and forms of the person's imagination, indicating much about their attitude about life. A large and heavy mount of moon usually indicates practicality in creativity. Sensitivity is also indicated by large moon mounts if it is elongated down toward the wrist. Whorl or loop patterns on the moon mount are signs of instability due to over-emphasis on the subconscious.

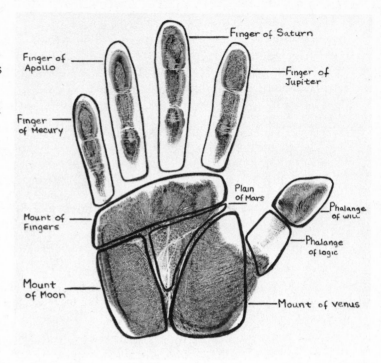

Magic

Magic is the channeling of available energies in the universe and study of their patterns and cycles in order to learn to transform oneself and others into successively higher more effective levels of consciousness. Magic is associated with the worship of the moon and the emulation of her patterns, as the moon symbolizes all the mysteries and powers of the unconscious and of the ungraspable which the magician, witch or sorceress is trying to join. As such, magic can communicate to us much about the nature of ancient moon study and worship as well as ways of living in tune with her principles. The moon as a goddess in magic has dark and light, black and white aspects, equally valued, with whose principles the initiate must become familar. Many magical ceremonies and festivals are held in the moonlight and the power which is being invoked is the energy and complicity of the moon. The practice of magic draws on many available systems or knowledge which conform to and enhance her patterns. The major lesson from the moon in magic is the complete equality of her dark and light aspects; elements are "good" or "bad" according to how one channels and understands them.

96

ANCIENT MYTHOLOGY
AND
FOLKLORE

ANCIENT MYTHOLOGIES

The beginning of the history of Egypt, Asia Minor, Rome and the Greek states is the story of the struggle between two world views, represented by the symbolism of the moon or of the sun. This struggle and change took place world wide. The earliest recorded myths are stories of the prematriarchal and matriarchal world; later ancient myths deal with the cultural strife resulting from patriarchal antipathy **to matriarchy and the eventual patriarchal take-over.**

Although many current scholars reject the evidence, extensive records of matriarchal cultures still exist. There are "myths" recording their stories as well as public documents. Hannibal's treaty with the Gauls stipulates that, in case of disputes, the interpretation of the treaty was to be made by a court of Gallic Matrons. These revered old wise women were later branded 'silly or evil old witches' to the political asset of the incoming patriarchies. Cretans refer to their country as the motherland. And the word 'matrimony' retains the echo of the time when the custom adhered to matrilineal ties. Bachofen is one of the few scholars who admits to seeing what these records show and wrote his book, MYTH, **RELIGION AND MOTHER RIGHT** to the dismay and disagreement of many **fellow researchers.** There are countless records of Queens such as the Celtic **Bridget** followers, African and Asia Minor Amazons, societies of supreme priestesses in India, the Americas, the South Seas and the Germanic Valkyries.

Understanding matriarchies requires some stretching of our imaginations and our memories, as they were not mere reverse images of patriarchies. From records we now have, it seems that matriarchies tended to be more peaceful communities than patriarchies concentrating their warrior skills not on conquest, but on defense of their motherland. Worship of the moon dominated, with priestess and fertility cults. Favor was given to the last born child. Lineage was indicated through the uterine line and illigitimacy of children not a concept. Matricide and crimes against women were the most loathsome transgressions.

Night and especially the midnight hour were considered the most important cosmic times. Meetings and councils were often held at midnight. Incest was not forbidden and polyandry allowed. Governmental intervention was minimal, as the society revered religious and magical laws and life progressed within loosely regulated principles.

Most myths related to the moon tell of an original time of total blackness out of which the life force molded a cosmic egg. This world egg split in two; one part remained in the sky to become the moon and the other became earth. These two parts of the mother egg have historically alternating sexes, but most often the earth is thought to be female as well as the moon, and the sun is male. At various times, the moon was thought to be male symbolizing either her independent wholeness or the struggle between the two principles for dominance. The story of the clash between the two world views is most often personified as strife in the relationship between the moon and the sun (thought either to be her husband or rebellious son-lover). The normal pattern of the story is that at one time, long ago, the sun and moon were of equal brillance and were one planet. They had a fight and split in two. Their spat continues (indicated in the heavens by eclipses, sunspots and moonmarks) but they visit now and then. When the moon is angry with the way the peoples of the earth are living she sends floods, but they are always followed by rebirth and resurrection. The moon is also said to rule the major sexual events of life: birth, puberty, and death. The moon is the home of unborn souls as well as of the dead.

The forms of most myths as we know them today are of more recent writing than the tales of the time of oneness, thus they are largely concerned with the story of the matriarchal-patriarchal struggle. As such, they are valuable documents which teach us of the reality of these issues and also of the dynamics of alternative social systems to existing ones. They are usually very moving and exquisite in conception, imaginative form, and complexity of psychological wisdom; as such, they are invaluable reminders of how arbitrarily and often wrongly we draw the line between the savage and the civilized.

The myths of the moon which follow were gathered from many sources. What they have in common is the taint of centuries of patriarchal revision. It is possible to read them as stories of the times of matriarchal-patriarchal struggle and after the firm establishment of patriarchy. It is equally crucial for us to open our collective memories in order to imagine what each story was when another mode dominated the earth's cultures and we lived our lives coherent with our deepest psyches.

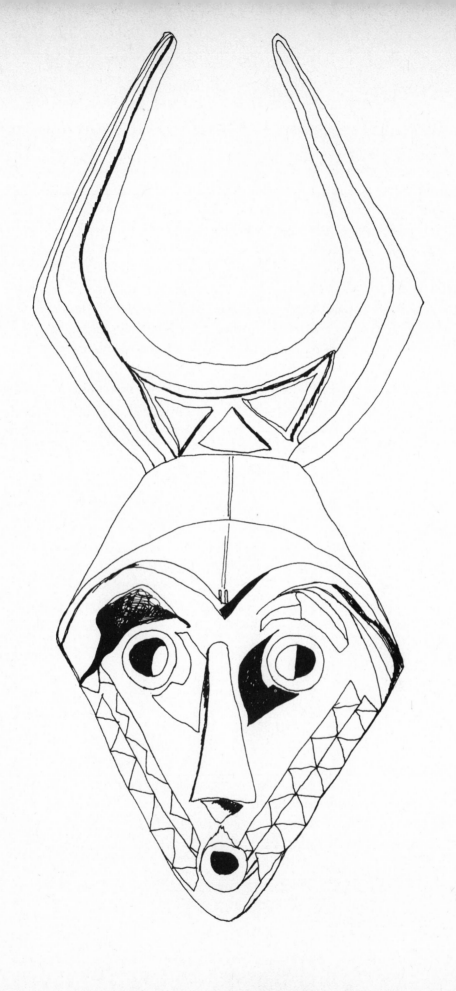

AFRICA

Fon of Dahomey

Mawu was the Moon, having control of the night and dwelling in the West. Lisa was male and the sun. Whenever there is an eclipse, the Fon say that Mawu and Lisa are making love. They were twins, and they were the parents of all the other gods.

The Gold Coast

If you see the new moon, blow ashes toward it and say, **I saw you before you saw me**. If you don't, as the moon grows to the full, your strength will fade. When the new moon is seen, one should turn all the money in your pockets, or show the newly minted coins to the moon; then, as the moon grows, the money will increase. Just as is true of the moment of the New Year, whatever you are doing when you see the new moon, you will do for the remainder of the month. Wishes on seeing the new moon will come true if they are not told, or if one kisses the nearest person. Pointing at the new moon brings trouble, as does seeing the moon in any phase, over the shoulder.

Kenya

It is thought that if the moon is disturbed or angered, it will send floods. Deluge floods symbolize the dark of the moon, and simultaneously rebirth and resurrection.

Chaga of Kenya

The Moon-Chief and his followers were more backward than the people on earth. A boy, Murile, invested his father's three-legged stool with magic and went up into the sky. He arrived at the Moon-Chief's village and was surprised to see people eating raw food. He saluted the Moon-Chief and asked why they did not use fires and was told they did not know about fire. He offered to show them and was promised many cattle and sheep in return. Then with two pieces of wood and some dry grass he lit a fire, and was hailed as a great magician.

Luyia of Kenya

God created the Moon first and then the Sun. In the beginning, the Moon was brighter and bigger, and the envious Sun attacked his brother. They wrestled till the Sun was thrown down and pleaded for mercy. Then they wrestled again and the Moon was thrown in the mud and splashed with dirt so that he was not so bright. God intervened to stop them fighting again, saying the Sun would be brighter thereafter and shine during the day for kings and workers. The Moon would only shine at night, for thieves and witches.

Ashanti

In Ashanti tradition Akua'ba is a lunar fertility figure. Women carry figurines of Akua'ba in their skirts at the small of their backs to aid fertility and to ensure well-formed children.

Baganda

In Central Africa it is a Baganda custom for a mother to bathe her newborn by the light of the first full moon following its birth.

Carthage

In Carthage, a Phoenician colony, the moon was connected to their two important gods, Baal Hammon and Tanit, his consort. Child sacrifice was practiced as a fertility rite.

Nigeria

The custom of maori moko (tattooing) recorded significant facts about the person and enabled the spirits to identify the dead and send them to their merited paradise. The symbol of eternity is a snake biting its own tail. The circle it makes stands for the two halves of the world united.

Zulu

There is in Africa a general belief in the life of souls after death and in nature gods. Magic is secret while religion is open. Zulus refrain from killing certain species of snakes because they are thought to be reincarnations of relatives.

Mozambique

A Zambezi myth: Formerly the moon was very pale and did not shine. It was jealous of the sun with its glittering feathers of light. She took advantage of a moment when the sun was looking at the other side of the earth, and stole some of his feathers of fire to adorn herself. But the sun found out, and in his anger splashed the moon with mud which remains stuck to it for all eternity. Ever since then the moon has been bent on vengeance. Every ten years she surprises the sun when he is off guard and cunningly spatters him with mud. Then the sun shows large spots and for some hours cannot shine.

Masai

The great god wished to protect the human race and advised Le-eyo, his favorite, to say when a child died, **People die and return; the moon dies and does not return.** Soon after a child died, but as it was not his own, Le-eyo did not trouble to utter the formula. He did not remember it until misfortune struck one of his own sons. But it was too late. Ever since then people have been subject to the law of death, and the moon to rebirth.

Bushmen of Southern Africa

They pray to the moon, sun and stars. The moon belongs to the praying mantis, who made it out of an old shoe.

103

Hottentots

The Khoi-Khoi, a pastoral people, have a cult of large stones and worship the praying mantis and a hero sorcerer who was born of a cow-virgin.

Congo

Long ago the sun met the moon and threw mud at it, thus making it less bright. When this happened, there was a flood and people were changed into monkeys.

Uganda

Sun and moon agreed to kill their children. Sun carried out his part, but the moon changed its mind and spared its descendants. So the sun has no children but those of the moon are innumerable—the stars.

The Nilotic Group

In Uganda the Nandi have a myth about the origin of death: a dog was told to bring people the message of their immortality. He thought he was not received with all the respect due a divine messenger, so he changed the tale and condemned humans to death saying, **All humans will die like the moon but you will not be reborn like it unless you give me food and drink.** People laughed and give him drink on a stool. The dog was furious at not being looked at as a man and said, **All humans shall die—only the moon shall be reborn.**

Akua'ba

104

Guinea and the Senegambia Group: The Serers

One day the sun's mother and the moon's mother were bathing naked in a little waterfall. The sun turned his back so as not to see his mother naked, but the moon looked very keenly at her mother. After the bath the Sun was called by his mother who said, My son, you have always respected me, may god bless you. You did not look at me in the waterfall. As you turned your eyes away from me i pray god will allow none to be able to look steadily at you. The moon was called in turn by her mother, who said, Daughter, you did not respect me in the waterfall. You stared at me as if i were some bright object, so i want everyone to be able to look at you without ever tiring their eyes.

Mawu, Congo

NATIVE AMERICANS, NORTH

Peyote Cult

Several of the features of the Peyote Cult which spread up into North America from Mexico give evidence of the basis of an older tradition that had much to do with the moon and matricarchy. Within the standard ritual of the Peyote Cults, a crescent-shaped altar is formed out of earth and is called a moon. In the Kiowa ceremonies, the horns face East. Along the crescent is a groove or "path" as it is called which stretches from horn to horn interrupted only by a flat space in the center where "father peyote" is laid on sage. This path represents the path from birth to maturity and wisdom to old age and death. It also represents the mountain range where in the origin myth, Peyote Woman found the first peyote. At midnight, the ashes from the fire are built into another crescent shape. It is said that Peyote Woman can be heard singing as a button is eaten.

According to some sources, in the Mescalero Apache version of the rites, ritual songs and designs employing the moon were much in use.

The Shawnee also say that if you listen you can catch the songs of Peyote Woman. The Kickapoo also have a tradition of a goddess who sings in the meetings when pleased.

Zuni

The moon is Moon Mother. Here is a Zuni prayer:

> Dawn old women
> Dawn matrons
> Dawn maidens,
> Dawn girls . . .
> Perhaps if we are lucky
> Our earth mother
> Will wrap herself in a fourfold robe
> Of white meal.

Athenesic, moon goddess

California Indians

They played with balls in order to stimulate the moon in its waxing period. They reported that their ball games had been originated by the "great rabbit," that is, the moon, using its eggs for balls.

General

Where the power of the egg prevails, there is always a matron as the spiritual and secular chieftain at the same time, as in the Great Mother clans of the North American Indians of former days. Under the domination of the egg, one usually finds a prevalence of peaceful, uterine life, satiated, comfortable, complacent, though determined in its defense against outsiders.

Hell

Unkatahe, goddess against disease

Oglala Sioux

In the Sun Dance ritual of the Oglala Sioux, according to the Medicine Man, Black Elk, a rawhide crescent is one of the things that must be made for the ritual because the moon represents a person, and also all things, for everything created waxes and wanes, lives and dies. The moon brings the light of Wakan-Tanka (the supreme diety) into the darkness.

Huron

Ball games arose from the egg cult. Hurons played a lunar ball game with rules akin to soccer whenever the chieftain became ill.

Algonquin

It is remarkable that in the language of the Algonquins of North America, the ideas of night, death, cold, sleep, water and moon are expressed by the same word. The Sun, armed with bows and arrows went hunting, but was away so long that his Sister became alarmed. She set out to look for him, and traveled for twenty days before She found him. Since then the Moon has always made journeys of twenty days across the sky.

Cree

The Cree people believe in twelve lunar spirits, one for each Moon and under which a person born in that month is protected. Some people had only one name for the winter Moon, grouping the four months together. The new Moon was a time for joyous celebration. The Sun and Moon were spirits who controlled the light of day and night travels. Many calendars began the year at the Moon of the Changing Seasons, or on the current date of Halloween.

Assinboin

The moon was thought to be hot and giving off its own light. Each month it was eaten by moles, moon-nibblers, whose teeth were burnt out eating the hot moon. They were punished by being sent to earth to burrow in the dry prairies, becoming the toothless moles which cover the West and North West. Other traditions have it that a bird, a crow, eagle, hawk or owl, eats the moon each month.

108

Maidu

A frog angry with the sun because it ate her children eats the moon. The shapes in the moon are sometimes attributed to the shadow of a girl under a shrub standing holding a pail.

Haida

The Haida of Canada see the moon as a masculine deity, Roong, who took a man from earth to keep him company. The captured man periodically struggles to get free and dumps his pail of water, making our rain.

Apache

The moon was an important symbol in Apache mythology and the Chief, Cochise, had a picture of the face of the moon painted on his shields. To the Lipan Apache, the Moon is Changing Woman, a very important diety.

Chukchi

It was thought that the moon if angered would lasso bad shamans and pull them up to the sky. Sacrifices of dogs were made to the moon, and supplications for good luck in weather and fertility were made on all fours.

Navajo

White belongs to the East and to the Moon. It is the cool and virginal character of the early softness of a breeze. White shell is its jewel and its meaning is purification. The feminine character of both white and blue is emphasized by the fact that probably the most divine member of the Navajo panteheon is Changing Woman whose jewel is turquoise. In myths in which she is dual, she is Turquoise Woman and White Shell Woman. The Egyptian Goddess was known as the Lady of Turquoise and there was a close connection between the East, Easter, dawn and Ishtar, the ancient goddess who descended to and arose from the Underworld.

Navajo: Changing Woman

Changing Woman is born with Darkness as her mother and Dawn as her father. Initially she calls First Man and First Woman her parents, but the winds tell her that this is not true. She is not like other children. Soon she refuses their food and eats only sacred pollen. After twelve days she is full grown and very wise. Her periods begin, and a Puberty Ceremony is given for her, in which First Man is assisted by Marsh Wren Woman and Bridled Titmouse Woman. First Man offers both White Shell and Turquoise, pressing them to the body of Changing Woman who thereby was made part of the sun.

Finally, Changing Woman quarrels with the First Man, First Woman and others from the lowest world, saying, **You are not my mother. Others took care of me. You had nothing to do with me.** She separates herself from them, setting up her own dwelling in the West, similar to the Sun's house in the East, guarded well, rich with the sacred stones. Her twins are born after she is well established in this place. Changing Woman is the favored figure among the Holy People. She had much to do with the creation of People and with the meeting at which they were taught how to control the wind, lightning, storms and animals, and how to keep all these forces in harmony. This meeting was a ceremonial of the Holy People and has become Blessing Way, a ritual which occupies a key position in Navajo religion. Changing Woman, ever young and radiant lives in a marvelous dwelling on western waters.

Changing Woman is the mother, transforming and releasing. She is the divine and eternal within substance. It is to Her that one may turn for sustenance, but always to be thrust out again into the flux. Changing Woman created Earth Surface People. She made our toes and fingernails of abalone shell, our bone of white shell, our flesh of red-white stone, our hair of darkness, our skull of dawn, our brains of white shell, our white of eye of white shell, our tears of collected sky waters, our pupils of shaken-off stone mica and rock crystal, our ear lobes of red-white stone. White shell oval beads make us hear; our nose was made of abalone, our teeth made of white shell. Straight lightning furnished our tongue, a rainbow our arms, plants of all kind furnished our pubic hair and skin pores.

Western Keres, Pueblo

There is evidence at the Laguna and Acoma pueblos the Creatrix of the World was Thinking Woman or Sitch-tche-na-ko. She created all the world and when She takes form She is Spider Grandmother, the beloved diety of Southwestern Indians.

110

Eskimo

The name of the Goddess is She Who Will Not Take A Husband. Arctic nights are longer so there is a great consciousness of the moon. Since moon light reflects off the ice, its light is greater and nearer our daylight, and so it does not seem to be the pale reflective light of the sun as it is in many other cultures. Fishing is a major source of sustenance and the people keep track of the fish through the moon. Their homes are circular also, and white is one of the primary colors of their universe.

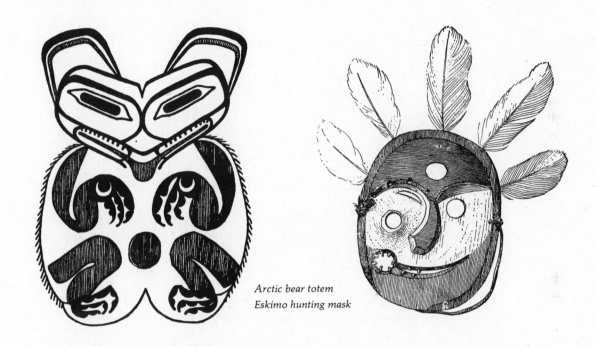

Arctic bear totem
Eskimo hunting mask

Taos Pueblo

My brother the star, my mother the earth,
My father the sun, my sister the Moon,
To my life give beauty, to my body give strength,
To my corn give goodness, to my house give peace,
To my spirit give truth, to my elders give wisdom.

We must pray for strength.
We must pray to come together.
Pray to the weeping earth
Pray to the trembling waters
And to the wandering rain.
We must pray to the whispering Moon
Pray to the tiptoeing stars
And to the hollering Sun.[9]

SOUTH AMERICA

Guatemala

There was a cult of the Sun and Moon, who were Grandfather and Grandmother respectively, Hun-Apu Vuch and Hun-Ahpu-Mtye, who were represented in human form, but with the face of the sacred animal, the tapir.

Peru and the Incas

Before the Incas arrived, the Quiches (ancient Peruvians) were totemistic to a large extent though they had a major temple dedicated to Mama-Quilla, their Moon Goddess, which was destroyed in Cuzco by the first invading Incas. Independent mountain tribes paid lip service to the new Inca solar cult, but continued to worship their Moon and maize mother. On the Peruvian Plateau, the Incas built a nunnery of pure gold, with golden furniture. Golden maize stood tall with golden leaves and ears and golden herdsmen with golden staffs guarded a golden herd on a golden pasture.

Vestals guarded the flame day and night. It was lit once a year, at the summer solstice, with a concave mirror, directly from the divine rays. There they wove the white woolen garments of princes and priests, prepared wine and bread for the religious rites and shaped and glazed the ritual vessels for their magic service in a procedure known only to themselves. They were called Mama-Cuna, but despite the solar flame and their betrothal to the fire and all the gold with which they were surrounded, they had remained Moon Women just as in times immemorial, and once a year they carried the image of their own Goddess, Mama-Quilla to the solar temple on their shoulders. Peruvians believed that their life and fertility were gifts from the Moon. Peruvians originally paid more attention to the rhythms of the Moon than to the fairly continuous sunshine in their countries. This adoration of the Moon is closely connected on the one hand with the relationship of the female cycle to the lunar one, and on the other hand to the reverence in which the art of pottery, a feminine art, is held among the Indians. According to popular opinion, every object manufactured by women absorbs their secret connections with nature. This opinion also explains the care with which Indians avoid impinging on female property rights.

Coatl serpent, Mexico

Brazil

The Jamunda have a myth in which the Moon is represented as a maiden who fell in love with her brother and visited him at night, but who was finally betrayed by him passing his blackened hand over her face. In another version, it is an unknown suitor who visits a woman secretly at night; the latter blackens her hands and smears the man's back. Later, she discovers her suitor is her brother. She flees and her lover pursues her; both rise to the sky where she becomes the Sun and he the Moon. Another tribe in Brazil, the Bakairi, believe that the phases of the Moon are caused by various animals which gnaw at it and finally swallow it. According to other tribes, the spots on the Moon are the marks of the beating received by the Moon when the Sun discovered the secrets of the initiation rites.

Quetzal

Mexico

The Mexican calendrical and astrological system is founded on a ritual calendar, the Sacred Calendar called the **tonalamatl** by the Aztecs and the **tzolkin** by the Mayans, of 260 days, based on the combinations of twenty holy symbols and the numbers one through thirteen.

As far back as archaeologists have uncovered appear the relics of the Mesoamerican civilization of the Olmec from approximately 1500 B.C.; the next more recent layer reveals relics of the advanced Mayans; then the enigmatic culture of Tectihuacan, next the Zapotecs, the Totonacs, the Mixtecs, the Toltecs, the Chichimecs and finally most recently before the current Spanish-Mesoamerican culture, the relics of the Aztec culture. Tezcatlipoca the Sun God (Smoking Mirror) was linked with the Moon diety, Meztli of the Evening.

More Recently

Dionicia Hernandez Castañon, mother of a friend, Marguerita Castañon-Hill, told Maggi that moon mythology persisted into her own adult life in her family and community. Of Mexican descent, Mrs. Castañon says,

My mother still believed in the power of the moon. When I was pregnant with Teresa in 1946 there was an eclipse of the moon; I wanted to go but she didn't want me to. When I insisted, she gave me a big wrench to tie on my waist over my belly; she said it would protect the child from the moonlight during the eclipse so the baby wouldn't come out with a cleft mouth or some other deformity.

CHINA AND JAPAN

China

Quan Yin is the ancient Chinese symbol of the World Mother, the feminine principle of creation, the Mother aspect of Deity. Chang-O is one of the names for the Goddess of the Moon. She was the wife of I, the excellent archer. She took up her abode in the moon in order to escape her husband's wrath after she had swallowed the drug of immortality which had been given to him by the gods. The couple were later reconciled, however, and he would visit her in the lunar palace. She was always portrayed as a very beautiful young woman.

Another version has it that the toad Heng-O was wafted to the moon after swallowing visionary pills. The toad coughs, spits up a pill and it turns into a rabbit. It is this rabbit that one can see in the dark maria shapes of the moon in China, and it is still living there grinding more elixir for pills. An old man also lives there to tend the acacia tree.

116

Moon Festival

The Festival of the Moon is one of the three great annual Chinese feasts and takes place on the fifteenth day of the eighth month at the full moon of the autumn equinox. It is a feast especially for women and children who buy little figures representing white rabbits and make them a sacrafice consisting chiefly of fruit. They offer a sacrafice directly to the moon when it has risen above the house tops, or before a large paper panel with a representation of the moon's palace with its inhabitant, the hare who makes the drug of immortality. The sacrafice consists of fruit, sweet cakes which are made specially for the occasion and a sprig of amaranth. Men never take part in this ceremony. The Goddess is also known as Heng-O and Shing Moo. The moon tree is the cassia, the tree of immortality, which grows on the moon. The fruit of this tree confers those who eat it immortality and transparency. Old Chinese maxim: **Love everything in the universe, because the Sun and Moon and Earth are but one body.**

Tao

For a long period of relatively recent history in China different religions co-existed: Buddhism, Taoism and Confucianism, the two first of which have their own temples and priests (the Bonzes and Tao-shih) while the last has temples without priests. Historical Chinese mythology was formed from a mixture of elements of these religions which suffered profound changes through the influence of literature.

From early times to the first years of the Chinese Republic the official religion was Confucianism. Each year the Emperor and his courtiers, in spring and autumn, made sacrifices to Heaven, the Sun, Moon, Soil, the god of War, Confucius, and the Ancestors, in their respective temples. Alterations occurred in the religions; thus certain Buddhist divinities are found under other names, while Taoism, to which Chinese mythology owes a large debt, was completely changed even to the personality of Lao-tzu, who is called its founder. In reality Lao-tzu was nearly a contemporary of Confucius and a philosopher. Popular legend endowed him with immortality and the power of conquering demons, claiming that he was the incarnation of the Celestial Master of the First Origin. After teaching and bestowing on his disciple, Yin Hsi, the Tao-te Ching or 'Book of the First Principle and its Virtue, he mounted a green ox and disappeared towards the West forever.

The actual founder of existing popular Taoism was Chang Tao-ling (second century A.D.) who was deified in the eighth century. After many exploits he ascended to heaven with his wife and two disciples, passing on his secret powers to his son.

Customs

The Chinese yang sun principle is male, hot, dry and active. The Chinese yin moon principle is female, cool, moist and passive. The yin principle shaped Chinese imperial ritual, ceremonial dress, architecture, standards of beauty and cuisine. Chinese houses have traditional auspicious 'moon' interior doorways. The traditional Chinese hump-backed bridge is semicircular in order to reflect itself in the water below, completing the moon circle. Not only did Chinese court beauties cultivate crescent 'moon' eyebrows, but imperial concubines were particularly chosen for their 'moon' faces, characteristically flat and circular. Yao Niang, the imperial concubine according to tradition, introduced the practice of foot-binding to shape her feet into crescent 'new moons.' Ritual robes of Chinese emperors were cut very wide in the sleeves so that when an Emperor raised his arms the sleeve-openings formed perfect circular shapes.

Fugetsu

Fugetsu comes from the term kacho-fugetsu which means literally, 'flowers-and-birds,' (or either one depicted separately) and 'wind and moon' (especially a breeze on a fine day and the full moon)—in other words, natural phenomena, and especially certain aspects of natural phenomena conventionally considered to be suitable subjects for art. The term also refers to the gently refined mind which finds pleasure in contemplation of flowers, listening to the song of the birds, gazing at the moon and generally giving itself over to contemplation of nature. As an extension of these senses, kacho-fugetsu comes to mean beautiful natural scenery, and still further, the refined, poetic way of life that finds its chief pleasure in the contemplation of beauty.

Himalayas

The Khasian people see the moon as a male god who will impregnate women who sleep in the moonlight.

Japanese Mythology

The great triad in Japanese mythology consists of Amaterasu, the Sun Goddess, and her two brothers, Susano the Storm God, and Tsuki-Yomi, the God of the Moon. The latter's name translates to "counter of the months" which links him with the primitive calendar. This god has shrines at Ise and at Kadono and in both these shrines is a mirror in which the god may manifest himself. The Japanese represent the Hare in the Moon pounding rice in a mortar. Pounding rice was a ritual done only at a new year. In Japanese, the word Mochi-zuki means to pound rice for cakes and it also means full-moon; although the ideograms with which the two words are written are entirely different, the identity of the consonants was enough to produce the image.

In Japanese folklore there is a tree called the **moon tree** which is a kind of laurel. It grows on the Moon and the spots on the Moon are the visible patches of those trees. When the Moon seems especially bright, the people say that the katsura tree is turning red or yellow.

In Japan at eclipse, they meditated with an honorific bow to cure ills. There is an older myth which tells of the order received by the last couple of seven generations of gods, Izanagi and Izanami. Izanagi washed his left eye and gave birth to the Sun, Amaterasu, and then he washed his right eye and gave birth to the Moon Goddess, Tsu yomi. To the Goddess of the Moon he entrusted the kingdom of the night. In Japanese art, the Sun and Moon are often depicted as two holy eyes. Kwannon, the Goddess of Mercy and Compassion, was also associated with the Moon.

Japanese family crests

The fundamental characteristic of true compassion is pure and fearless openness without territorial limitations. There is no need to be loving and kind to one's neighbors, no need to speak pleasantly to people and put on a pretty smile. This little game does not apply. In fact it is embarrassing. Real openness exists on a much larger scale, a revolutionarily large and open scale, a universal scale. Compassion means for you to be as adult as you are, while still maintaining a childlike quality. In the Buddhist teachings the symbol for compassion, as I have already said, is one moon shining in the sky while its image is reflected in one hundred bowls of water. The moon does not demand, "If you open to me, I will do you a favor and shine on you." The moon just shines. The point is not to want to benefit anyone or make them happy. There is no audience involved, no "me" and "them." It is a matter of an open gift, complete generosity without the relative notions of giving and receiving. That is the basic openness of compassion: opening without demand. Simply be what you are, be the master of the situation. If you will just "be," then life flows around and through you. This will lead you into working and communicating with someone, which of course demands tremendous warmth and openness.

—Chogyam Trungpa, 1974[10]

Kuan Yin, goddess of mercy & protectress of children

NEAR EAST

Assyrian Moon Tree & Nisroch

Chaldea

The name Chaldean means "moon-worshippers." The shepherds of Chaldea would sit and look at the moon seeing it as a mirror in which the earth was reflected. After Calvary it was thought one could see the figure of Judas in the moon, suffering exile for his treason.

Assyro-Babylonian Myths

At the month's beginning to shine on earth
Thou shalt show two horns to mark six days.
On the seventh day divide the crown in two;
On the fourteenth day, turn thy full face.

Sin, the Moon God, occupied the chief place in the astral triad. Its two other members were his children Shamash, the Sun, and Ishtar, the planet Venus. In physical aspect he was an old man with a beard the color of lapis lazuli and wearing a turban. Every evening he got into his barque—which appeared to mortals as the crescent moon—and navigated the vast spaces of the nocturnal sky. But one day the crescent gave way to a disk which stood out in the sky like a gleaming crown. There could be no doubt that this was God's own crown, and then Sin was called Lord of the Diadem. These transformations gave Sin a certain mystery thus was he called He-whose-deep-heart-no-god-can-penetrate. He was also the measurer of time by the lunar calendar.

Sin dispersed evil and darkness and was the source of dreams and prophesies. The Sumerians, credited as being the inventors of the wheel, were moon worshippers. Ishtar was goddess of love and fertility. Her statues are found carved in alabaster, a gold crescent on her head, and rubies in her eyes and navel. Ishtar was also the goddess of water, sender of the moisture of fertility or the floods of destruction. Some very ancient texts tell a story of a flood sent by Ishtar in her rage at the people's disregard for her laws.

Noah, in the Old Testament story, is probably a form of Nuah, a Babylonian moon goddess. Like Ishtar, Noah saved a remnant of the world from destruction an ark, a moon boat. When the waters subsided, Noah, taught by a dove, the bird of the moon, went onto the land. The earth was repeopled from him and his family and the animals he had taken along in the ark.

I the mother have begotten my people and like the young of the fishes they fill the sea.

—Ishtar's Song

Turkey

The Saracens called the Moon Cabar, the Great; and its crescent is the religious symbol of the Turks today. Tradition says that Phillip, the father of Alexander, meeting with great difficulty in the siege of Byzantium, set the workmen to undermine the walls, but a crescent moon discovered the design which miscarried; consequently the Byzantines erected a statue to Diana, and the crescent became a symbol of that state.

Another legend is that Othman, the Sultan, saw in a vision a crescent moon with its horns extended from east to west and he adopted the crescent for his standard.

Arabia

The cult of the moon prevailed over sun-worship. Mohammed forbade the use of any metal in amulets except silver. In the shrine at Mecca is the Ka'aba, a meteorite: inside the dark hall, there are three columns holding up the roof which has a number of silver and gold lamps hanging down from it. The floor is of marble tiles. In the eastern corner some five feet above floor level, is the famous black stone (al hadar alaswad) sealed off. The stone is attended by men called the Beni-Shaybah or Sons of the Old Woman. There is a cleft-of-Venus in the stone, suggesting that it was a venerable stone that was once an object of worship as the lunar great mother. The moon was associated with Cancer's sign and considered to be a female deity. If born under influence of the moon a person will be pale with red cheeks and a round face, not serious, talkative, fun-loving and should be careful of falling.

123

Moon as sign of Cancer, Arabia

Ardvi Sura Anahita

The Avesta, sacred writings which Ancient Persian tradition attributes to Zoroaster, devotes an entire chapter to Anahita. Her full name means the High, Powerful, Immaculate. Her sanctuary at Erez in Akilisene contained her golden statue and the daughters of noble families of Armenia used to prostitute themselves there to strangers before marriage, in submission to her ultimate rule over their sexuality. Also the Goddess of War, she rode in a chariot drawn by four white horses, Wind, Rain, Cloud and Hail. The moon was associated with Persian royalty who wore crowns surmounted by the lunar crescent and disc. The moon god's name was Mah.

Asherath in Israel

The worship of Asherath seems to have been introduced into the ritual of the Royal Court by a Sidonian princess, Jezebel. As bride of King Ahab, she influenced him to make an image of Asherath, ca. 873-853 B.C. The images themselves seem to have been made of wood and their bases were implanted into the ground. Later a statue of Asherath was set up in the temple of Jerusalem itself.

The moon was created for the counting of the days.

—Midrash Text

124

Astarte and Anath

Both Astarte and Anath were moon goddesses, as well as a third goddess derived from the Canaanite-Syrian Pantheon, Qadesh, who bore the Egyptian title Queen of Heaven.

There is historico-mythical account of a city called Asheroth-Qarnaim, Astarte of the Two Horns. The original meaning of the name Astarte was womb, or that which issues from the womb.

In Ugaritic mythology, Anath is the most important female figure, goddess of love and war; wanton, amorous, as well as given to uncontrollable rage and cruelty. She is the daughter of El, the god of heaven, and his wife, Asherath of the Sea. She has so many features in common with the Sumerian Inanna and the Arkadian Ishtar that one must regard her as their heiress.

Anath was called Lady of Heaven, Mistress of All the Gods. She loved gods, humans and animals. Her foremost lover was her brother Baal. When she approached, Baal dismissed his other wives, and she, in preparation for the union, bathed in sky-dew and rubbed herself in ambergris from a sperm-whale. The intercourse with him is described graphically in ancient Near Eastern texts. In a place called Dubr, Baal lay seventy-seven times with Anath who assumed the shape of a cow for the occasion.

These adventures in love pale next to Anath's exploits in war and strife. No Near Eastern goddess seems to have been as bloodthirsty in later mythology. She was easily provoked to violence, and once she began to fight would go berserk smiting and killing with pleasure.

Lilith

In Hebrew legend, Lilith was the first woman and wife of Adam. She was banished for infidelity and became a night phantom. In patriarchal revisions of the myth she became symbolic of the Terrible Mother enemy of the newborn, and closely related to the Greek figure of Hecate with her demands for human sacrifice. In fairytales her imagery is transferred to that of the wicked Stepmother and bad Mother-in-Law.

Do you not see what they do in the cities of Jerusalem? The children gather wood and the fathers kindle a fire, and the women knead the dough to make cakes to the Queen of Heaven and pour out libations to other gods, in order to anger Me.

—Jeremiah

Hathor, goddess of the sky, of love and beauty

EGYPT

The barque of the Moon, Yâåhu Aûhû, in some places called the Left Eye of Horus, comes out of the door of the east every evening. On the 15th day of each month a sow attacks it and after a fortnight's agony and increasing pallor, the moon dies and is born again. If the sow manages to swallow it altogether this causes an eclipse.

The frog was an attribute of Herit, the Goddess who assisted Isis in her annual resurrection of Osiris. The little frogs which appeared on the Nile several days before it overflowed to enrich the soil were regarded as heralds of fertility.

The moon was also thought to be the carrier of the souls of the dead over waters to the sun.

With the rise of patriarchal sun cults in antiquity, men created the egg of the phoenix, a counter egg to the female one. At the beginning of every new epoch, this gold and purple magic bird appears with an egg in his beak and places it on the altar of the sun at Heliopolis. It is a hollow egg formed of myrrh, which is also a sarcophagus. He places his father's body inside. In flaming myrrh, the father's carcass is burned on the sun altar to ensure new life. The phoenix-rejuvenated flies out of the ashes into the solar year as herald of its beginning. Thus the material egg form was retained, but without the original purpose. Fertilization is mythologized to occur by contact with the power of fire. Father became born from sun and son from father by the light rays of the sun, immaculately conceived and without a mother.

The Veil of Isis is the flesh or human form which must be lifted to find spirit; it is the door of every mystery.

Nut is the Goddess whose star-spangled torso forms the sky. Each evening she is swallowed by the sun and born anew each morning.

The Greeks thought the Egyptians were "backward" because they conceived of the sky as a woman and the earth as a man. Heaven has usually been

the goddess Nut holding up the sky

considered, except in Egypt, part of the masculine or aggressive etheric principle, associated with things of the spirit and with the number three; the earth has usually been related to the feminine, receptive or material principle, and the number four.

The Moon in Egypt

The moon in Egypt was known by as many titles as there were names and conquerors. Among the very earliest names were Thot, Aah, and Khons. The name of Thot appears on palettes of pre-dynastic times and into the First Dynasty. He took form as a cyncocephalus, or baboon. The priest, Horapollo says of the Baboon-God:

. . . He rejoiceth at the coming of the moon, for then he stands up, lifting his forefeet toward heaven, wearing a royal ensign upon his head. And he hath much sympathy with the moon, that when she meets the sun, as betwixt the old and the new moon, so that she gives no Light, the male, or he-cynocephalus, never looks up, nor eats anything as bewailing the loss of the moon.

Very early there is also a trace of a Goddess, symbolized by a star on a pole, surmounted by inverted horns. Her name was Seshat, Goddess of Learning and Temple Building.

As Briffault says in THE MOTHERS,

Nowhere can a primitive solar cult be found unpreceded by a lunar cult. All solar mythologies exhibit the inconsistencies which reveal the clumsy adaptation of lunar attributes by which they have been produced. They are invariably the products of priesthoods and sacred monarchies; they are never the spontaneous outcome of popular religious ideas. Therefore, as we shall see, almost every major Egyptian god identified with the sun cult has vestiges, if not outright attributes of lunar mythology. It is not hard to image that perhaps these male lunar deities were themselves makeovers of originally matriarchal deities.[11]

Among the most famous of these "sun" gods is Ra. At Thebes, where he was worshipped as Amen-Ra, he was joined to the local god, Ammon. His name means the **hidden** or **The Obscure**, hardly a name for the solar disk. His image as a frog was held sacred at Thebes which is also a singularly unusual symbol for a sun deity. He was the Horned God, famous even among the Greeks. Even older than his association with Ra, was his association with Min. Amen-Min is the Fiery Bull, Lord of the New Moon, who becomes the Full Moon who shines at the beginning of each month.

J. Norman Lockyer, an English astronomer had a theory that Osiris, the mate of Isis was a Moon deity of the Nubian peoples who came from the Libyan desert into Egypt. He postulates that around 6400 B.C. the divine dynasty of Osiris began with a lunar calendar of 360 days. They built temples at Amada, Semneh, Philae, Edfu and Abydos. These Osiris temples were used to find the sun's place at the Autumnal Equinox, the beginning of the lunar year.

All this seems quite possible as there are numerous inscriptions which call Osiris Lord of the Moon. Also one of his names was The Great Hare. In the famous Isis/Osiris myth he was cut up into 14 pieces, the number of days of the waning moon. There are pictures which show him at the top of a staircase of fourteen stairs which was another way of representing the waning moon. When it was the moon specifically, it was depicted as the Left eye of Horus. An inscription from the Old Kingdom reads, **Salute to Thee, Osiris, the Master of Eternity. When Thou art in the sky, Thou appearest as the Sun, and Thou appearest again in thy form as the Moon.**

Horus, the son of Osiris and Isis was given the place of honor at Heliopolis as the Rising Sun. But very often he was regarded as consisting of a head and face only. One of his titles was Lord of the Transformations, and he was spoken of as the "Old Man who becomes a Child again." One of his feasts under his title of He-Who-Renews-Himself-and-Becomes-Young-Again was celebrated on the last day of the month, or the New Moon. The left eye of Horus was one of the most common symbols of the Moon and the God. In Panopolis he was worshipped as the Moon and his temple was called Temple of the Moon.

Khons, a lunar deity, was an exorcist and a healer.

Thoth, the name Dejhuti or Zehuti took in Graeco-Roman times, was identified by the Greeks with Hermes, Messenger of the Gods. He was worshipped in Egypt as a lunar patron of science, literature, wisdom and inventions, spokesman of the gods and keeper of records. Djehuti seems merely to mean **he of Djehut**, the old province in Lower Egypt whose capital, Hermopolis Parva, probably was the cradle of Thoth's cult before his principal sanctuary at Hermopolis Magna in Upper Egypt. Thoth is ordinarily represented with the head of an ibis, often surmounted by a crescent moon, or at times as a dog-headed ape. According to theologians of Hermopolis, Thoth was the true Universal Demiurge, the divine ibis who had hatched the world-egg, who had accomplished the work of creation by the sound of his voice alone. When he woke in the primordial void he opened his lips and from the sound that issued forth four gods materialized and four goddesses. These eight deities sang hymns morning and evening to assure continuity of the sun's course.

In the Books of the Pyramids, Thoth is sometimes the oldest Son of Ra, or the child of Geb and Nut, brother of Isis, Set and Nephthys. Usually, however, he is not part of the Osirian family but is the vizier of Osiris and his kingdom's Sacred Scribe. Thoth remained faithful to his murdered master and contributed powerfully to his resurrection, thanks to the trueness of his magical voice and to the thoroughness with which he purified the dismembered Osiris.

When Horus resigned earthly power Thoth succeeded him to the throne, for three thousand two hundred and twenty-six years the model of a peaceful ruler. Endowed with complete knowledge and wisdom, Thoth invented all the arts and science and above all writing without which we would run the risk of forgetting his doctrines, losing the benefit of his discoveries of infinite power.

After his long reign on earth Thoth ascended to the skies where he became the moon-god or the god in charge of guarding the moon: Thoth played draughts with the moon and won a seventy-second part of its light from which he created the five intercalary days. The moon as the left eye of Horus is watched over by either an ibis or a dog-headed ape. A passage in the Book of the Dead tells us that Ra ordered Thoth to take his place in the sky while he **lighted the blessed in the underworlds.**

Thoth made nocturnal voyages in his lunar barque and was devoured slowly by monsters each month. Various defenders of the moon then made the monsters disgorge it which enabled it to appear once more whole. The Ibis-headed god had his primary festival on the nineteenth of the month of Thoth which was a

few days after the full moon of the beginning of the year. His followers gifted each other with honey, figs and sweetmeats and greeted each other with the words, **Sweet is the Truth.** His statues were often blue ceramic topped by a crescent containing a mother of pearl full moon disc.

Ptah, the great god of Memphis, was known as the Lord of Thirty Years which seems to be identical with the local moon deity of Cochin, China. He was often referred to as the Two-Faced God, and the God of Multitudinous Forms. Neither of these terms fit the solar deity he was later supposed to be as the Father of Ra at Heliopolis. Also he was called Ptah the Embryo and Ptah of the Beautiful Face, again two names which indicate lunar rather than solar associations. He is also credited with being the egg of the Moon.

Finally, we see the moon imbedded in what is now probably, after Ra, the most solar-connected symbol of all, the Scarab. The Egyptian priest, Horapollo burst this final stronghold for us when he said that the scarab propagates itself by

the Lotus of the Earth

Mneuas

Moon Ark

131

Fertility Scarabaeus   Mut, nature   Isis, motherhood & fertility

depositing its ball of ox-dung in the earth for 28 days, after which the scarab emerges; he adds: The second species is that which is horned and bull-formed and is consecrated to the moon.

As for female moon dieties (other than the horned and disked headresses worn by Isis) Hathor and almost every other Egyptian goddess of any note were allied with the moon from time to time, from earliest pre-dynastic Egypt before any records were kept.

In Egypt, by assimilation with the Sky Goddess, Hathor became the Celestial Cow, bearing the moon between her horns and spangled with stars. Her legs were called the four pillars of Heaven and kings of later days are portrayed between her forelegs as if within a gate above which the moon disk is raised upon her horned crown. Hathor is sometimes a pillar with a horned head as a capital. She is also portrayed between cleft mountains, the horned gate that divides cleft

Bast

Khensu the Moon

132

Neb-Thet, the family

Hathor, the sky

mountains, the horned gate that divides death-sleep and the waking of the sun. She is the mountain enclosing the cave tomb.

The Egyptian title for Isis means **moisture**. In written history, Isis is mostly identified with Sirius, called by the Egyptians, Sept. She is occasionally identified with the moon until Ptolemaic times with the influx of Greek thought and religion.

In the texts of THE EGYPTIAN BOOK OF THE DEAD it is the role of a woman called the **Tcherauur,** who personifies Isis, to whisper in the ear of the deceased, at the door of the tomb, **Behold, thy lips are set in order for thee, so that thy mouth may be opened.**

Neith and her predecessor, Hathor, are identified with the Milky Way, though both wear the lunar horns, probably left over from their supreme rule as Mother Moon before the foreign and official cult of the Sun moved in.

Maat, law & justice

Net, the hunt

NORTHERN EUROPE

I am the womb of every holt,
I am the blaze on every hill,
I am the queen of every hive,
I am the shield to every head,
I am the tomb to every hope.

—Irish Song of Amergin, 1268 B.C.[12]

Europe

The name Europe comes from that of the Greek moon goddess Europa, which means White Face. At first she rode her lunar bull over the seas and through the world. Then, with patriarchal revolt, he raped her and became instead her abductor.

Celts

Matriarchy was the basis of the Celtic civilization. Both Ireland and Scotland were named after women, Erin and Scota. The Queens, such as the famous Celtic Boadicea, leading their tribes into war, would raise their arms in supplication to the heavens to the Goddess Andraste, before entering battle.

Irish and Gaelic heroic clans took the names of the mothers. They and the Celts of Britain retained matrilocal marriage up to and including, the age of chivalry.

Druids, the high priests of their religion, were always pictured with crescents in their hands. In Meath the temples of Fleachta were sacred to the Moon. The cosmic hour was midnight, the male day being enclosed by two female nights,

Albrecht Durer, Virgin on the Crescent

and time division was by the night. Temples of the Druids in Ireland were decorated with figures of the sun, moon and stars.

The Celtic land of Faerie is a female universe. Fairy tales and folklore of the Celts are filled with crowned birds, coming and going between the earth and the enchanted kingdoms, voicing wisdom as oracles. Lunar women's graceful movements were responsible for the rotation of the stars. In the silvery moonlight naked and woad-painted priestesses danced in Gaul and Britannia.

The major Goddess was Brigit who was originally a triad: Brigit of Poetry, Brigit of Healing, and Brigit of Smithcraft. In Gaelic Scotland, her symbol was the white swan and she was known as the Bride of the Golden Hair and the Bride of the White Hills. Her Aegean prototype seems to have been Brizo of Delos, a moon-goddess to whom votive ships were offered. This brings to mind the legends of the glass boat or **lunette** which the Druids used in the celebration of their mysteries.

The Moon herself was the Goddess of time and bestowed sonambulism.

Stonehenge

Recorded history starts approximately 5000 years ago. In 1900 B.C. Stonehenge, the most extraordinary ancient temple of lunar and nature worship in Northern Europe was constructed with several revisions over centuries. Here Druidic priestesses and priests later calculated the cycles of the moon, sun and stars in order to predict seasonal phases and natural events and to provide a center of worship of the natural order. The tremendous stones framed spectacular moments in the paths of the moon and sun. Stone megoliths and lintels are universally holy constructions, symbolizing the os and womb, the sacred doorway, the center of the universe, the dwelling place of the life force.

Lunar Connections

In Europe, there is widespread belief that sleeping in the moonlight results in insanity, lunacy, moon-madness.

Bad luck is thought to come from seeing the moon over the left shoulder. Ominous too is a halo around the moon which means rain. If there are stars in the ring, it will rain for as many days as there are stars, or the rain will come after that number of days. If there are five stars in the ring, the weather will be cold; if fewer, it will be warm. Sometimes the number of stars within the ring indicates the number of friends to soon die.

The waxing or waning moon has its sympathetic influence on sublunary affairs. Shingles, for example, laid in the waxing of the moon tend to swell as the moon grows. In Devonshire hair was cut in the waning moon, in Worcestershire in the waxing moon. The new moon is thought to be the most powerful phase of the waxing moon because it has further to grow.

The Celts had many names for the goddess. Among them are Ceridwen, Ked, Sidee, Devi, Andraste, Esaye and Isi.

In later days in Northern Europe, the moon remained connected to the forest and the hunt. There was even a particular hunting called **mooning:**

All the excitement of the expedition may be said to lie in this "mooning." If the dark object which the hunter fondly imagines to be an opossum lie higher than the line of the moon, he must perforce fix his eyes on it and walk steadily backwards until the moon is directly behind it. . . . The beast can obviously be mooned from one spot only at any given moment.

—1898 Encyclopedia of Sport

Honeymoon

This is the name for the month after a wedding during which, in Teutonic custom, the community celebrates by drinking honey mead for thirty days.

The Teutonic word **mona** was simultaneously the name of their moon goddess, the word for moon and the word for month.

Does

The prestige of the deer in symbolism in Europe is not simply connected with its beautiful appearance and agility, but also with the phenomenon of the cycle of regeneration and the growth of its antlers. The northern people still believe (in the hunting stage, as in Lapland) in the mother of the universe as a doe-elk or wild reindeer doe. Myths speak of a pregnant woman who rules the world and looks like a deer, covered with hair and with branching deer's horns on her head. The body of the doe of Muldava is decorated with crescents: hence the animal is shown to be closely related to moon symbolism.

Moonraker

Moon'rak''er, 1 munrek or; 2 moon'rak'er. n. 1. Naut. A sail carried above the sky-scraper. 2. A foolish person; specif., a native of Wiltshire, England; from the story that some Wiltshire rustics, seeing the reflection of the moon in a pond, tried to rake it out, thinking it a cheese. According to the Wiltshire version, the men were raking a pond for kegs of smuggled brandy and deceived the revenue officers with the cheese story. 3. A smuggler.

Germany

In war, every ancient German army had a prophetess, without whose advice nothing was attempted. At home, the seeresses were more respected than their male counterparts, as were the priestesses. When it came to war hostages, it is said that the Germanic chiefs preferred to give away themselves or send their sons, rather than part with their daughters. In old German poems of the third and fourth centuries the women woo the men.

The uterine line was preferred long after Romanization set in. In the time of Frederick the First (1152-1190) the children took on the status of the mother.

Lombards, Visigoths and Astrogoths

The Lombards, or Langobards, were named after their ancestress, Gambara. Visogoths and Ostrogoths always moved into the homes of their wives; their properties and titles were inherited only through the wives. Hence, in Saxony, it was not uncommon for a ruler on his deathbed to instruct his son to marry the widow after his death. Heirs apparent did not feel legitimate until they possessed the Queen.

Frigg-Freya, dawn & fertility

Fro-Freyr, growth

Scandinavia

Until the eighth century the succession went from mother to daughter and only through her could be inherited by the husband.

The shapes on the moon are traditionally said to be a girl and a boy holding a pail of water which they periodically spill. Our **Jack and Jill** folktale comes from this belief. The moon is often thought to be a repository for the cast-offs of earth, such as broken vows, misspent youth and useless tears.

Greenland

It is believed that the moon is a male god who will impregnate women who sleep in the moonlight, unless they take the precaution of spreading some spittle on their bellies.

138

Finland

Kuu is the name of the moon.

Romania

The Moon is the Sun's sister. But the Sun lusts for her and so she hides when he rises and comes out only when he sets.

Serbia (Yugoslavia)

The Moon was The Bald Uncle and his name was Myesyats. Although the name is masculine, in some legends the Moon is represented as a feminine beauty whom the Sun marries in summer, abandons in winter, and returns to in Spring. The divine couple of the Sun and Moon give birth to the stars. When the pair is in a bad mood and not getting on well together, an earthquake results.

In some legends, the Moon is masculine and is married to the Sun who is a woman.

Even in modern Yugoslavia certain expressions dedicated to curing illness beseech the Moon for help, starting out Pretty little moon. . . .

Werewolves and Witches

It is a ubiquitous European folk belief that if a man falls asleep in the moonlight, especially on a Friday night on open ground with the light shining on his face, he will turn into a werewolf. There are similar thoughts on vampires as both are night creatures who prey on the blood of the innocent. But there are some significant differences. Vampires seem to be richer, usually living in castles. They also are often men and women, whereas werewolves are almost always men.

Vampire legends seem to come from two sources: the real reigns of terror by several berserk Germanic tyrants who literally "fed" on their serfs, and ancient cults which believed in the healing powers of blood and which invented various constructive or destructive rituals.

Becoming a vampire or a werewolf is a form of ritual initiation, and automatically separates the Christians from the non-Christians. These blood and wolf initiations have their roots in the very ancient animal cults of Europe and elsewhere. Two of the critical steps in almost all ritual initiations are animal

siren merman harpy

communion and blood passage. All ·over the world ancient peoples practiced puberty and religious initiations which included isolation of the initiate into the forest for reversion to the ways of animals. (Leopard cults in Africa, bear cults in Italy, buffalo and polar bear cults in North America, bird cults in South America.) For the initiate this animal apprenticeship was to be a temporary slip back into pre-tribal consciousness to learn the raw secrets of nature, before being re-born as an adult back into the community.

Some of the initiates, however, did not make the necessary re-entry. Not all were mentally or spiritually strong enough and some were lost forever to adult human life. Romulus and Remus are two famous initiates who succeeded in re-entry after being "raised by wolves." Cannibalism or eating raw meat was often part of being animal-raised and the initiates who didn't make it died or sometimes **remained living their forest life, occasionally venturing out to attack people in the community.**

These "werewolves" were greatly feared by villages because they were lost souls who could not make civilized transitions and with whom one could not reason. Later, to the Christian Church, these people were doubly outcasts because it was clear that not only were they uncivilized in the ways of humans but they had also adhered to pagan religions. The Church probably magnified the horror of these legends to emphasize the need to ally oneself with it for salvation. One charm which will stop a vampire in its tracks is a cross. Other repellents are garlic and wolfbane herb. The cross and herbs were probably initially part of the more ancient religious rites, being the cross of the tree of life, the symbol of the goddess, into whose cult they were being initiated. Later it seemed that the only thing that could save was the cross of Christianity.

140

In another aspect, the tales of werewolves and vampires particularly reflect the religious struggles between male secret societies and female ones, between patriarchy and matriarchy. In the greater percentage of legends, vampire and werewolf alike are male feeding on women and children. These stories reflect an era in which one of the focuses of the male cults became terrorizing the female societies in power struggle. At first the attacks were organized. When male power began to overthrow the female cults, organization was less necessary and the earlier practices turned into generalized license for men to assault women. Wife-beaters and rapists are the modern day werewolves. Societies of women are once again organizing to protect themselves from these tactics.

Psychic werewolf and vampire states (usually attributed to the influence of the moon) are also indications of our cultural unfamiliarity with unconscious states and our general discomfort with the instinctual. Because of this fear, violence has been substituted for passion and repression for initiation.

Women have a little less of these perverted substitutions because they have been permitted to remain "emotional creatures" and, therefore, less thrown off-balance by intensity of feeling. This discrepancy is reflected in the legends in which women rarely become werewolves (and only become vampires if they submit to male dominance) and are not considered to have the same kind of vulnerability to moon light. Werewolves and vampires are tortured, remorseful creatures. What most Moon women become in legend is witches, who are usually portrayed as happy in their craft.

Wyfe, I weene thou art dronke or Leunitike.
Nay husband, women are never moon sicke.

—Epigram, 1867

Celtic witch's foot

Gypsies

The majority of Gypsies, apart from the Mussulmans, have a very defined female cult. **De Develeski** is the Divine Mother, the Mother of us All, who has always existed (even prior to O Del, the god). O Del made O Cham the Sun and O Shion, the Moon.

Although a solar cult among the Gypsies is often mentioned, it is difficult to study because precise documents are lacking. This is one series of cultures in which there is more information on the cult of the Moon. On the nijako-staff of chiefs of tribes, the Sun had right to second place. This staff is a silver stick, on top of which is an octagonal disk, red tassel, battle axe, sun, moon, star, and cross, in that descending order.

Many Gypsies take off their clothes to the Moon. Kalderash Gypsies recite to the New Moon:

The New Moon has come out—May She be lucky for us—She has found us penniless- —May She leave us with Good Fortune—And with Good Health, and more.

The second most important person in the tribe next to the Chief is the Phuri Dai. She is a wise old woman whose opinion is taken by the Chief and who is in charge of women and children.

There is a cult within Christian Gypsies that is devoted to the Black Virgins. Most of these are the Virgin Mary, but one is known as Sara the Kali (Kali meaning the Black Woman in Gypsy). One of the people of the Belgian Gypsies who received the first revelation was Sara Kali. She was of noble birth and was chief of her tribe on the banks of the Rhone. She knew the secrets which had been transmitted to her. Near the Rhone the tribes worked in metals and engaged in commerce. The Rom at that time practiced a polytheistic religion, and once a year took out on their shoulders a statue of Ishtari and walked into the sea to receive benediction there.

An important Gypsy time of celebration are the days from May 24 to 25 on which is held the pilgrimage to Sainte-Marie-de-la-Mer. The people walk to the church in that village where they spend the night in the crypt in which a statue of Sara Kali is kept, along with an ancient altar said to be an old blood sacrifice altar of the Mithraic cult (as well as a 3rd Century Christian altar). The statue of Sara la Kali is not an ancient one; it is plaster, painted black several times over, from the eighteenth century, but evidently modeled on an earlier wooden statue. The Gypsies keep watch in the crypt and devote themselves to two acts of ritual, touching and hanging up garments. The women in particular stroke the statue, and kiss the hems of its many garments. Like the Virgin of the Spanish Gypsies, the Virgin of the Macarenas, she wears seven petticoats. They also hook up clothes beside her that they have brought, handkerchiefs, silk bodices, slips, silk kerchiefs. Finally they touch the statue with objects, photographs, medals, and clothing, representing those absent or sick. In the practices they are like the Dravidians of Northern India who have trees or images, covered with rags of clothing, they call Chitraiya Bhavani, **Our Lady of the Rags**. The last aspect of their ritual devotion is a procession to the sea and symbolic immersion.

Gypsy Ritual Dances

In Yugoslavia, Gypsy women dancers, or dodole, serve by their rhythms to prevent sterility in herds of cattle. The ground on which they have danced is said to cure warts and gall stones. In Bulgaria, the dancers are sprinkled with water to bring rain.

In Romania, Gypsy women have long danced a very ancient dance which served to create collective ecstasy. They also perform a Snake dance, often confused by outsiders with belly dancing because of the undulations.

One of the indications of their old matriarchal tradition is that lineage was formerly through the mothers only.

The Magic Flute

Mozart's opera tale **The Magic Flute** comes from very old European folktales. In the current version of the story the Queen of the Night is mourning because her daughter has been abducted by the Sun King. The three women attendants to the Queen find a beautiful young prince who falls in love with a picture of the princess and agrees to go set her free.

Do not tremble, my dear son.
I see that you are gentle, wise: the one
The fates have sent to take my part
Avenging, yes, avenging mine, a mother's ruined heart.
A villain, ah, a demon, wicked, a magician
Stole from me, my daughter, my loved child.
You have come to bring her back to me again!

For protection on his journey the prince is given a magic flute. He locates the Palace of the Sun, but is won over by the appeal of the order there, called the Order of Reason. Aided by the magic flute he and the princess successfully undergo trial by fire and emerge into the council of wise old men into the Light of Reason. In the final scene, the mother Queen of the Night makes a last attempt to retrieve her daughter but is repelled by the forces of reason.

This is clearly an allegory of initiation recommending father-sun worship and portrays mother-moon as a conniving weaker witch. It indicates the matriarchal-patriarchal struggles which persisted up to very recent European times telling of the change in dominance of Father Reason over Mother Feeling. At the grief of the banished mother, not only is the son sun-initiated, but also the daughter as well.

Germanic magic fire eye

A right jolly moon am I.
I'm fixed far up in the sky.
But I see much fun when the day is done,
That I cannot be sad if I try!

—English Rhyme, early 1900's

Mother Goose

Mother Goose is a comparatively modern fairy tale version of the witch-moon-goddess, lover of children and women, who rides through the air on a white bird. The songs and rhymes in the Mother Goose collection are largely secularized poems recording ancient sacred mythologies describing the seasonal celebrations.

Old Mother Goose

Old Mother Goose when
    She wanted to wander,
Would ride through the air
    On a very fine gander.

Mother Goose had a house,
    'Twas built in a wood,
Where an owl at the door
    For a sentinel stood.

The Man In the Moon

The Man in the Moon came tumbling
    down,
    And asked the way to Norwich;
He went by the south, and burnt his
    mouth
    With eating cold pease porridge.

Old Woman, Old Woman

There was an old woman tossed in a basket,
    Seventeen times as high as the moon;
But where she was going no mortal could tell,
    For under her arm she carried a broom.
Old Woman, old woman, old woman, said I,
    Whither, oh whither, oh whither so high?
To sweep the cobwebs from the sky;
    And I'll be with you by-and-by.

Selene going down into the sea

GREECE AND ROME

Medusa

Crete

One of the most salient features of the Minoan moon goddess was her three-fold representation of the dove. Sometimes the doves were shown atop three columns, a symbol of divine fertility in Crete. Often she is shown wearing the calendar necklace of twelve lunar discs or a similar headdress. These representations are found from the earliest times to the middle of the 7th century B.C. The Cretan goddess was closely associated with the goat, the pig and the dove. When the Dorians invaded Crete, the people fled to Kaphri which became a secluded mountain enclave of Minoan culture, in an effort to preserve the civilization. The triple-goddess became the three graces or muses. Helen-Dendritus was a pre-Hellenic goddess of Nature associated with the three phases of the moon. She was usually depicted wearing a crown.

The Aegean

Medusa and other Greek goddesses of the old Titan generation were established in Greece and the Aegean long before the Hellenes appeared. They exhibit every possible sign of an original relationship to an extremely early neolithic, perhaps even mesolithic, lunar serpent-pig context, represented in the myths and rites on the one hand of Melanesia and the Pacific, and on the other, of Celtic Ireland. The usual form in which Medusa is shown squatting, arms raised, tongue hanging, eyes wide—is a pose that is characteristic of the guardian of the other world in the pig cults of Melanesia.

In Troy, paintings have been found of a pig dotted with stars representing the sky woman as sow.

147

Cadmus, founder of Thebes, was led to the site of Thebes by a cow with a moon-sickle whom he then sacrificed to the Goddess.

Among the Hittites, the Moon was called Arma, meaning big, pregnant.

Selene drawing the moon across the sky

Greece

Endymion the shepherd,
As his flock he guarded,
She, the Moon, Selene,
Saw him, loved him, sought him,
Coming down from heaven
To the glade on Latmus,
Kissed him, lay beside him.
Blessed is his fortune,
Evermore he slumbers,
Tossing not nor turning,
Endymion the shepherd.

In Greek religion, in the very earliest days there was only Selene, the Moon. Then came Aphrodite the Bright Moon and Hecate the Dark Moon. Later still there were three-headed Artemis, the Crescent Moon; Selene, the Full moon; and Hecate, the Waning moon. Often they were depicted as Maiden, Mother, and Crone. This carried into the Demeter myth, where even though the mythological personages are tainted with patriarchal themes and attitudes, we still find traces of moon mythology. In the three main characters we see the three aspects of the Goddess: Persephone the waxing moon, Demeter, the full moon and Hecate, the waning moon.

The myth, upon which the Eleusinian Mysteries are based goes like this: One day, while picking flowers in a meadow, the Kore (maiden, in Greek) was horrified when the earth opened up near her and Hades, the God of the Underworld came out on his stallion, grabbed her and took her into his terrible kingdom. The ground sealed up after him so there was no trace left to show where she had gone. Only Hecate, the Moon had observed them. Demeter came looking for her daughter. When she called and there was no answer, she became afraid. She went all over the world trying to find her, but none had seen her. Demeter's grief was so great that she laid the earth waste; nothing would grow. Finally she questioned Hecate and the Moon told her what she had seen. Demeter went to Zeus and demanded that his brother return her child. Seeing that she would kill everything that grows and that all humanity would die, Zeus sent Hermes to Hades' kingdom to demand the return of the Kore; she could only return if she had eaten no food from the kingdom of the Dead. Hermes went down and demanded the girl. Hades had made her the Queen of his kingdom and her name was Persephone, but she was so unhappy, she had only cried and refused to eat. Hermes started to lead her back into the world, to her Mother, but the gardener of Hades came forward and swore that he had seen her eat seven pomegranate seeds (or three in some versions). Because of this, she could return to her Mother, but must spend part of each year in the Underworld.

Seven is the number of moons that a farmer must wait to see the growth of his corn. Three is the number of months to the season of Winter when Demeter is mourning and will let nothing grow.

In Greece also was the worship of Aphrodite Eurynome, a moon goddess, whose statue was a mermaid carved in wood in her temple in Phigalia in Arcadia. Sacred to her were the murex, the myrtle tree, the palm tree, the dove, the tunny, the sturgeon, scallop, periwinkle, and the colors white, green, blue and scarlet.

The Willow

In Greece the willow was sacred to Hecate, Circe and Persephone, all dark aspects of the Triple Moon Goddess worshipped by witches. The willow (helice) gave its name to the Helicon, abode of the nine muses, the orgiastic priestesses of the Moon Goddess. The willow is sacred for many reasons. It is the tree that most loves water and the Moon Goddess is the giver of dew and moisture. Its leaves and bark, the source of salicyclic acid, are sovereigns against rheumatism formerly thought to be caused by witchcraft.

A Greek Sculpture of the Goddess with moon-disk head is now in the Louvre. The Goddess of Ascalon was variously called Atargatis, Derketo, Athara, and frequently represented as half-woman, half-fish.

Sparta

The Spartans missed the battle of Marathon because the moon was not in the right quarter for starting battle.

The Dorians

The Dorians named themselves after the moon Goddess, Doris. Dorians and Ionians both claim descent from Helena-Selene, the Moon Goddess. Spartus, or Spurius means **mother's sons**, or swamp plants procreated fatherlessly by an unknown planter. Spartan girls, prior to marriage, enjoyed freedom over their bodies and sexuality. No difference was made between legitimate and illigitimate children.

The Virgins

The Greek word **parthenos**, refers to Virgin Artemis and, translated correctly, means unmarried woman, the initial meaning of the word virgin. Therefore, Artemis is the goddess of fecundity, not wedlock, and all virgin goddesses were originally fertility goddesses before their patriarchal redefinition. **Parthenioi** means **virgin born**. This correct ancient translation explains some of the seeming contradiction of the **virgin births** of later religious mythology. **Parthenoioi** was applied to the children born of holy fertility rituals.

Artemis

The Amazons built a temple at Ephesus to house an image of a goddess later identified with Artemis. This temple was destroyed by Barbarians in the middle of the 7th Century. About 100 years later King Croesus erected a temple there which became one of the Seven Wonders of the World. The chief object of veneration, mentioned in the Acts of the Apostles, was a palm wood statue of Artemis. This temple was the recipient of rich gifts, often gold and silver awnings or garments for the statue which were changed at intervals. To some of these were attached large golden sculptured dates, giving the appearance of clusters of breasts. On the head of the Goddess was a shrine which probably contained the diopet, the most ancient and sacred thing in the temple. This was a small stone, possibly a meteorite from neolithic times thought to be thrown by Zeus, which had been venerated at Ephesus since long before the Ionians came.

The temple continued in fame and splendour until the second half of the 3rd Century A.D. About the year 400, the statue was smashed by a Christian who boasted on an inscription that he had wrecked the "demon" Artemis. It is said that the diopet was saved and hidden; and it is quite possible that it is an object now in the Liverpool City Museum.

Rome

One day while Diana the Moon was bathing at a pool with her attendant nymphs, a Prince by the name of Actaeon came upon her and saw the Goddess naked and he desired her. She spotted him and turned him into a stag, whereupon he bolted away and the hounds of his father chased him down and killed him. Diana felt this was just punishment for a mortal to look upon a Goddess as he would a woman and not give her the worship she had right to.

She was also known by the name Juno Lucetia, a moon goddess, and in this aspect was the feminine principle of light, and the female counterpart of Jupiter who was the masculine principle.

Because wild animals live by the moon, Diana is their Goddess. And because human hunters depend on the moon to light their way, they must appeal to her for guidance. The moon is the hunter's companion.

Diana was portrayed as the friend of the deer and as the hunter of evil men. She allowed men to hunt in her forest, unless they broke her laws.

Diana was the Roman-Italian version of Artemis. There is a legend that she was brought to Italy in a bundle of faggots. This is based perhaps on the symbol of the flame that is latent in wood, as the Goddess is frequently portrayed as a flame. Diana is thought of as the Goddess of the Woodlands. Her sanctuaries were commonly in groves and she is often associated in dedications with the forest god Sylvanus.

Diana was conceived as the moon and especially the yellow harvest moon. She filled the farmer's grange with goodly fruits and heard the prayers of women in travail. In her sacred grove in Nemi she was worshipped as a Goddess of Childbirth who bestowed offspring on men and women. Her sanctuary on the Aventine in Rome reveals her in an image copied from the many-breasted idol of the Ephesian Artemis of Fecundity.

The Cult of Diana

In ancient Italy her oldest and most famous place of worship was at Aricia, near the modern Nemi. Here a volcanic lake called the Mirror of Diana, is surrounded on all sides but one by precipitous, densely wooded slopes. In a grove, Nemus, on the only accessible shore was the sanctuary of Diana, said to have been founded around 500 B.C., although the cult itself had far older origins.

Diana was worshipped as Goddess of fertility and childbirth, of hunting, of wild and domestic animals. She had three natures, thus called Triformis and was sometimes represented with the heads of a horse, dog and bear. She was Luna the moon in heaven, Diana on earth and Hecate in the infernal regions. In the latter character she presided over enchantments, and was also called Trivia, Ruler of Crossroads.

In historical times, the priesthood of Diana at Nemi was without parallel. The priest, or the King of the Grove, was always a runaway slave who, coming to Nemi, had to pluck a bough from a certain tree and engage the current priest in single and mortal combat. Victorious, he then lived in perpetual expectation of challengers, one of whom in due time would overcome him and succeed him in his priestly duties and terrors.

This **laying on of hands**, was an echo of more ancient ritual human sacrifices.

Slaves had a holiday on Diana's principle festival in mid-August, which was transformed by the Christians into the Feast of the Assumption of the Virgin Mary, also venerated as patroness of outlaws and thieves.

There are records in the 10th Century which refer to wicked women who attended meetings by night with the pagan Goddess Diana, the twin sister of Apollo. Diana was known for her liking for exclusively female society, her savagery toward certain men and toward her female attendents if they involved themselves with men; her folk cults were associated with gynandry.

152

INDIA

Shakti is the root of all that exists; it is out of Her that the Universes are manifested; it is She who sustains them and, at the end of time, it is in Her that the worlds will be reabsorbed.

—The Tantratattva

Soma

Soma was a sacred plant, an essential part of ancient Indian sacrificial offerings. The god, Soma symbolizes immortality and victory over death to all who drink of him. Frequently he symbolizes the Moon. In the Puranas (later Vedic Hymns) Soma's qualities appear:

May the god Soma, He who is called the Moon, liberate me. . . . Thanks to Soma the Adityas are powerful; thanks to Soma the earth is large; and Soma is placed in the midst of the Stars. When the plant is crushed, they who drink of it consider it as soma, but no one can drink what the holies consider soma.

Soma was born from the churning of the sea. The twenty-seven lunar stations are his wives, the daughters of Daksha. The waning of the moon is sometimes explained by the fact that the gods are drinking the soma it contains. Another legend has it that Soma sprang from the eye of the wise Atri, son of Brahma. His other names are Candras and Indus. The words for cow and moon are both gaus in Sanskrit.

154

Kundalini Yoga

The two spiral channels on either side of the central channel of the spine, up which the serpent power is supposed to flow through a control of mind and breath, are called the lunar and solar channels.

Sarasvati

She was originally a water deity and later identified with Vach, the Goddess of Speech, who invented Sanskrit and discovered soma in the Himalayas, bringing it to the other gods. She originated in the ocean and was the power behind all phenomena and mistress of all. She is goddess of all the creative arts and in particular poetry, music, learning and science. She is represented as a graceful woman with white skin, wearing a crescent moon on her brow. She rides a swan or a peacock or is seated on a lotus flower. It is said that the full moon is in the center of the lotus.

Five Nations of Vedic Aryans

They are descended from the five Jayati sons, tracing themselves back to Ita, their creatress and the source of their name, as did the first Indo-Aryan dynasts, the Moon or Parava rulers.

Brahmans

The greatest and most powerful enemy of women's free participation in the affairs of the world in India was the Brahman priesthood after its victory over the warrior caste of the Kshatriyahs. Brahmans excluded women from all religious and official actions, and women were no longer allowed to even read the sacred writings, which they had helped to write. In the **Mahabharata**, Pandy says to Kunty, his young wife:

Hear then O woman of the beautiful face with the sweet smile, that formerly the women were not locked in the houses dependent on husbands and relatives. They were accustomed to walk freely where they pleased, amusing themselves as best they could. In no way, thou woman of wonderful character, were they faithful to their men, and they were not adjudged guilty for that reason, for this was the accepted custom of the times. . . . Truly that custom, so indulgent with the women has the blessings of vurnerability. The present custom, on the other hand, that they are bound to one man for life, was established a short time ago.

Tantra

Tantra equates the male ejaculation to oil being poured out in sacrifice; the friction of the sexual organs with the rubbing of sticks to light fire; the vagina of the female companion (who should for the extreme left-hand ritual, be menstruating so that her own vital energies are at their peak) with the altar onto which the sacrifice is poured; the fire with the enjoyment; and the woman with the Great Goddess. The White and the Red were thus combined, an important symbolic conjunction throughout Tantra.

Indian tradition has it that on different days of the month a woman's sexual sensitivity, which is related to cosmic movements by her own periods, needs to be triggered by special attention to different parts of her body. Ancient diagrams illustrate these trigger points and relate them to phases of the moon. Ritual sexual acts are preceded by the annointing of different parts of the woman's body with differently perfumed symbolic oils.

Important was the idea that divination can be performed by a member of the opposite sex who has already been raised to a high spiritual level, and thus has the capacity to initiate. The women were called Dakinis in Buddhism; they have more recently been converted into fantasy figures called Dutis.

It is probable that in ancient times the special potency of Tantra was transmitted along a female line of power holders; initiation was by ritual sexuality with them. Some scholars have identified them with a mysterious old sect of women called the Vrayas. This connects with what can be learned about archaic cult practices among early paleolithic peoples. It also accounts for the way in which female energy symbolism has survived in later religions such as Tibetan Buddhism and Brahmanical monasitic Tantra, which were male oriented and not at all likely to have discovered the female principle for themselves. Female transmission was bound to be entirely outside the caste system, which depended on strict rule and custom. Such female transmitters became outcasts, and as sexual partners, defiling. To seek an initiation with them would have placed the sadhaka beyond normal society. Most Bengali erotic poetry, both Buddhist and Krishna-Hindu, makes a point of the fact that the beloved (outer and inner) is of degraded caste!

There has been much dispute as to whether the rite worked better if the couples were or were not married to each other. On the whole the weight of opinion favored ritual intercourse outside the marriage bond, and in the cakra couples could split to pair with the husbands or wives of the others. The rite could be preceded by the adoration of one or more virgins through whom the presence of the Goddess was invoked. It is also probable that in some versions of the rite a human initiated Dakini played the role and some form of preliminary intercourse was had with her by male participants. At a high level of practice, with participants of Vira, or heroic status, other things were practiced.

Time is always the field of the Goddess. Her most important name is Kali Time. It is important for sadhana to incorporate a comprehensive imagery of Time. This can be done by meditating on and making a special kind of yantra.

There is a description of the moon in a yantra described by Shiva in the **Mahanirvana Tantra**:

Encircling the moon, a crowd of stars. . . . The Moon is white. . . . The Moon should be visualized as holding nectar in one hand, and giving with the other.

Prakraty, Vedic-Hindu Power of Manifestation

Durga

The Hindu goddess Durga is brave, powerful and strong. A beautiful, black haired woman clothed in red and gold, she rides a ravenous lion and holds a weapon in each of her eighteen hands. She is a warrior goddess, embodiment of angry, affirming strength. Her image can be seen all over India today.

Fire

The first fire came from the woman in the Moon rubbing her genitals.

The cosmic force has been personified as the great goddess since neolithic times in India; tantra is the surviving fertility cult. Because the kundalini energy is warm inside one, it is associated with fire, the gift of the moon. Shakti, the great goddess is supposed to be born of the anger of the gods at injustice in the universe; their anger heated to such a great force that it bore Her, and she crushed the monster who was endangering the universe. This birth by fire is seen as the minor gods giving back their power and allegiance to the Source and thereby restoring the primitive state of balanced universe. The religious power in people is felt/conceived as heat in the body; a power which one needs to learn to channel, for comfort. So the power over one's circulation and body temperature is considered a sign of religious quality. Possession by something sacred causes heat in the body; **shanti**, sanskrit for **peacefulness**, comes from another sanskrit root word which means **cooling down**. These two temperatures suggest the cycle of religious awakening. The religious creative cycle is supposed to be the pattern for all other creative processes, the imitation of the creation of the world.

Parashakti, Brahmanic-India tripartite mother

The Lotus

The highest spiritual body center is the thousand petalled lotus called the place of the hidden moon.

The Garland of the Divine Mother Goddess is made of many moons representing various aspects of her power as one moon reflected in countless waters (Brahmabindu Upanishad).

158

Chandra

Chandra is a moon god who rides in a chariot pulled by antelope-deer. He is consort to 27 beautiful women who are stars. He protects the world from chaos and ignorance.

Moonstone

A whitish, cloudy feldspar gemstone which is said to contain an image of the moon. The Hindus believe this stone was formed by the congealing of the moon's rays. A moonstone owned by Pope Leo X (1475 to 1521) was said to wax and wane in brilliance with the moon. Held in the mouth at the full of the moon it will reveal the future. It is well thought of by lovers since it evokes tender passions. It brings luck to its owner, cures epilepsy, nervousness, has a cooling effect and makes trees fruitful. There are large moonstone mines in India and Africa.

Jotma, Might, India

Burma

A grandmother who lay dying had but one thing to leave her grandson: a pestle. After she died, he carried it with him everywhere for he knew that if she left it to him it must be valuable. One day as he was carrying it, he met a snake and the snake asked to borrow the pestle. When the young man asked why, he said it was for his dead mate whom he wished to restore to life. The man professed he knew nothing about such magical properties in the pestle, but the snake insisted and took him to its mate. There the snake bade the young man put the pestle to the nose of the dead snake. When he did so, the snake came back to life. The other snake thanked him and said, Now you know how to use it. But make sure you never tell anyone how you do it or the secret will no longer work. The young man returned to his village and lying outside the village was a dog that had died many days before and was putrifying. He held the pestle up to the nose of the dog and it immediately came back to life. He called it Master Putrid and kept it for his own pet.

159

Thereafter he healed many dead people and brought them back to life. Soon the King heard of it. He summoned the lad and bade him restore his dead daughter. When he did so, the King gave her to him in marriage. The young man did not even tell her of his secret pestle.

One day, he thought to himself, If this magic pestle will restore life, might it not give everlasting youth if used on live people? So at night, after his wife was asleep, he put the pestle under her nose and under his own and within several weeks he saw that the pestle conferred eternal youth upon them.

Now it happened that the Moon which shone down every night in full splendour, noticed this too, and was very jealous. All things grow old and die, said she. Even the sun which shines so splendidly by day turns red and fades by night. I will steal that magic pestle from him. It is not right that a mortal should have it.

One day when the young man had washed the pestle and put it on the lawn to dry, the Moon thought she might have her chance. All day he guarded it, until his wife chided him for being so silly. Even then, he was reluctant to leave. So he had his faithful dog, Master Putrid guard it for him. The moon came down by day to steal it so she was invisible, but the dog smelled a strange scent and was alert. The Moon stole the pestle and ran away with it, but the dog smelled the scent of the pestle and chased her even though she was invisible. Thus each evening the dog is chasing the Moon. Because he is always sniffing the pestle he remains eternally youthful and immortal. Sometimes he catches the Moon and swallows her, but he always must throw her up again as she is too big for his throat. When the Burmese see an eclipse of the Moon, they say, Master Putrid has swallowed the Moon again.

Cambodia

The moon was held to be ruler of everything that grows on the earth, protector of all living things. Its waning was considered to be a sickness. The full moon marked the turning point for good luck, the summit on which all changes stood in balance.

Maja, Vedic-Hindu Allmother

OCEANIC ISLES

Hina-who-worked-in-the-moon floated as a Bailer,
She was taken into a canoe and called Hina-the-bailer,
She was carried to the shore and put by the fire,
Coral insects were born, the eel was born,
The sea-urchin was born, the volcanic stone was born,
So she was called HINA-from-whose-womb-came various forms.

—Cumulipo Chant[13]

Hawaii

In Hawaii, the Moon's name is Hina and there are as many creation myths about the sun and moon as there are islands. In the Gilbert Islands, the Sun and Moon are the children of the first man and woman created by Na Reau. He forbade them to have children. When they did he picked up his club and went to their island to punish them. In terror, they threw themselves at his feet. They begged him to spare their children because the Sun enabled them to see and when he was resting, his brother, the Moon took over. Na Reau left without hurting them.

In the Celebes, the Moon, Sun and stars make up the body of a heavenly woman. In Nias, Sun and Moon were formed from the eyes of the armless and legless being from whose heart sprang buds which were the origin of gods and humans. In the Cook Islands, Sun and Moon are the eyes of Valca. In the Society Islands, Samoa and New Zealand, they are the children of heaven placed in the sky as eyes.

In Queensland, the female Sun was made by the Moon. In the Palau Islands, two gods made the Sun and Moon by cutting two stones with an adz and throwing them to the sky. In the Admiralty Islands, two mushrooms were thrown into the sky. The one thrown by First Man became the Moon; the one thrown by First Woman became the Sun. On Woodlark Island the only person possessing fire originally was an old woman. Her son stole it to give to mankind. In rage the woman took what fire she had left, divided it and threw both parts into the sky, where the larger became the Sun and the smaller the Moon. The Arunta of Australia believe that the Moon was the special property of a man of the Oppossum totem. It was stolen. The Oppossum man was unable to catch the thief so he shouted to the Moon to go into the sky.

Papua

A man dug a deep hole one day and discovered a small bright object. When he picked it up it began to grow. Slipping out of his hands it rose into the sky and became the Moon. It would have been brighter if it had stayed in the ground until it was born naturally.

Moonblink

Moonblink is a term which refers to a condition of temporary blindness supposed to be brought on by sleeping in moonlight in tropical climates.

162

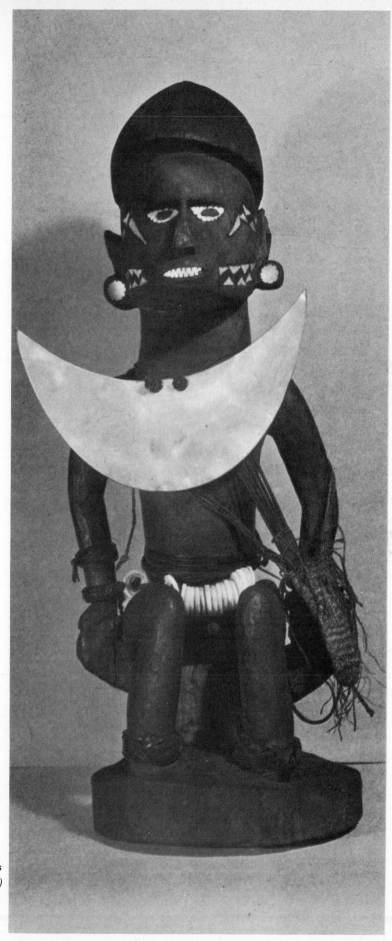

Moon Spirit, Solomon Islands
(wood & mother-of-pearl)

Moonspots

In New Guinea the moon was in the beginning hidden in a pitcher by an old woman. Some boys noticed it and opened the pitcher. The Moon came out and rose into the sky. The spots on the Moon are the marks of the boys' hands trying to hold it back.

In the Cook Islands the Moon fell in love with a pretty girl, came down to earth and eloped with her back to the sky. She is still there and you can see her with her heaps of leaves for the oven and her tongs to settle the embers.

In Maori myth a man went to the Moon in search of his wife. He and the Moon man spend their lives eating each other, which is why the Moon diminishes.

To the Wongibon of New South Wales the Moon is an old man who before going to heaven hurt his back by falling off a rock. He walks bent over which is why the Moon has a bowed back each month as it appears.

Australian Aboriginies

Wuinpranili is Sun Woman with Moon Man of Japara. They carry torches of flaming bark. When they reach the Western Horizon, they extinguish the torches using the smouldering ends to light their return eastward through the darkness of the underworld. In the morning the fire lit by the Sun Woman to prepare her torch of bark creates the first light of dawn. She achieves the Western horizon at sunset. Before she returns to her camp, she paints herself with red ochre causing the beautiful colors of the sunset.

Java and Bali

In Java it was customary to burn the bodies of princes in coffins shaped like bulls to take them to the moon spirit.

Malay

In Maylayan mythology the shadows on the moon are a hunch-backed man sitting under a banyam tree.

164

New Guinea

For the Papuans the moon is a girl's first husband. They assume that menstration is proof of the relations between women and the moon.

Mother Moon and Father Sun watch over the sky. Moon fertility figures are made for many uses. Some double as fishing net holders and fertility charms to enlist the grace of the moon to guide the fish into the net. (See illus. page 217). The image of mother and child is a sympathetic image of multiplication. There is also a belief that the moon was originally a child's ball which the sun god Waneka tricked some children into throwing up to him. He was tired of working both night and day and used this ball to light the nights.

Queen Pomare and her daughter

Polynesia

Maui, the Maori hero returns, at the end of an adventurous life, to his native country to the house of his grandmother Hinenui-te-po, the Great Lady of the Night. She is sleeping. Quickly throwing off his clothes he prepares to enter the giantess' body. He is attended by birds which he forbids to laugh before they see him come out victorious. The birds are silent as long as Maui is passing through the body of his grandmother; when they see him half-way out of her mouth the birds burst into laughter, and the Great Lady of the Night shuts her teeth on him, cutting him in two, so that he dies. That is why we are mortal. If Maui had managed to emerge unscathed from his grandmother's body, we would have gained immortality.

Hina, the woman who beats tapa cloth in the Moon, has a dual nature. She is first woman and Goddess of the Land of the Dead, life-giver and life-destroyer. Tane is both her father and lover. She is involved in the firewalkers' fertility ceremonies.

Tahiti

On the Tahitian island of Moorea a stone moon temple or **marae** still stands from the sacred rituals of long ago. It is made of many stone spheres, all about the same size, creating a low step pyramid. Close to it is another temple consisting of a rectangular space marked out in the forest by a low stone wall enclosing an area of grass peppered with irregularly placed stone slabs. These were markers of special meditation spots for worshippers. In front of these temples the mountain drops off at a steep incline opening before you the immensity of the clear blue sea, defined at the island by the beautiful crescent bay of Moorea. Legend about these temples is very awesome to the Tahitians and no one dares to disturb the area. Occasionally a tourist will remove a spherical stone from a temple wall and, as the stories go, disaster and the revenge of Tupapau always follow this violator of the place of the gods.

Tahiti, one of the most famous matriarchies existing today, has long been known as a **paradise on earth**, a land of luscious fruit, sweet flowers, clear blue lagoons and happy beautiful people. The person we have most records of today who was prominent in Tahitian history is Queen Pomare Vahine IV who ruled from 1827, at age 14, to 1877, the year of her death. She was known for her

Queen Pomare

practicality, her dignity and her joyousness, as well as her exasperation of missionaries who attempted to restrict her sexual habits and convince her to be "serious."

Even after Tahiti became a French protectorate, Queen Pomare was supported by the people and was kept in office as head of state. Her daughter-in-law attested Pomare remained **Tahitian in her soul** paying some tribute to the Europeans but basically disregarding their ways. She had an entourage of ladies in waiting, elderly relations, old nursemaids and **tahua** or high-priestess witch-healers. Maidens massaged her while she slept. She lived most of the time on the island of Pepeete in an oval-shaped palm house.

Though with the establishment of the French and other outsiders in Tahiti it has become harder for the people to **remain Tahitian in their souls**, the cultures of the islands still seem remarkably un-westernized. From what i know from my own visit there in 1974, it is a place to go and stay, to get to know as much as one can today, some of the experiences of a matriarchal culture.

RITUAL
AND
INITIATION

RITUAL AND INITIATION

An initiation is an event which marks, or causes, a change in level of awareness. Ritual is the methodology by which this change is achieved. Every culture at every stage seems to have the phenomenon of these ceremonies, whose purpose is to facilitate and celebrate significant growth. Initiations vary in content according to what facts or states the initiate is supposed to realize, but the basic structure of the ritual seems to be universal: (1) Separation of the individual according to sex from the rest of the community (into a hut in the woods, a cave, an official secret place). This symbolizes a return to a primal state, infancy, the womb. (2) Physical and spiritual tests, such as fasting, meditation, torture, riddles, which prove one's fitness for 'graduation.' Psychological dismemberment of the person's normal (and now former) mode of thought and behavior leads to symbolic 'death' to the former mode. (3) Education into the original, sacred, "higher" modes, through tutelage of people representing the gods, the ancestors, the initiated. (4) Vows of secrecy of the sacred process. (5) Ending with ritual rebirth to community life, by a new code of behavior, and often under a new name.

The purpose of initiation rituals is to teach several significant things: how to confront crisis and survive; how to contact deeper layers of awareness; how to distinguish the sacred—in other words, how to implement a system of regeneration. One of the most universal patterns of learning this skill is to imitate the original behavior of significant ancestors (personified as gods, animals or humans). The process is supposed to work on all levels. As the individual is regenerated, so is the community and the cosmos (hence the possibility of a savior or a scapegoat). The basic order of the universe is reenacted and, therefore, confirmed and resuscitated.

Initiation ceremonies are important because they instruct what values are considered 'higher.' In old-fashioned terms, they defined for a community what was religious. And from this definition of the sacred, all priorities followed. For

170

instance, if the ceremony taught the initiate that Jesus of Nazareth was the significant ancestor, then one would try to imitate his behavior in all modes of one's current life. Imitation of the 'perfect' life pattern of an ancestor is common to all initiation rituals. If one thought that the great ancestor was personified as a bear, as in some religions, then deification and imitation of its behavior took place. Initiations also determine which behavior codes are considered 'civilized.' Remnants of the ancient religious significance of these cults survives in the level at which people of different cultures regard the 'manners' of their culture as indicative of a person's spiritual level; everyone is a barbarian outside their own code.

There is a recognized era in which the activities of initiation societies reflected the struggle between matriarchy and patriarchy and were altered to promote the primacy of one or the other:

The morphology of men's secret societies is extremely complex. As to their origin, the most generally accepted hypothesis is the one originally suggested by Frobenius and revived by the historicocultural school. According to it, the male secret societies, or Societies of Masks, were a creation of the matriarchal cycle; their object was to terrify women, primarily by making them believe that the masks were demons and ancestral spirits, to the end of undermining the economic, social, and religious supremacy of woman which has been established by matriarchy.

—Eliade[14]

Religious power struggles occurred simultaneously with military struggles to determine what mode was to be considered **the establishment.** Although obviously in most countries partiarchy has been the dominant structure for centuries, the struggle has never stopped, and the issues are current in attempts to enforce patriarchal laws through The AMA, The Church and The Law.

It seems that women need female initiations and men need male ones, for to each of us what is a sacred mystery is largely determined by our attempt to understand our own sexual essence. The important initiation ceremonies of ancient peoples, as well as forms which still exist today, are timed by the major sexual changes, the onset of menstruation for girls, puberty for boys, marriage and birth. Some of the initiations celebrated by women have been: birth, menstruation, marriage, childbirth, divorce, physical or artistic prowess, death, rebirth.

In most ancient cultures, the pattern of the initial menstruation ritual is the same. At the sign of the first menstrual blood, the girl is separated from the community and educated. Among the Swahili in Africa, the girl is taken to an isolated place in the forest. In the customs of Brazil, the New Hebrides, the Veddahs, some African tribes and most North American Indians, the girl is confined to a special cabin. She is allowed to only associate with other women, not to see the light of the sun and is under the tutelage of older tribal women. She learns from them the secrets of sexuality, fertility, the customs of the tribe, religious traditions and is prepared for her innate role of the creatress. There are usually special dietary restrictions and special dress. At the end of the isolation period, often three days, the girl is decorated by the other women as well as painted red with ochre to simulate the regenerative female blood. Then she is led to a fresh water lagoon to be ritually cleansed. After this there is ecstatic, orgiastic celebration, song and dance, and she is taken back to the community to assume her role and responsibilities as an adult woman. Often she visits the houses in the village to receive gifts. The celebration culminates in a communal dance in the village.

For women, initiation is an introduction into the mystery of blood, their own miraculous blood, which is the source of life and fertility. This is different from the experience of male initiation, although many of the male initiatory rituals attempt to imitate female blood rituals as symbols of their change into adult sexuality, by either drawing blood from a part of their body, sacrificing an animal or by a ritual of subincision as practiced in Australian tribes, in which the young men's penises are split open to simulate the female genital opening and the flow of blood. There is also mutual imitation of the other sex: in some period of the initiation the boys are dressed as girls and the girls are dressed as boys, to symbolize their becoming whole persons in all aspects. For men, the initiatory ritual seems to be focused on learning invisible **secrets**, such as the ways of the sky god. Conversely for women, initiation is based on visible **miracles**, for women were originally worshipped because they could produce life, food and could bleed without dying. To both women and men initiation symbolizes return to the Great Mother, as the huts and dark caves are symbols of the womb, and a path of spiritual rebirth into a new and adult mode of heightened consciousness.

There is an almost universal mythology connected with initiation rites which tells of how in the beginning women possessed all cult secrets and sacred objects, and later men stole them. This seems to corroborate anthropological evidence that matriarchy or Great Goddess worship is the oldest form of social structure, and also that each culture went through a period of power struggle between the worship of the moon and sun, the dominance of matriarchy or patriarchy. There are myths in Japan, (where originally the moon was personified as a woman and has become a male god) which tell of the men and their gods attacking the meetings and spinning gatherings of the women. Mt. Sinai translates as **Mountain of the Moon**. In Babylonia **Sin** is the name of the moon deity who wrote down the laws from the sky; one of the laws passed on was the measuring of time by the moon. The religious calendar of the Jews is still a lunar calendar, as are most religious calendars. It seems that all religions were originally fertility religions, based on the birth power of women, so that most of the initiation symbology

172

comes from this cycle. The huts and retreats are wombs, as are all whales and monsters who swallow people and disgorge them; the experiences of the initiatory period represent the otherworldly experiences of pre-natal consciousness and closeness with the secrets of the universe; return to the community symbolizes rebirth, the second coming reacquaintance with the source mysteries of life as an adult.

I tried to think what remnants there are today of these patterns of initiatory rituals and cults for women in the Western world. Some that come to mind are: Christian baptism and confirmation, Sweet Sixteen celebrations, debutante coming-out parties, sororities, Daughters of the American Revolution, marriage, childbirth, death and the cult of the psychoanalyst. Most initiations have the possibility of repeating the patterns as the person attains higher levels of development, as exemplified, supposedly, in the HS, BA, MA, PhD system of exams and certificates. Graduates of initiatory trials usually come out with a renunciation of the old way of life, a new name, a new language, a new consciousness and the responsibility of teaching the uninitiated. M. Esther Harding, in WOMAN'S MYSTERIES, says that the process of psychological analysis has become the modern equivalent to the process of initiation to the moon goddess. Primal Scream Therapy has one of the more obvious initiation patterns. And the psychological process certainly has most of the earmarks of the mystery initiatory cults: separation of the patient from the community, return to infancy, focus on ancestors, dream study, secrecy of the process, tearing down and rebuilding the personality, and hopefully the rebirth of a more functional adult into the community. The modern day 'trials of the hero on the quest' seem to have narrowed down to studying, facing one's unconscious and paying the bills.

A flaw with this replacement of psychology for initiation to the mysteries of the moon is that few people seem to get 'reborn.' Freud himself claimed this as one of the flaws of his system, but this doesn't seem to daunt most analysts! One only has to think on the success ratio of the cases in mental institutions as well as the legendary lengthy process of analysis to wonder at the effectiveness of this mode as the major growth process. I see these processes as especially detrimental to women, as the creators and perpetuators of the systems are mainly white men, who, therefore, have no firsthand knowledge of the female psyche or feeling for what the importance of female experiences of reality are. Psychology may be an appropriate development process for men. I don't know. Jungian psychological theory and practice come closer to the scope of the broad social initiations of the ancients, but they still seem to me to perpetrate a very secondhand interpretation of the female. Some women Jungians, such as M. Esther Harding, Emma Jung and Irene de Castillejo, have written clarifying material in this area, though the Jungian definition of the feminine principle still dominates and, to me, distorts their insights. In this complex area, of course, nobody is totally pure and clear on what the female essence is, so an eclectic approach to the subject probably comes closest to truth. (You'll probably even find some confusions and contradictions in this area in my own theories! I hope you can correct them!) So it is important to explore different people's attitudes and findings at all levels of 'enlightenment.' It seems to me that the process of feminism is becoming the significant process today of female initiation. Feminist consciousness raising process contains the basic pattern of ancient lunar initiation: the initiates are separated by sex into education groups (CR); we are re-educated to the ways of our ancestors (herstory); often women take on new names; we learn a new language; and we are initiated back into the community as adults. The goal is viewed as the renaissance of the purer primal knowledge of the female essence.

Ancient female initiation patterns were supposed to imitate the maternal birth process as well as the process of eternal rebirth exemplified by the moon. The lesson of the lunar cycle is the lesson of the continuous growth cycle: beginning, fruition, death and beginning again. The message is a hopeful one and the rituals were usually ecstatic, peaceful and life-oriented.

In an era when mechanization has been so thorough, when the inclusion of subjective factors is considered a hinderance to the search for truth, when emotional and sensual development are sacrificed to industrial development, we have all but lost our capacity for planetary and personal rebirth—our capacity to contact the moon principle within ourselves and to integrate it into our lives. We need to relearn her invocations. We must relearn to be familiar in our unconscious and our emotions and to respect the powers of value we have abandoned because they are impossible to learn on a linear level. Many people in groups and as individuals are involved in this process. I am not suggesting any object or person (such as the moon or a goddess) be literally 'worshipped,' but what seems relevant and vital for us today to learn from these ancient customs is their respect for and powerful knowledge of the capacity for community and individual regeneration. Formed rituals are a way of contacting normally inaccessible levels of consciousness; initiations are celebrations of major changes in these levels. We can make our initiations today conscious, and nurture and develop our patterns of rebirth.

The next chapters contain ancient moon rituals from different cultures, then modern rituals being developed today. The hope of this information is that it will throw light on those connections which have persisted but are not recognized and encourage us to reestablish those connections which need to exist.

174

AFRICA

The aim of all religious and magical acts is to align ourselves with the essential energy of creation. The origin of symbolic religi-magical elements came from the most basic elements of life and fertility—flesh, blood, seed and sweat, which became bread, wine, water (or seeds) and salt. The circle—around a table, around a holy chalice, around a tree, around the open center—is the basic ritual form, and seasonal moon patterns the basic timing. Sometimes it was thought that to ensure fertility of crops and the community it was necessary to trade a life, in the form of plant, animal or human sacrifice, for the perpetuation of all life. It was thought that the more sacred the life given up, the more exquisite the life energy given back from the Creator. Thus the tradition of royal sacrifice (the king must die, Sang Real, Blood Royal, the yearly sacrificed priest, the Holy Grail, Jesus Christ, the saviour) the son of the Mother who dies yearly for the world but is constantly reborn, by the grace of the universal life force. These beliefs appear symbolically in rituals the world over.

Southern Rhodesia

Ancient Zimbabwe people painted and carved the lunar cycles of fertility on cave walls. Their king scheduled his public appearances according to the phases of the moon, which also governed his time of marriage, his sexual relations and his ritual time of death.

Pygmy

The feast for the new moon among African Pygmies takes place just before the rainy season. Pe, their moon goddess, is believed to be the principle of generation and the Mother of Fertility.

Moon, O Mother Moon, O Mother Moon,
Mother of living things,
Hear our voice, O Mother Moon!
O Mother Moon, O Mother Moon,
Keep away the spirits of the dead,
Hear our voice, O Mother Moon,
O Mother Moon! O Mother Moon!

—A Gabon Pygmy song

Guiana

Sir Walter Raleigh described Amazon customs of Guiana. The women met with men once a year. At that time all the kings of the borders assembled with the Queens of the Amazons. After the Queens had chosen, they cast lots for their valentines. For one month they feasted, danced and drank wines in abundance. When the Moon was done, they departed to their own provinces. If any of them gave birth to a son, they returned him to the father; if they bore a daughter they nourished and retained her.

Bavenda, South Africa

Fertility through cosmic harmony is achieved by the **Deumba** or python dance in which young virgins of the Bavenda tribe identify with the serpent force. After the rains, during ceremonial days, the old women initiate the virgins, conduct the ceremony and act as the pivot around which the dancers spiral in rhythmic movements simulating the coils of the python. Collapsing and reviving, they dance like the forces of nature in the seasonal round of death and rebirth.

Hottentots

The people throw mud balls at the moon for charms. At the new moon, the people go cry to the leaders that their community has been renewed. The women tend the sacred water supply and the eternal fire, for the benefit of the whole tribe. To encourage rain, dew and fertility, ceremonies of water or milk pouring are conducted. Torches, candles and fires are burned to stimulate fertility; they are extinguished and rekindled as symbols of rebirth.

Okondia

In the Lisimbu society among the Kuta of the north, a great part of the women's ceremony takes place near, or in a river. Aquatic symbolism is present in almost all the secret societies of this part of Africa. In the river itself, they build a hut of branches and leaves. It has only one entrance, and the top of the hut is hardly a yard above the surface of the water. The candidates, who age from twelve to thirty-two years, are brought to the shore. Each is under the supervision of an initiate, called **the mother**. They advance together, walking in the water, crouching down with only head and shoulders out of the water. Their faces are painted with **pembe**, and each holds a leaf in her mouth. The procession goes down the river and, on arrival at the hut, they stand up suddenly and dive into the opening. Having entered the hut they undress completely, and dive out again. Crouching down, they form a semi-circle around the entrance to the hut to perform their fishing dance. One of the mothers afterward comes out of the river, tears off her loin-cloth and dances an erotic dance. Then the candidates go into the hut. It is here that their first initiation takes place. The mothers take away their clothes, plunge their heads under water to the edge of suffocation, and rub their bodies with rough leaves. Then the initiation is continued in the village. The mother beats her daughter, holds the latter's head close to a fire (on which they have thrown a handful of pepper). At last, the initiate makes her own dance and passes between her mother's legs.

Two months later, another initiation is held on the bank of the river. In this case the neophyte undergoes the same ordeals, and her hair is cut all round in the distinctive fashion of the society. Before going back into the village the organizer breaks an egg over the roof of the hut, to ensure that the hunters will catch bountiful game. When back in the village, each mother rubs the body of her daughter in the **kula**, divides a banana in two, gives one piece to the novice and they eat the fruit together. Then the daughter bows down and passes between the mother's legs. After a few more dances, some of which symbolize sexual acts, the candidates are considered initiated. They believe that the ceremonies of Lisimbu exert a favourable influence over the whole life of the village; the plantations will give a good return, the hunting and fishing expeditions will be successful, epidemics and quarrels will be averted.

Orinoco

During an eclipse of the moon the Orinoco used to bury lighted brands in the ground. They thought that if the moon were extinguished all fire on earth would be extinguished with her except that which was hidden from sight.

Gaboon

In the Gaboon, there are women's societies called **Nyembe** or **Ndyembe**, which celebrate their secret ceremonies near a stream of water. In the initiatory ordeals a fire must be kept burning continually, and the novices have to venture alone into the forest, often during the night or in a storm, to gather wood. Another ordeal is that of staring at the burning sun, while a song is being sung. Finally, each novice has to plunge her hand into a snakehole, catch a snake, and bring it into the village coiled around her arm. During the initiation, members of the sisterhood perform nude dances, singing obscene songs. There is also a ritual of death and initiatory resurrection which is performed in the last act of the mystery: the leopard dance. It is executed by the leaders, two and two, representing the leopard and the mother. Around the latter a dozen of the young girls are assembled and 'killed' by the leopard. When it is the mother's turn, she attacks the leopard and 'kills' it.

Cameroons

The harvest is celebrated with festivals of sexual license in the Cameroons, in the Congo. In British Central Africa, among the Kaffirs, the Hottentots and the Bantu, the harvest festivals are very much like the feasts of Bacchus. The only restriction on behavior seems to be that no one at the festival is allowed to have intercourse with their partner.

Sierra Leone

Among the Grebo people of Sierra Leone there is a pontiff who bears the title of Bodia. He is appointed in accordance with the council of an oracle and is in charge of public talismans and idols to which he feeds rice and oil every new moon. He is expected to bring forth abundance, to keep the people healthy and to drive away war.

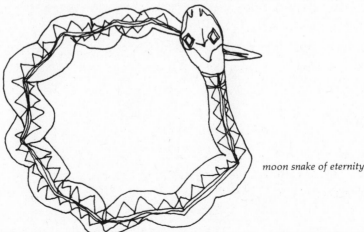

moon snake of eternity

moon shield

NATIVE NORTH AMERICAN

The Shields that men carry, and the Medicine Belts of the women, are called Mirrors or Hearts. These Mirrors are their Names and are the Morning Star. I am a Man of the Shield. It is my Medicine Gift to Teach in this Way, the Way of the Shields.[15]

Algonquin

Not long after the world was formed, a great conjuror or **angikak** became so powerful that he could ascend to heaven when he pleased. On one occasion he took with him a beautiful sister whom he loved very much, and also some fire, to which he added great quantities of fuel and thus formed the sun. For a time the conjuror treated his sister with great kindness, and they lived happily together; but at last he became cruel, ill-used her in many ways, and as a climax, burnt one side of her face with fire. After this last indignity she ran away from him and became the moon. At new moon, the burnt side of her face is toward the earth. At full moon, it is turned away.

Ottawa

Two Indians found themselves in a beautiful country, lighted by the moon, which shed a mild and pleasant light. They could see the moon approaching as if from behind a hill. They advanced, and the aged woman spoke to them; she had a white face and a pleasing air, and looked rather old. She spoke to them very kindly. They knew from her first appearance that she was the moon. She asked them several questions. She informed them that they were halfway to her brother's (the sun), and that from the earth to her abode was half the distance.

Other Indians have a tradition of an old woman who lived with her granddaughter, the most beautiful girl that was ever seen in the country. Coming of age, she wondered that only herself and her grandmother were in the world. The grandma explained that an evil spirit had destroyed all others; but that she by her power had preserved herself and her granddaughter. The young girl thought that surely some survivors might be found. She travelled till on the tenth day she found a lodge inhabited by eleven brothers, who were hunters. The eleventh took her to wife and died after a son was born. The widow then wedded each of the others, beginning with the youngest. When she took the eldest, she soon grew tired of him, and fled away by the western portal of the hunter's lodge. Tearing up one of the stakes which supported the door, she disappeared in the earth with her little dog. Soon all trace of the fugitive was lost. Then she emerged from the earth in the east, where she met an old man fishing in the sea. This person was he who made the earth. He bade her pass into the air toward the west. Meanwhile the deserted husband pursued his wife into the earth in the west, and out again in the east, where the tantalizing old fisherman cried out to him, **Go, go; you will run after your wife as long as the earth lasts without ever overtaking her, and the nations of the earth will call you Gizhigooke, he who makes the day.** From this is derived Giziz, the sun. Some of the Indians only count eleven moons, which represent the eleven brothers, dying one after the other.

Zuni prey god fetish

Zuni

Women are given bowls of sacred water by men who have cleaned the sacred spring. The women pour the water, decorate the bowls and leave them on the spring ledge to bring rain.

Pueblo

A rain dance called the Snake Dance is done by men headed by an elder around the sacred rock, holding serpents in their mouths. Women say prayers and sprinkle maize flour over animals and men. The snakes are thrown to the ground and the women sprinkle them. Operations are performed by women, and the invention of agriculture is traditionally ascribed to women.

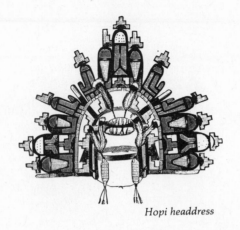

Hopi headdress

Navajo

The first woman holds it in her hands,
She holds the moon in her hands,
In the center of the sky she holds it in her hands.
As she holds it in her hands, it starts upward.

Pawnee

It is there that our hearts are set,
In the expanse of the heavens.

Pima

Arctic "butterfly" basket

According to the Pima Indians, during the time of the creation the Earth Doctor made a song as he created each thing. The following is an adaptation of the ancient moon-creation song of the Earth Magician:

I am making the Moon!
I am making the Moon!
Here I throw it to the directions.
Here I throw it to the directions.
Throw it to the east direction-
There it comes up correctly.

Mexican calendar stone

SOUTH AMERICA

Chile

The only beneficent deity among the Araucanians was Auchimalgen, the moon. She protected the Indians against disasters, and drove away evil spirits by the fear she created. A red moon was the sign of the death of some great person.

The Incas

Among the divinities Mama Quilla the Moon, came immediately after the Sun, her brother and husband. Her image was a silver disk with human features. She was the protecting goddess of married women. Other planets and stars were thought to be ladies-in-waiting to Mama Quilla.

Amazon Jungle

Uaupes people burn a corpse one moon after its death, pound the ashes, mix with special fermented drinks and then drink it ceremonially.

Central America

With the peoples of Central America, on the night of the planting of the seed, certain people were appointed to perform sexual acts at the precise moment when the seed was deposited into the ground.

Mayan idols from Yucatan

Peru

Among Puruvians the festival held at the ripening of the **palta** or alligator pear was preceded by a period of fasts and abstinence. Men and women gathered together naked, a signal was given and a race was run. Every man who caught a woman had intercourse with her. Similar festivals were held in Chile, Nicaragua and tribes of Northern Mexico. The care and regulation of rain was in the hands of sacred women and priestesses of the moon.

Where the sacred fire of the Moon is tended by vestal priestesses, they are usually responsible also for the rain rituals. This was the case in Peru, where the priestesses of Mama-Quilla were vestals and also rain makers.

186

CHINA AND JAPAN

Queen of Heaven

On a gold throne, whose radiating brightness
　　Dazzles the eyes—enhaloing the scene,
Sits a fair form, arrayed in snowy whiteness.
　　She is Chang-O, the beauteous Fairy Queen,
Rainbow-winged angels softly hover o'er Her,
　　Forming a canopy above the throne;
A host of fairy beings stand before her,
　　Each robed in light, and girt with meteor zone.

Ch'ang-o or Heng-O, Chinese Moon Goddess

At the full moon of the autumn equinox, women and children buy little figures either representing a white rabbit or a helmeted soldier dressed in armour with a face like a hare, and make them a sacrifice consisting chiefly of fruit. They offer a sacrifice directly to the moon when it has risen above the house tops. Sometimes the sacrifice is made before a large paper panel with a representation of the Moon's palace with its inhabitant the Hare who makes the drug of immortality. The sacrifice consists of fruit, sweet moon cakes which are made specially and sold for the occasion and a sprig of red amaranth. Men never take part in this ceremony, for in the popular mind the hare is the symbol of women, children and the oppressed and is considered their patron.

　　The Moon is also inhabited by a Moon Goddess. She is the wife of I, the excellent archer, a mythological personage who brought down nine suns with his arrows one day, when the ten suns of primitive times took it in their heads to rise together and threatened to shrivel up the world.

187

Autumnal Full Moon

This moon is the time of one of the three great annual festivals of the Goddess Heng-ugo. Sacrifices of fruits, crescent-shaped moon-cakes and flowers are given. The moon is the essence of yin and the ruler of water. The moon symbolizes happiness and reunion. According to the Chinese lunar calendar, the festival is calculated on the 15th day of the 8th month or August 15th. The cakes are made of lotus flowers.

My Tai Chi teacher, Li Li-ta, and his wife, Ai-Ling, gave an autumnal full moon party last year. The party was to be outside, and began when the moon rose. We celebrated with lotus moon cakes, some round orange ones with yellow spheres in their centers, and wine and fruit—and demonstrations of the lovely art of Tai Chi.

Seed Rituals

Rites pertaining to forebears, harvests and the erotic life are considered inextricably linked. The conjugal bed used to be placed in the darkest corner of the room, where seeds were kept and above the spot where the dead were buried.

Tao

Rituals of light therapy were prescribed: men were to stand nude in the sun for certain periods holding a sun symbol; women were to stand naked in moonlight holding round colored yin shapes. These light exposures were thought to balance our psyches.

Japan

Both the sun and the moon are traditionally Goddesses in Japan: Amaterasu is the Sun and Tsuki yomi is the Moon.

Spring Moon Watching

The Empress leads her court and the people outside and onto her palace roof to watch the new spring moon. Moon meditations are a regular part of the culture, thought to clear the mind and calm the soul.

Tsuki Ga Deta

Meditations

A friend of mine, Kiyomi Ota, was taught by her family that when one is troubled one should go outside into the moonlight, bow three times, meditate until calm, then bow three low reverent bows when cured. Yone Ota, her grandmother, who is in her 80's and performs with the Japanese Kubuki Theater, taught her about lunar mythology and customs. She says that the Japanese customs came from the Chinese and that until very recently the moon was always female. The song above is The Moon Came Out. A summary translation is:

The moon came out and it is round, full and pure, like a mirror without clouds, shining and protective like the essence of the buddha.

New Year

Mochi-zuki is rice-pounding with stone pounders done at the new year (same as Chinese New Year) to make flour for rice cakes. It is thought that the rabbit in the moon is also mochi-zuki.

Tibet

The Tibetan new year begins with the new moon which appears about the fifteenth of February. For 23 days afterwards the government of Lhasa, the capital, is taken out of the hands of the ordinary rulers and entrusted to the monk of the Debang monastery who offers to pay the highest sum for the privilege.

Korea

In the Korean language the word for month, is the word moon. Each moon has a particular holiday associated with it and many of the customs are connected with children.

Everybody in Korea celebrates their birthday on the first of February, the First Moon. The birthday cakes all have twelve candles, one for each moon. March, the Second Moon, is associated with cold stormy weather and considered a good story-telling time. The Third Moon, April, is giving time. May, the Fourth Moon, contains the Feast of Lanterns. On May 24, everyone hangs lanterns in their yards high on polls, hoping the flame will burn brightly for a long time to signify a good year.

June, the Fifth Moon, is associated with romance and particularly with a folktale of an inventive young commoner who used her swing to catch glimpses of a prince she loved over his high palace wall. Now every June a contest is held to see which girl children can swing the highest.

July, the Sixth Moon, is the moon for the Yuda party. People go out on picnics and eat round geodan rice and honey cakes and five-colored spaghetti balls called yudu gog. Then everyone bathes in a stream and washes their hair. All these are good luck charms.

August, the Seventh Moon, contains a celebration of the bridge of friendship. On the seventh day of the Seventh Moon, one remembers the legend of the magpies who flew up and built a bridge along the Milky Way for two separated stars.

September, the Eight Moon is the moon of the Harvest Festival. Jack-o-lanterns are made of hollowed out turnips. Everyone feasts on pine-nut cakes in the shape of half-moons.

NEAR EAST

Babylonia

Ishtar is referred to as **Sharrat Shame**, Queen of Heaven. A Babylonian hymn to Ishtar mentions the **kamanu** sacrificial cakes offered her.

A writer of the 10th century, Abu-Su'id Uahb Ibn Ibrahim, described a feast (at the Christian time of Lent) of the Moon-god in Harran: In the middle of the month is the feast of Al-Bayât (Mourning Woman) and this is the Ta'uz feast which is celebrated in honour of the God Ta'uz. The women bewail over him, lamenting that their Lord has been cruelly slain. They grind bones in the mill and scatter them to the winds. The women during the feast abstain from work and from food during the period of seven days of the lamentation for Tammuz.

An archaeological find at Nahariah in Israel, north of Acre, on a bamah (high place), a stone mould was found dating from the 17th Century B.C. The mould was used for casting small figures of the Goddess Astarte, her identity clearly indicated by the two horns which protrude to the right and the left over her ears. She is Astarte of the Horns standing naked except for her tall, conical headdress, looking down at her protruding navel, with an enigmatic smile on her lips. It could be that such moulds were used to bake cakes in the shape of Astarte, to be either eaten by the celebrants (perhaps as a precursor of the Christian Holy Communion in which the Host is actually supposed to turn into the body of Christ) or burnt on the altar.

The Moon Queen of Heaven fell into the waters of the Euphrates at the end of night and was brought ashore by fishes or water gods. This (abridged) hymn, sung in her honor, is from the Seven Tables of Creation which date from the seventh century B.C. The hymn is probably much older. Ishtar is Diva Astarte, Divine Astarte, the power, the life, the health of men and gods, and the opposite of this which is evil, death and destruction:

I pray unto thee, Lady of Ladies, Goddess of Goddesses!
O Ishtar, Queen of all peoples, directress of mankind!
O Irnini, thou art raised on high, mistress of the spirits
   of heaven;
Thou art mighty, thou hast sovereign power, exalted is thy name!
Thou art the light of heaven and earth, O valiant daughter
   of the Moon-god.
      Ruler of weapons, arbitress of the battle!
      Framer of all decrees, wearer of the crown of dominion!
O Lady, majestic is thy rank, over all the gods it is exalted!
Thou art the cause of lamentation, thou sowest hostility
   among brethren who are at peace;
Thou art the bestower of strength! (friendship)
Thou art strong, O Lady of Victory, thou canst violently
   attain my desire!
O Gutira who are girt with battle, who art clothes with
   terror,
Thou wieldest the sceptre and the decision, the control of
   earth and heaven!
Holy chambers, shrines, divine dwellings and temples worship thee!
Where is thy name not (heard)? Where is thy decree not (obeyed)?

            o   o   o

At the thought of thy name the heaven and earth quake.
The gods tremble, and the spirits of the earth falter.
Mankind payeth homage to thy mighty name,
For thou art great, thou art exalted.
All mankind, the whole human race, boweth down before thy power.
Thou judgest the cause of men with justice and righteousness;
Thou lookest with mercy on the violent man, and thou settest right
   the unruly every morning.
How long wilt thou tarry, O Lady of Heaven and earth, Shepherdess
   of those who dwell in human habitations?
How long wilt thou tarry, O Lady, whose feet are unwearied, whose
   knees have not lost their vigour?
How long wilt thou tarry, O Lady of all fights and of all battles?
O thou glorious one, that ragest among the spirits of heaven,
   that subduest angry gods.

Thou hast power over all princes, that controllest the sceptre of kings,
That openest the bonds of all handmaids,
That art raised on high, that art firmly established, O valiant
   Ishtar, great is thy might
Bright torch of heaven and earth, light of all dwellings.

              o   o   o

O goddess of men, O goddess of women, thou whose counsel none
   may learn,
Where thou lookest in pity, the dead man lives again, the sick
   is healed,
The afflicted is saved from his affliction, when he beholdest
   thy face!
I, thy servant, sorrowful, sighing, and in distress cry unto thee.
Look upon me, O my Lady, and accept my supplication,
      Truly pity me and hearken unto my prayer!
Cry unto me It is enough! and let thy spirit be appeased!
How long shall my body lament, which is full of restlessness
   and confusion?
How long shall my heart be afflicted, which is full of sorrow
   and sighing?

              o   o   o

Unto thee therefore do I pray, dissolve my ban!
   Dissolve my sin, my iniquity, my transgression and my offence!
Forgive my transgression, accept my supplication!
   Secure my deliverance, and let me be loved and carefully tended!
Guide my footsteps in the light, that among men I may
   gloriously seek my way!
Say the word, that at thy command my angry god may have mercy
And that my goddess who is wroth may turn again.
   Thou art the ruler, let then my torch flame forth!
   May my scattered strength be collected.

              o   o   o

Let my prayer and my supplication come unto thee,
And let thy great mercy be upon me,
That those who behold me in the street may magnify thy name,
And that I may glorify thy godhead and thy might before mankind!
      Ishtar is exalted! Ishtar is Queen!
     My Lady is exalted! My Lady is Queen!
Irnini, the valiant daughter of the Moon-god hath not a rival.
O exalted Ishtar, that givest light unto the (four) quarters of the world![16]

Arabia

The three daughters of Allah have retained the ancient names of the three aspects of the Arabian moon goddess: Al-Uzza, the black mother stone at Mecca; Mamat, time, fate; Al-Ilat.

Armenia

The Armenian translation of the word **Amazon** is **Moon-woman.** The Amazons at one time ruled over much of Asia Minor and North Africa, founding the cities of Ephesus, Smyrna, Cyrene and many others. They reckoned descent only through the mother, and their queen, Lysippe, decreed that the men were to perform all household tasks while the women fought and governed. Amazons were armed priestesses of the mother goddess; their emblem was the moon. Zeus carried a thunderbolt by permission of his Cretan mother goddess, Hera, who gave it to the Amazons in the form of the labrys, or double axe.

Pigs and the Moon

Wherever the eating of pork is forbidden and the pig held to be unclean, we may be sure of its originally sacred character. (Erich Newmann, **The Origin and History of Consciouness**, 1954). This refers to the very early association of moon goddesses with pigs which were called **the uterine animal.** This is also true of sacred cows.

And it came to pass, as soon as he came nigh unto the camp, that he saw the calf (golden), and the dancing: and Moses' anger waxed hot, . . . and he took the calf which they had made, and burnt it in the fire, and ground it to powder, and stowed it upon the water and made the children of Israel drink of it.

Exodus 32:19-20

Syria

At Carrhae near Edissa the moon was thought to be an androgynous deity and was worshipped as Lunas and Luna. Even today the peasants of Anatolia and Syria have their sacred trees, and in Arabia the annointing and circumnabulation of monolithic stones were practised until fairly recently. (This is also true of Modern India and the Far East, and of many localities of Western Europe where stones set up for ancient rites still stand and are still tended.)

The Sabbaths

The Biblical name Shabbath (Sabbat), designating the seventh day of the week, seems to have had some connection with the Akkadian shabattu, the name for the feast of the full moon.

The Hebrew Moon Goddess

Anath the Victorius is a woman acting as a man clad as a male and girt as a female. In Jeremian, people tell the Prophet, **But since we ceased burning incense to the Queen of Heaven and to pour Her libations, we have wanted everything and have been consumed by sword and famine. To these words the women added, Is it that we alone burn incense to the Queen of Heaven and pour Her libations? Is it without our husbands that we make Her cakes in Her image and that we pour Her libations?** This passage allows us a glimpse of the actual ritual of the Hebrew Astarte worship. The rites were led by the kings of Judah and the princes; participants were the men, women and children of the people.

One of the most important Jewish religious symbols is the seven-branched candlestick. This semicicular candlestick forms the lower half of a moon shape, an upper half-circle being devoutly completed in the beholder's imagination to form the perfect full moon.

Do you not see what they do in the cities of Jerusalem? The children gather wood and the fathers kindle a fire, and the women knead the dough to make cakes to the Queen of Heaven and pour out libations to other gods, in order to anger me!

—Jeremiah

Omen Chant of Ishtar

(To be sung while twirling silver and blue ball.)

**To give oracles do i arise,
Do i arise in perfectness.**

Assyro-Babylonian cylinder seal

The left Eye of Horus, the Moon

EGYPT

Rituals of Osiris and Isis

The religious ceremonials of Egypt were concerned with the happenings of the myth. The death of Osiris was enacted each year, and the wanderings of Mother Isis and her lamentations played a conspicuous role exactly as the mourning of Ishtar for Tammuz and of Aphrodite for Adonis did in Arabia and the Grecian Isles. The final mystery of his resurrection and the public display in procession of the emblem of his power, the image of the Phallus, completed the ritual. The phallus was carved from wood and was sometimes a couple of hundred feet long. In the myth, Osiris' penis was swallowed by a fish and that is why a carved wooden one is used.

It was a religion in which the emotional participation in the grief and joy of Isis played a prominent part. In later days it became one of the religions in which redemption was achieved through the emotional ecstasy by which the worshippers felt themselves to become one with the deities.

Once a year the Egyptians sacrificed pigs to the moon and to Osiris and ate their flesh, though on any other day of the year they would neither sacrifice nor eat them.

Winter Solstice

November is the month of Hathor and public festivals to the Cow-Goddess are conducted. There are processions involving the carrying of sacred statues of the the cow and the phallus preceded by a water vase. At the winter solstice late in December a golden cow in a black robe is carried around the "dead" Osiris three times.

197

Magic Lamps

Ancient Egyptian trance techniques usually involve staring into a lit lamp (the Arabian magic lamp) after annointing your eyes with sacred ointment to prevent eye strain. If you have a question for the deity of the lamp, you say, **I pray you to reveal yourself here tonight and to speak with me to answer the questions I ask.** As you pronounce the spell you will see a sacred figure standing behind the lamp who will respond to your questions. An alternative ritual is to lie down on green reeds, having abstained from sexual communion, with your head southward, your face looking north toward the lamp.

Possession

A priest or priestess is to bring a statue of the healing moon-deity Thoth, the presence of which will exorcise the demon. The techniques of religious magic were preserved by the priesthood and the mystery cults of the pyramids and sphinx.

Water Ceremonies

A vase of water was carried in the annual procession of the Phallephoria, in front of the image of the phallus which represented Osiris. Water jars and water pourings played a large part in the worship of moon deities, givers of rain and dew.

Water is poured out to induce the Goddess to send rain, a suggestion of mimetic magic. Her powers are felt to be increased by the service given, by the water poured out. The rite is thought to be especially efficacious when water is scarce and, therefore, a costly sacrifice. Sometimes, indeed, in severe drought a more costly fluid still is dedicated to the Goddess. A cow is led out to the fields and there milked, the milk being poured out on the parched ground. This sacrifice is felt to be particularly pleasing to the Moon Goddess, who is also the Heavenly Cow. Water is fertilized by plunging in a lighted candle.

Rose of Isis

For those who endure the moon goddess initiation without collapsing, they become Moonmen or Daughters of the Moon and are awarded the Rose of Isis.

Isis-Nephthys was the humanized, deified form of the holy-bird. In ceremonial dress, the body of the priestess is enfolded by the bird's two wings. The bird-head appears above her headdress, and in her hand she holds a bird. The coloring of the feathers is a dark vivid blue.

NORTHERN EUROPE

Boys and Girls, Come Out to Play
Boys and girls, come out to play;
The moon doth shine as bright as day,
Leave your supper and leave your sleep,
Come with your play-fellows into the street.
Come with a whoop, come with a call,
Come with a good will or not at all,
Up the ladder and down the wall
A penny loaf will serve us all.
But when the loaf is gone,
    what will you do?
Those who would eat
    must work, that's true.

          —Mother Goose

Virgin Mary

Egg Lore

Mythological European lore has it that the reason men have to take their hats off to honor something and women don't is because women already **are** eggs.

Spinning

Spinning was a magical act, recorded in the symbolism of European fairy tales such as **Sleeping Beauty** and **Rumplestilskin**.

    The moon spins time, fate and the lives of mortals. Spinning is a sacred female initiation act. Later men's societies at times attacked the spinning huts. Then spinning became a dangerous ritual, eventually lost. The link between feminine initiation, spinning and sexuality, however, has persisted.

199

Witches

There are women's associations for enacting the mysteries in Africa and the Weiberbünde, or in antiquity the closed groups of the Maenads. We know that some sisterhoods have taken a long time to disappear—such as those of the witches of the Middle Ages in Europe, with their ritual reunions and orgies. Medieval trials for sorcery were in most cases inspired by theological prejudice, and it is probable that orgies of witches took place, not with the meaning ascribed to them by the ecclesiastical authorities but in the first, authentic sense that they were secret reunions including orgiastic rites—that is, ceremonies related to the mystery of fertility.

The witches, just like shamans and mystics of other primitive societies, were concentrating, intensifying or deepening the religious experience revealed during their initiation. Witches were dedicated to a mystical vocation which impelled them to live, more deeply than other women, the revelation of the mysteries.

Scotland

In the Orkney Islands the stone circles are still known as Temples of the Moon.

Ireland

It is an Irish custom that on the waning moon, people say the charm: **Leave us as well as you found us.**

Fire Rituals

Tuathal, the Irish Prince to whom the estates, circa A.D. 106, swore allegiance, erected a magnificent temple called Flachta, sacred to the fire of Samhain, and to the Samnothei, or priests of the moon. Here on every eve of November, the fires of Samhain were lighted. With great pomp and ceremony, the monarch, the Druids, and the chiefs of the kingdom attended. From this holy fire, and no other, was every fire in the land first lit for the winter. It was deemed the highest act of impiety to kindle winter fires from any other; and for this favour the head of every house paid a Scrubal, or threepence tax to the Arch-Druid for Samhain.

Other Irish moon-gods are mentioned such as St. Luan, alias Molua, alias Euan, alias Lugidus, alias Lugad, alias Moling. The foundations with which St. Luan under aliases is connected extend over eight countries in the provinces of Ulster, Leinster, and Munster. Luan to this day is the common Irish word for the moon, worshipped as the symbol of female nature.

Russia

In the Ukraine, women lift their skirts to their waists to jump over a fire. It is said to be "burning the hair of the bride," and to benefit the whole community for marriage.

Carnivals of Fertility

The Carnival is the license festival May Day celebration. In Russia promiscuity took place as late as the 16th century at Midsummer Day and Christmas.

The Fete des Fous, persisted in France until the 17th Century, with general license.

The operation of divine generative power which brings about the fertility of nature and animals and women is believed to be stimulated not only by sexual intercourse, but also by any act or speech of a lascivious and sexual character.

Assumption

August 15 is the Feast of Assumption of the Virgin Mary. Its original purpose was to assure a good harvest free of storms. Many torches and fires were lit. It was thought to be the day she was carried to Heaven to become Queen. At Candlemas, February 1, the fires of the world were renewed.

Siberia and the North

The Altaic peoples of Siberia salute the new moon and ask for happiness and luck. Estonians, Finns and Yakuta celebrate marriages only at the New Moon.

Mary

Mary was called the Many Breasted Mother of All, the All-Dewy-One, of fertility. A dew bath was a medieval love charm, as in the tropics sun is the enemy of vegetation. Grotto water temples were her special homes.

Saxon Death Rituals

One moon after a death, friends would gather and drink ceremonially to the deceased. It was called ceremony of month's mind.

The shamans of Lapland, during their trances, are supposed to enter into the intestines of a big fish or a whale. One legend tells us that the son of a shaman awakened his father, who had been asleep for three years, with these words:

Father! Wake up and come out of the fish's guts; come out of the third loop of her darkness.

The Runes

Before the Burning Times, in each area, witches had their own similar Wiccan languages. The symbols here are Celtic. Witches were afraid to use them so the languages died out. Try using the symbols for special labels, or journal keeping. Any spells written should definitely be in runes. The witches code is, Harm none, and do as thou wilt.

Tree Ceremonies

On Christmas Eve, a log is brought into the house, an invocation is sung and it is burned on the fire. The ashes, which were preserved and thought sacred, were scattered over the fields to ensure fertility in districts of Germany. In Montenegro they are put around fruit trees for the same purpose. In France they are mixed with the fodder of cattle in order to make them calve. In Italy they are scattered over the fields for the same purposes.

202

Deck The Halls

Traditional

Old Welsh

1. Deck the halls with boughs of hol-ly,
2. See the blazing Yule be-fore us,
3. Fast a-way the old year pass-es, } Fa, la, la, la, la, la, la, la, la.

'Tis the sea-son to be jol-ly,
Strike the harp and join the cho-rus,
Hail the new, ye lads and lass-es, } Fa, la, la, la, la, la, la, la, la.

Don we now our gay ap-par-el,
Fol-low me in mer-ry measure,
Sing we joy-ous all to-geth-er, } Fa, la, la, la, la, la, la, la, la.

Troll the an-cient Yule-tide car-ol,
While I tell of Yule-tide treasure,
Heed-less of the wind and weather, } Fa, la, la, la, la, la, la, la, la.

GREECE AND ROME

Minerva-Athene, wisdom and the arts

The spiritual societies of ancient Greece are some of the best documented and most commonly known remnants of purely matriarchal goddess worship in Western civilization available to us today. Yet even these are shrouded in mystery and underplayed in historical importance. They are significant to current Western culture because in their stories we can see some of the phases of transition from matriarchy to patriarchy—which led to our social structures of today. And we can learn much more about the practice and theology of their female spiritual groups. We must use our collective knowledge to fill in the record gaps.

Ancient Greece and Western Anatolia

In Greece, as in India, the Great Goddess survived superimposed Indo-European culture. A predecessor of Anatolian and Greek Artemis-Hekate, the Goddess lived through the Bronze Age, Classical Greece, and even into later history, despite transformations of her name and outer form.

Artemis is known from Greek, Lydian and Etruscan inscriptions and texts and on very ancient tablets from Pylos. Artemis and Hekate, as two Goddesses or one, belong to the moon cycle: Hekate, awesome and death-linked and Artemis, youthful, beautiful, reflecting the purity of nature and linked with unmarried motherhood.

In Caria (Western Turkey) Hekate was the primary Goddess. Mysteries and games were performed in her sanctuary at Lagina. In Colophon, dogs were sacrificed to her and she was thought to be able to turn into a dog. Hekate and her dogs were supposed to journey over the graves of the dead and above sacrificial blood. In the days of Aristophanes and Aeschylus she was the Mistress of the Night Road, of fate and of the world of the dead. As Enodia she was the guardian of crossroads and gates; her sanctuaries stood at the gates of hill-forts and

204

entrances to homes. Pregnant women sacrificed to Enodia to ensure the Goddesses' help at the entrance of birth. Clay figures of the Goddess seated were sacrificed to her. A terra cotta medallion found in the Athenian Agora portrays a triple-bodied Hekate-Artemis with stag and dog flanking her; she holds a torch, whip, bow and arrow. Hekate is responsible for lunacy and is the Giver of Visions. Well-bred girls of Athens of marriageable age danced as bears in honour of Artemis of Brauronia becoming bears or **arktoi**. In vase paintings, the dancers of Artemis wore animal masks. The girls and women of Lakedemonia performed orgiastic dances to glorify her.

Offerings to Artemis include phalli, animals and fruit, as she was the protector of all life, bestowing fertility.

The sacrifice of any living thing to her was appropriate. According to the legend adapted by Sophocles, the most beautiful girl of the year, Iphigenia, had to be sacrificed to the Goddess.

In nearly all shrines dedicated to Artemis, spindle-whorls, loom weights, shuttles and kallatoi have been found and from inscriptions in sanctuaries it is known that woolen and linen clothes and threads wound on spools were offered to her as gifts. On Corinthian vases, Artemis and her priestesses are seen holding spindles.

She appeared at births as the birth-giving Goddess, Artemis Eileithyia (Child Bearing). Diana also presided over childbirth and was called **Opener of the Womb**. Tithenidia, the festival of nurses and nurslings in Sparta, honored her name. Artemis Brauronia aroused madness and her anger could cause the death of women in childbirth.

In her various manifestations the Great Goddess existed for at least five thousand years before the appearance of Classical Greek civilization. Village communities worship her now in the guise of the Virgin Mary. The Goddess in bear form was deeply ingrained in mythical thought and survives in contemporary Crete as **Virgin Mary of the Bears**. In the cave of Acrotiri near ancient Kydonia, a festival in honor of Panagia Arkoudiotissa (Mary of the Bear) is celebrated on February second. In Athens, Artemis was honored with round cakes, called **selenai**, representing the moon.

At the various temples of Aphrodite at Corinth and in Cyprus she was served by sacred prostitutes; and at Abydos there was a temple of **Aphrodite Porne**, Aphrodite the Harlot. This connection with ritual prostitution attests Aphrodite's eastern origin, for the custom prevailed at the cult centers of many eastern goddesses.

Various animals were connected with her, including doves, sparrows, swans, dolphins; also mussels and forms of vegetation, such as roses, myrtle, cypress and pomegranates.

Rites of Hecate

The rites of this Goddess were performed at night and were especially concerned with placation in order to turn aside wrath and evil. She is Dea-Triformis of the Cross Ways who leads travellers astray. As Queen of the Ghosts, she sweeps through the night followed by her dreadful train of questing spirits and baying hounds. Even as late as medieval times witches were thought seen flying through the air headed by Hecate herself. She is Goddess of Storms, of destructions, of terrors of the night.

The August 13th festival of Hecate in Greece was a moon festival to request protection of the harvest.

Hecate's Circle, a gold sphere with a sapphire in its center and hung on a thong of oxhide, was used for divination. It was spun, and where and how it moved and stopped indicated one's fate.

The Temple of Diana at Ephesus

Ephesus, even before recorded history, was the site of temples dedicated to Diana and Artemis. The first temples were burned around 356 B.C.

The second temple was 425 feet long by 220 feet wide, and was ornamented with 127 columns, each of which was the gift of a king, according to the account of Pliny. These columns were very large, and made of beautiful marbles, jasper, and other fine stones. Some of them were carved in elegant designs, one being the work of Scopas, who is believed to have made the Niobe group. It required 220 years to complete and the necessary money was so difficult for the people to obtain that even the ornaments of the women were given to be melted down in order to add to the fund (and yet, when Alexander offered to pay for the temple if his name should be inscribed on it, they refused his aid).

When it was completed, many works by the best artists were placed therein. The Ephesian artists were proud to do all they could for its adornment, without other reward than the honor of seeing their works in so grand and sacred a place. The great altar was filled with the sculptures of Praxiteles; a painting by Apelles, called the "Alexander Ceraunophorus," was there, and was a celebrated picture; and it is probable that many other artists were employed in its decoration.

This great temple was plundered by the Emperor Nero; the Goths carried the work of its destruction still farther in 260 A.D.; and, finally, under the Emperor Theodosius, A.D. 381, when all pagan worship was suppressed, this temple was destroyed, and now almost nothing remains at Ephesus to remind one of its past grandeur. It is probable that the materials which composed the temple, and other noble buildings there, have been carried to Constantinople or other cities, and much may still be hidden beneath the soil.

Albania

In the temple of the Moon the Albanians of the Eastern caucasus kept a number of sacred slaves. When one exhibited more than usual symptoms of inspiration or insanity, the high priest had him bound with a sacred chain and maintained him in luxury for a year. At the end of the year he was anointed with unguents and led forth to be sacrificed.

Thessaly

Thessalonian sorceresses, witches in the esquiline country, with bare feet, loose hair, and robes tucked up around their waists, gathering bones and herbs in the cemetary by the light of the new moon became well-feared in ancient Greece. They were perennially charged with attempting to draw down the moon from the sky (which means that they were unlicensed devotees of the moon Goddess, Isis or Nut) and of having great powers with herbs.

Moon Foods

The hot cross buns of good Friday, at first sight, have little relevancy to moon worship, and those who eat them suppose they were originated to commemorate the Christian sacrifice; but we know that the cross was a sacred symbol with the earliest Egyptians, carved upon their imperishable records. Bun itself is ancient Greek, confirmed by discoveries at Heraculaneum of two perfect buns, each marked with a cross. The boun described by Hesychius was a cake with a representation of two horns, a crescent. It is what we know as a croissant.

The Three Marias

The three Marias of Greece were Virgin Mary, Mary Magdalene and Mary Gypsy.

Crete

The rites centered on the Goddesses were formally ceremonious. Those enacted out of doors in the fertility and vegetation cults were ecstatic and mystic. The Greeks came to associate the island of Crete with mystical religion, and the Cretans themselves claimed that they had enacted in public those Mysteries which at Eleusis were veiled in utter secrecy.

Scenes engraved on gold signet rings and seal stones show the Goddess sitting below a tree, dancing in flowery meadows or occasionally lamenting at a shrine or over ritual jars. She is attended by female votaries, or, where boughs and trees are being plucked, she is accompanied by the young god. In vegetation rites the dancing is often ecstatic or frenzied. Ritual meaning was expressed in positions of the arms. The goddess is often shown with arms bent and raised above the head, or extended before her. A common position of worship was with the right hand clenched and pressed against the forehead. Conch shells were blown, perhaps in order to summon the Goddess.

In tree worship, associated with the moon and the Mother, trees, columns, pillars and obelisks are all substantially one. The tree cut down becomes a pillar or obelisk, and though dead it does not lose its sanctity. All trees are sacredly possessed by an unseen life, but above all fruit trees are sacred. Earth sends up fruits, with the help of the moon.

Stones, also thought to be the residence of special cosmic life, are also connected to moon/tree worship. Monolithic stones are altars. The communication between a worshipper and the divine spirit was affected by physical mediums such as oil, as refinements of the tree's fertility, and blood, as the sharing of life.

Within the palaces of the Cretan towns and in many private houses, rooms are discovered to contain the bases of vanished wooden columns, before which simple tree worship rites seem to have been performed. The floors of the rooms always rest upon the heavy pillars of windowless crypts and these pillars have trenches cut around them for libations. Occasionally the horns or bones of sacrifice or a ritual vessel are found nearby. The symbol of the double axe was incised on the wooden pillars.

The gem cult of the Moon in Crete in Minoan days is a fact clearly established. On a certain day a gem worshipper would go to a Mycenaean sanctuary, a walled enclosure within which grows an olive tree. In the sanctuary where the rites are performed is a large crescent moon.

The Pandroseion in Athens is in all probability a moon-shrine, with its Dew-Service, or Hersephoria. Minoan mythology tells of the Moon-Queen, Pasiphae, she-who-shines-for-all, mother of the holy horned bull-child. The Dew-Service is at the full moon in the shrine of the All-Dewy-One.

The coinage of Athens reminds us that the olive is associated with the moon. Ancient statues of Athena's maidens carry moon haloes and Athena on her shield carries for blazon the full moon. We have the direct statement of Plutarch that according to Orphic tradition, the oracle of Delphi in the temple of Apollo was held by Night and Moon. The priestesses wore blue bird robes, the robes of the Egyptian Goddess Isis. In the **Clouds** of Aristophanes the Moon complains bitterly of the neglect into which she has fallen.

Cretan Bull Dancing — Maggy Anthony

There is a paucity of scholarly material dealing with this aspect of Minoan life, although there is much art work concerned with it in frescoes, figures, and pottery dating from the Pre-Palace times.

Minoan Civilization was based on close links between humans and nature, felt to resemble those between a child and its mother. Sensitivity, one of its predominant features, was expressed in art, in a feeling for grace, a love of movement and energy, and a taste for refinement and sumptuousness. The fear of death was almost obliterated by the ubiquitous joy of living. The whole of life was pervaded by an ardent faith in the goddess Nature, source of all creation and harmony. This led to a love of peace, a horror of tyranny, and a respect for the law. Even among the ruling classes personal ambition seems to have been unknown. Nowhere do we find the name of an author attached to a work of art nor a record of deeds of a ruler. The important part played by women is discernible in every sphere, and there is no doubt that women—or at least the influence of female sensitivity—made major contributions to Minoan Art. One finds in the archaeological literature a tremendous reluctance to speculate on whether the bull games and bull dancing had any religious significance, so we must find sources in the literature of people who have no academic stake in it. The best source seems to be Mary Renault, whose historical novels about the ancient world have been praised because of her careful scholarship.

In her novel **The King Must Die** (Phantheon, 1958), Ms. Renault describes the Knossos finds and the certainty that the Cretan bull-ring equalled that of Spain in popular esteem. Leading toreros enjoyed tremendous prestige and might even become a princess' lover. She also describes the preparations that went into the training of bull-dancers and life in the rings.

Before the dance the toreros stood before the shrine, and dedicated themselves to the Goddess-on-Earth in ritual words, stretching their hands palm down toward Mother Dia to purge them of impiety. From anywhere in the bull court, you could see the Bull of Daidalos. It was named after its creator, though every part of it

209

had been reworked, save for the bronze horns worn smooth with unnumbered hand grips. Everyone said the horns were Daidalos' own handiwork. There was a perch in the hollow body between the shoulders, where the trainer's boy would sit to work the levers which made the head swing or toss; the toreros would dance and sway out of the way. After bull dancing came bull-leaping. Here on the wooden bull it was a mime of what only the living beast gives meaning to, and few students would achieve. No team had many bull-leapers, some teams only one, but they were the Princes and Princesses of the Bull-Court. The bull-leapers strolled up idly, sparkling and tinkling, and gave a loose seal bracelet on their wrists to someone to hold. Then they ran to the lowered bull horns and, as they tossed up, swung themselves to a handstand. At the pinnacle, they let go, their flight still curving on, till their toes touched the bull's back. Then they bounced off. When the bull is alive, if the leapers want to live too, they had better land on their feet.

All the great bull-leapers had tricks of their own by which they were known. The names of these great women and men were remembered for generations.

On the practice Bull of Daidalos dancers learned how to save each other and themselves: how to twine the bull's horns with their arms and legs so that he could not gore them; how to grasp the horns from before, behind and sideways in leaping on and in getting away; how to confuse him by covering his eyes. They were not allowed to harm the bull, even to save their lives, for he was the dwelling place of the goddess.

The Eleusinian Mysteries—Maggy Anthony

What little we know about the Cult and religious rites at Eleusis is taken from historical accounts of the public rites, archaeological evidence and descriptions of similar religions. We do know that it was based on the legend of the abduction of The Kore to the Underworld by Hades, Lord of the Dead. The three central figures of worship were The Kore; Demeter, The Mother; and the Crone or Moon in the person of Hecate. The core of the idea has grain and motherhood as its natural sheath and disguise. Somewhere in the rites a single ear of corn was shown and reaped in silence. There are connections of the abduction of Persephone and her descent to the underworld, with the idea of her as the grain that is sowed and dead in the soil, then returns in the flowering. This idea is universal and is carried in the Christian New Testament in John 12:24:

Verily I say unto you, except a grain of wheat fall into the ground and die, it abideth alone; but if it die, it bringeth forth much fruit.

The major rite celebrated was the Initiation. Any person, free or slave could be an Initiate as long as they were free of another's blood. There was a prescribed period of fasting for about two weeks before the rites. Only fermented barley water could be taken to slake the thirst, in addition to water, and these in small amounts. Then, all met in Athens where they bathed in the sea ritually and performed sacrifices of pigs to the Goddess. When three days of rites were performed, they then set out one morning, by foot, to Eleusis, which is about a day's walk from Athens. Arriving in the evening they went straight to the temple where the secret rites began. At this point, our ignorance and their pledge of secrecy pulls the shutters together; we have only the voice of some illustrious Initiates to tell us of the quality of those rites:

Homer: Great awe of the gods makes the voice falter. The essential gift of the ceremonies no man may describe or utter.

Blessed is he among men on earth who has beheld this. Never will he who has not been initiated into these ceremonies, who has had no part in them, share in such things. He will be as a dead man in sultry darkness.

Sophocles: Thrice blessed are those among men who, after beholding these rites, go down to Hades. Only for them is there life; all the rest will suffer an evil lot.

Cicero: We have been given a reason not only to live in joy, but also to die with better hope.

The rites were awesome but not violent. An interesting incident that has been documented occurred in 20 B.C., when a holy man from Indian was invited to

211

participate in the rites. When the part that concerned the fire came, the holy man, as a gesture of disdain, annointed his body with oils and jumped into the fire to burn alive under the horrified gaze of the others. His last words were to the effect that in his country they put their whole soul into their religion and were not satisfied with symbols.

We know that the final mystery shown was called the Opening of the Eyes, which was like a second birth of sight. We also know that fire was an essential part of the rites as Persephone was looked upon as a Goddess of Fire. We know too that two men had positions of meaning in the rites. One was the Hierophant (he who sings the holy words, etymologically) and the other was the Psychopompos, who was a guide or Hermes figure. Kerenyi, a Jungian scholar, says that to enter into the figure of Demeter means to be pursued, to be robbed, raped, to fail to understand, to rage, to grieve, but then to get everything back and to be born again.

As far as the Moon is concerned, these three figures of the Goddesses could certainly be viewed as the three major phases of the Moon as they were early in Greek religion: Persephone the Waxing Moon, Demeter the Full Moon and Hecate the waning Moon. In the original myth, Hecate, the Moon was in her cave when the abduction took place and heard the cries of the Kore. In other versions of the myth, it was Hecate who went to the Underworld and found the Kore. Unfortunately, most of the writings we have now come from patriarchal times in Greece. The reason for the secrecy of the rites might have been that they were supermatriarchal and put the Moon above the then flourishing worship of Apollo and Zeus.

o   o   o

The Stages of Initiation

The initiation process of the followers of the Goddess is one of the best kept secrets of history although countless devotees were initiated into the cult, including such public and relatively talkative Greek philosophers as Pythagoras and Plato. It seems that the rites were of such an impressive order and the vows to secrecy taken so solemnly that the veil around the mysteries has remained. We have only a slight outline sense of the stages of the initiation and must guess the rest from our collective unconscious.

The initiation began in the sacred lake with a journey in a crescent boat through the waters to a region where one went through rituals of warmth and emotion. After secret and awesome events the sacred vessel was presented for the

212

initiate to see with a spear and blood in it carried by attendants. The initiate is supposed to know at this point to ask, **What do these holy vessels mean and whom do they serve?** If the initiate has passed through the trials well, a celebration follows and she is awarded the Roses of Isis, to become a Daughter of the Moon. She is also thought to have become married to the moon and, therefore, a whole and independent person, knowledgeable in the highest secrets of the natural order. The following chant is the initiate's confession sung in recognition and rejoicing of the event:

> I have eaten from the timbrel
> I have drunk from the cymbal,
> I have borne the sacred vessel,
> I have entered into the bridal chamber.[17]

Rome

The moon, this other, celestial earth, is androgynous, Luna and Lunus in one, feminine in relation to the sun, but masculine in relation to earth; but its masculine nature is secondary, it is first woman, afterward man. It is fecundated by the sun and passes this fecundation on to the earth. Thus it maintains the order of the cosmos; it is the interpreter between mortals and immortals.

—Plutarch

Vestal Virgins

The Vestal Virgins, priestesses to the Goddess, tended Rome's eternal fire and sacred vessel, a vase containing water, wine and milk with fruits, grains and candles in the center. The priestesses gave oracles and conducted the celebrations performing holy sexual rituals on specified days. On March 24, Cybele's grief for the death of her son is honored. Originally castration was required of her priests; later this became circumcision or celibacy. August 13th in Rome was the festival of Diana Moon to ask for no storms and protection of the harvest. The Romans had their mid-winter festival at the winter solstice on December 23rd. The Vestal Virgins, guardians of the sacred fire of Vesta, performed a ceremony at the Ides of May, the time of the full moon, to regulate the water supply. This included throwing twenty-four mannikins into the Tiber, a substitute for the human sacrifice, which had formerly been made to the river.

The shrines of the Moon Mother were usually in groves, where there was a spring, often in a grotto where the water trickled directly out of the rock, while ceremonies of water drawing and pouring were a constant feature of her service.

INDIA

Tantra

In the middle of the lotus is the full moon enclosing a triangle. It is here that the final union of Siva and Sakti; the goal of tantric sadhana, is realized and it is here the Kundalini ends its journey through the six chakras.

The conception of sexual union as a spiritual union between the aggressive and receptive principles is represented by the union of the sun and the moon.

All of the sadhaka's efforts are directed toward unifying the moon and the sun, for to do so is to take the middle way. A number of yogic and tantric practices are explained by the intention to homologize one's body and life with the celestial bodies and cosmic rhythms, first of all with the moon and sun. This rhythm is shown especially by the moon, for the moon measures time and makes contrasting realities into parts of the same complex. A considerable portion of Indian mystical physiology is based on the identification of suns and moons in the human body.

Women's Rituals

At the onset of menstruation, girls are individually separated from their community. In isolation they are given religious instruction. The period of isolation varies from three days in most of India to several years in Cambodia. Eventually the initiated women form a group.

The tribes of Muzaffarpur, on the Ganges have women dance naked at night in the fields around a clay image which they make and sing lewd songs to stimulate the god of fertility. Often naked sorceresses draw a plough across the field.

In Southern India, when rain is wanted, the women make a clay figure of a moon and carry it from house to house singing obscene songs and then place the figure in a field. Sometimes in other areas a frog is carried to the same ritual.

Throughout India sexual license which marks the agricultural festival is well known.

In Kundalini yoga, in the first millenium A.D., the two spiritual channels on either side of the central channel of the spine, up which the serpent power is supposed to flow through a control of mind and breath, are called the lunar and solar channels.

Ritual to Destroy Time

In the commentary on Kanhupada's **Dohakosa**, it is said that the moon is born of the semen virile and the sun of the ovum. The common names for **ida** and **pingala** in Hindu and Buddhist tantras are **sun and moon**. The essence of the moon is blood. The Sammohana-tantra says that the nadi on the left is the **moon** because of its gentle nature; the nadi on the right is the **sun** because its nature is aggressive. The Hathayoga pradipika compares them to night and day. Ida and pingala convey the prana and the apana. The former is Rahu, the Asura who swallows the moon. Apana is the **fire of time**, Kalagni. By using the specified ritual principle **breaths** and the principle **subtle channels**, one can destroy time.

Cambodia

In Cambodia the expulsion of evil spirits took place in March. Bits of broken statues and stones considered as the abode of demons were collected and brought to the capital. Here as many elephants were collected as could be got together. On the evening of the full moon volleys of musketry were fired causing the elephants to charge and put the devils to flight.

Kholarion Tribes of Bengal

The intercession for rain is the concern of the women. They ascend to the hills and pray to Mrong Buru to send rain.

In Indian ritual, grains of rice serve to represent the seed of fertility.

A Hindu festival of great antiquity was the **pole-planting** fertility rite, which took place at the time of the first new moon preceding the vernal equinox, when the pole was crowned and worshipped.

The soma plant in India is plucked by moonlight and cleansed in milk and water. It swells as it is washed. It is yellow and identified with moon tree fruit used for sacred rituals. It is supposed to inspire genius, immortality and ecstasy.

OCEANIC ISLES

Polynesia

In Polynesian mythology the moon is thought to disappear each month because it is being eaten, bite by bite, by a monster. This is typical of many moon myths conceptualizing the moon being consumed or fragmented, as in the myth of Osiris being chopped up: from this concept comes the concept of the necessity of a ritual death to ensure rebirth-fertility. The one who dies for the fertility of the community is considered a heroine, a savior. There are also frequent symbolic marriages between the moon-husband and his earthly wives.

Firewalking is universally considered a sign of great spiritual accomplishment. The Polynesian firewalking ceremonies were offerings to the moon goddess for fertility of crops and the people.

Hawaii

Hina the moon goddess was considered the goddess of light and the hearth. Her ceremonies involved burning wood (at a time when that was the only earthly way known to make light), carrying torches, burning candles and consecrating the hearth in one's home.

New Guinea

The people of New Guinea reckon months by the moon. To accelerate its progress or to hasten the return of their friends, they throw spears and stones at the moon.

Bali

It is thought that periodic expulsion of demons is necessary or the island would become uninhabitable. The main ceremony is the day of the dark of the moon in the ninth month.

Java

To ensure fertility of the rice fields, men and women have sexual intercourse in the fields in seasonal ceremonies.

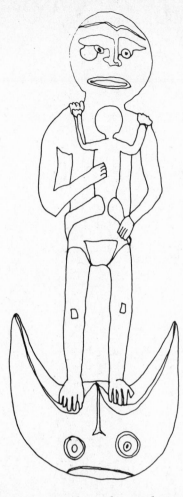

Mother Moon, New Guinea

Trobriand Islands

When the women are planting, they have the right to attack and overthrow any man who comes too near their work. Several types of secret women's associations have remained in being to this day. Their rites always include fertility symbols. In the secret society of women among the Mordvins, men, unmarried girls and children are excluded. The mascot of the association is a hobby-horse, and the women are called **horses**. They suspend from their necks a striped bag full of millet, representing the horse's belly, to which they attach little balls representing testicles. Each year, in the house of one of the old women, the association holds a ritual feast. As the young married women enter, they receive three whips from the old women, who call out: **Lay an egg!** and the young women produce cooked eggs from their bodices. The banquet, to which every member of the society has to contribute victuals, drinks and money, becomes orgiastic. At nightfall, half the members pay a visit to the other half—for each village is divided between two parties; this is a raucous procession of drunken women bestriding hobby-horses and singing erotic songs. When the two halves of the society are reunited, the uproar grows. Men dare not venture out into the streets. If they do, they are attacked by the women, stripped and bullied, and made to pay a ransom before being released.

Black Madonna

MARY   THE MOON OF OUR CHURCH   OUR MOON

THE SPIRITUAL MOON   THE PERFECT AND ETERNAL MOON

STAR OF THE SEA   RULER OF THE OCEAN   RULER OF

THE NIGHT, TO WHOM WE APPEAL IF WE HAVE LOST THE GRACES

OF THE DAY   NOTRE DAME   MOTHER OF GOD

MOTHER MOON   QUEEN MARY   THE VIRGIN

HOLY MOTHER   THE BLACK VIRGIN   VIERGE NOIRE

DARK OF THE MOON

THE BLACK VIRGIN

Black Virgins appear all over the world. Their phenomenon is baffling to many modern scholars and tourists. There are paintings, statues and stories galore which attest to the importance of the Black Virgin and to her antiquity. She is connected in ancient folk tales to her healing powers and her love of water and the dark. Her shrines are often in underground grottos close to a water source.

One of the explanations of the origin of the Black Virgin is that she came from African Christian cultures. There are records of many Black saints. Monastery life and work are thought to have been developed in North Africa and African Christian missionaries were sent into pagan Europe. At least three Popes are known to have been Black.

Black Virgins appear in Moorish, African and South American countries where it seems logical that the native peoples with dark skin would paint and carve their goddesses in their likeness. But to confuse matters, she also appears in Scandinavia and all over Northern Europe. Thus, attributing her color to racial ties seems to be only part of the explanation of her origin.

Some people say that the Black Virgin of Chartres is the Virgin Mary. But this theory is also unsettled by the knowledge that a stutue of her stood in a shrine at that location way before Christians came to the area and the gypsies of Eastern Europe have long held her as a special patroness.

Jacques Huynen has written a book on the puzzle called **L'Enigme des Vierges Noires** (Lafford Publications, France). It seems clear from his work, from the research of women today into matriarchal religion, and from the still-existing beliefs of many Black Virgin worshippers that for her origin we should look to lunar sources. She is the **Queen of the Night**, the **Lady of the Underworld**. She is the Dark of the Moon. Her worship comes from a time when her dark and light aspects were equally valued. This balance today has been broken and her origin seems like fantasy.

Chartres

During the French Revolution, a wooden image of the virgin Paritura, or **Virgin about to bring forth**, was hauled out of the crypt of the Cathedral at Chartres and ceremonially burned. This was one of the oldest statues of the Goddess in Western Europe. Fortunately, it was well documented and there are many copies of the original and descriptions of it. It was a statue carved in the hollowed-out-trunk of a pear tree, of the Goddess, pregnant, and with a child between her legs. A stone carving on the front of the Cathedral is supposed to be a copy of it and it shows a crowned woman (with the high Asiatic type crown which was seen on the Diana at Ephesus) with a child sitting between her two legs, looking rather pregnant.

Chartres itself, built on a mound, was a place of pilgrimage of the Early Christians. But before the Christian era, there was evidence that it was a place of pilgrimage of the Gauls, and before that of the whole Celtic world.

When Christian pilgrims arrived, they were received by the Hopitallers of the Benedictine monastery which is now the Church of St. Peter. After hearing mass, they went up singing psalms to pay honor to Our Lady of Under-the-Earth, the Black Virgin. After this visit to the mound, they went by a passage leading to the crypt, to visit a grotto underneath the church where the sacred statue was to be seen. They made their devotions here and were sprinkled with holy water from a well in the crypt, emerging out another exit in procession.

Black Virgin of Montserrat

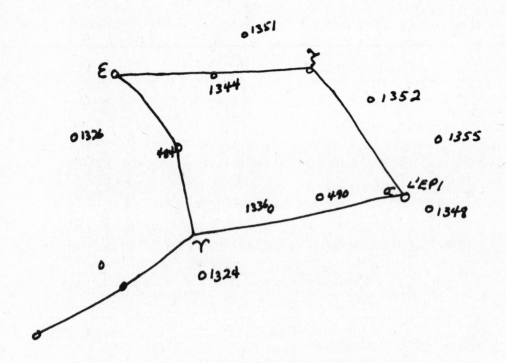

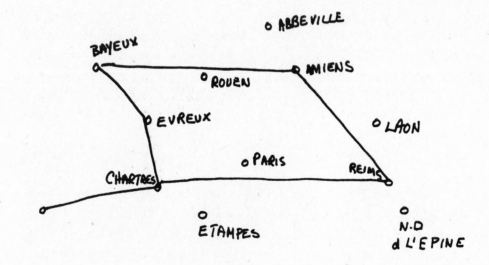

*The constellation of Virgo and the
pattern of Notre Dames in France.*

Black Virgin, San Francisco church

Black Virgin of Montserrat

The Lady in the Grotto was most definitely a goddess. If we are to believe Louis Charpentier (**The Mysteries of Chartres Cathedral**), she could be Belisama. This was the name of the wife and sister of the god Belin. Belin took his name from the fact that the Sun was in the constellation of the Ram at Spring Equinox. Most probably Belisama was there before Belin, some two or three thousand years earlier.

A familiar expedient in the early, struggling days of Christianity was to appropriate celebrated pagan shrines and their tutelary deities. This is supported by archaeological evidence of such a shrine on the site of the Cathedral and by frequent juxtaposition of sacred wells and images at Gallic sanctuaries. The original wooden image of the Patroness of Chartres, bore a striking resemblance to the Mother Goddess figures of the Gallo-Roman era. Chartres is also traditionally claimed to predate the Christian era which is explained as an example of prophetic worship of the Virgin.

It is not only in Chartres that we have this carry-over from the Mother religion into the strongholds of Christianity. In certain shrines of Mary, Mother of God, Moon of the Church, the image of Mary is black. These shrines of the Virgin are all wonder-working, highly esteemed and visited by pilgrims from far and wide. The Church of Notre Dame de la Recourance in Orleans has a statue of the Black Virgin, which is considered miracle-working and particularly holy. In times of calamity it is carried through the streets in procession. A statue of the Black Virgin in Notre Dame de Monserrat, Spain, depicts both Virgin and Child as black. In the north rose window of the Cathedral of Notre Dame at Chartres, the Virgin is dark and her child is fair. The shrine of a Black Virgin at Einsiedem, Switzerland, depicts her standing on a moon.

o   o   o

o   o   o

[Here Mr. Carmichael, who was reading Virgil, blew out his candle. It was midnight.] . . .

But what after all is one night? A short space, especially when the darkness dims so soon, and so soon a bird sings, a cock crows, or a faint green quickens, like a turning leaf, in the hollow of the wave. Night, however, succeeds to night. The winter holds a pack of them in store and deals them equally, evenly, with indefatigable fingers. They lengthen; they darken. Some of them hold aloft clear planets, plates of brightness. The autumn trees, ravaged as they are, take on the flash of tattered flags kindling in the gloom of cool cathedral caves where gold letters on marble pages describe death in battle and how bones bleach and burn far away in Indian sands. The autumn trees gleam in the yellow moonlight, in the light of harvest moons, the light which mellows the energy of labour, and smooths the stubble, and brings the wave lapping blue to the shore.

—Virginia Woolf,
To the Lighthouse[18]

o   o   o

Shine on, shine on Harvest Moon
　up in the sky
I ain't had no lovin'
　Since January February June and July . . .

HARVEST MOON   HUNTER'S MOON   BLOOD MOON

FULL MOON   NEW MOON   OLD MOON   CRESCENT

MOON   WAXING MOON   WANING MOON   BLUE

MOON   DARK OF THE MOON   SAILOR'S MOON

HONEY MOON   ROSE MOON   MOON WHEN THE DEER

SHED ANTLERS   BIG WINTER MOON   GREEN GRASS

MOON

Young Moon

Word and music by
Malvina Reynolds

Young moon, small moon, lit-tle girl moon,

Po-ny tail moon in the sky -- -- --

Tho you are far and a-lone, Just for this

mo-ment you are my own. Young moon,

small moon, lit-tle girl moon, Some day I'll look by my

side, -- -- -- -- And I will see some-one

there and I'll wonder where I've seen her be-fore, So

young, so soft-ly bright, And then I'll re-mem-ber this

night, Young moon.

LUNAR CALENDARS

A lunar month or lunation is the period from one new moon to the next. As far back as 32,000 years ago, humans had lunar calendars. On all the famous prehistoric sites, there have been found hitherto undecipherable markings on pieces of bone, stone and other objects that were formerly thought of as 'man's urge to decorate,' or as doodles, which have been found to be ways of marking lunar sequences.

As far back as 30,000 B.C., the Ice Age hunter of western Europe was using a sophisticated system of notation that seems to have been thousands of years old by that point. Lunar notations were also in use by other peoples such as Combe Capelle of the East Gravettian culture in Czechoslovakia and Russia and by subcultures in Italy and Spain. The tradition seems so widespread that scholars guess its beginnings go back to the period of the Neanderthals.

The seven day week, the 29-30-31 day month and the 365½ day year are a result of relatively late cultural divisions developed by the first agricultural civilizations of the Middle East and the Nile about 5,000 years ago.

It seems that the Ice Age hunters were not much interested in an abstract number system or in keeping records in a modern sense. They kept a lunar notation because with the phases of the moon they told stories, held rites and structured practical, cultural and biological aspects of the community. The notations were **remembering marks** for well known stories. This notation skill probably developed after the observed astronomical lore and perhaps for teaching.

On many of the female figurines, these same marks appear; on some of them, these marks are clearly lunar notations. Breast images were both used and worn by women, or by a ritual official performing for women, helping them to participate in the story. These female images are thought to have been used for group ceremonies and the rites of the goddess to be one of the threads leading to and preparing the way for agriculture. The notations are ritual lunar calendars.

Egypt

An official dynastic Egyptian calendar, introduced about 3,000-4,000 B.C., was based on a solar day count and a stellar astronomy. The start of the solar year of 365 days was the morning on which Sirius, the brightest star, first appeared in the eastern dawn sky around July 19. There is an ancient, pre-dynastic lunar calendar in Egypt whose tradition is lost but whose remnants are implied in the ritual, symbolism and religious calendar. The first calendars of Mesopotamia are lunar, also with additions of solar, stellar and planetery observations. The evidence reveals an ancient lunar tradition, with a month that begins with the observation of the lunar crescent.

China

The early Chinese calendar contains observations of both the sun and moon but is based on an ancient tradition that is primarily lunar. The lunar month in China began with the new moon.

The lunar calendar was used also in Japan, Korea, and Vietnam. According to Buddhists, Buddha meditated under the Bo tree for 28 days.

India

The early Hindu calendar was lunar, describing the 28 mansions of the moon, still used today. Each lunation was divided by the days of the new moon, amavasya, and the days of the full moon, purnamasi. These two parts were called the bright one, sukla, which was the fortnight of increasing light from the new moon onward, and the black one, krishna, which was the decreasing of the light after the full moon.

Near East

The Babylonians had twelve lunar months of 354 days, but they reckoned their years as having six months which might account for the phenomenal length of life of certain individuals in the bible.

The Chaldeans discovered the saros, a repeating pattern of eclipses which occurs in cycles of 18 years, 11 ⅜ days. The earliest known Chaldean calendar was lunar with alternate months of twenty-nine and thirty days.

228

Moslem years and months are lunar. According to the Koran, Moslems must see the new moon with their naked eye before they can begin their fast in Ramadan. The Mohammedan calendar is figured on the lunar month. The months progress through the seasons, since the calendar does not take into account the earth's rotation about the sun. The Islamic year is, therefore, only 354 or 355 days long. The religious festivals, such as the fast of Ramadan, occur at various seasons of the year, since they are fixed by the month. This reckoning is the origin of **movable feasts** whose dates change according to the moon.

Jews today use a religious luni-solar calendar which came originally from a lunar one. The years are solar, but the months are lunar. The length of each month was determined from observation of witnesses who reported having seen the new crescent moon and were carefully questioned by authorities. The Hebrew word for month, **Yera**, comes from their word for moon. Jewish Passover is celebrated at the full moon.

Greece and Rome

The Greeks attempted to combine in a single system the lunar year of twelve months totaling 354 days, and the solar year of 365.25 days. The only real requirement was that each month must begin with a new moon.

The very earliest Roman calendar was lunar. It contained ten lunations from March to December, and then had a two lunation gap in winter. The first day of each month was the proclamation of the new moon known as **Kalendae** or **callings**. At that time, sacrifices were offered to Juno.

The Greeks around 400 B.C. discovered that 19 solar years equal 235 lunar months. In 46 B.C. Julias Ceasar revised the calendar; and it was altered again in 1582 A.D. by Pope Gregory XIII into its present form.

Northern Europe

According to Pliny, the calendar of the Celts was lunar. In Caesar's **Gallic Wars** he writes of the Celts, **They reckon all time not by days, but by nights.** Thus the modern expression **fortnight** which is a lunar measurement.

> And thirtie dozen moones with borrowed sheene,
> About the world have times twelve thirties beene.
>
> —Shakespeare, **Hamlet**, 1602

All kinds of omens are associated with the different phases and appearances of the moon. A crescent moon of which the rest of the circle is visible as a dark shadow is thought to be an omen of disaster.

> Late late yestreen I saw the new moone,
>   Wi the auld moone in hir arme,
> And I feir, I feir, my deir master,
> That we will cum to harme.

> —the sailor, in the
> Ballad of Sir Patrick Spens

In 1793 France adopted a revolutionary calendar. It dated from September 22, 1792, the beginning of the new republic (also the fall equinox). The year had twelve months of thirty days each with five extra days at the end and six at leap year. Each month had three decades of ten days with numerical names. All Christian elements were eliminated. Festivals were held to observe such things as hatred of tyrants and traitors, Supreme Being, Nature and Benefactors of Mankind. Leap Day was known as the Day of the Revolution. The calendar was abandoned in 1805 because Napoleon needed a favor from the Pope for which return to Christian time was the price.

At the beginning of every almanac is the fashion to have the body of a man bitten and shot at by wild beasts and monsters. This fellow they call the moon's man.

> —Calendar, 1609

> The fair maid who, the first of May,
> Goes to the fields at break of day,
> And washes in dew from the hawthorn tree,
> Will ever after handsome be.

> —Mother Goose

South America

Though the official, priestly calendar of the Central American Mayans was solar, there are indications of a basic, earlier lunar calendar in South and North American Indian traditions.

The Mayan calendar was comprised of a 260 day year which corresponded to their ritual calendar. The day one was the day of the Moon Goddess.

According to Mayan tradition, there is a natural rhythm to apocalyptic events. One of the functions of a precise calendar is thus the prediction of these cycles to aid in the preparation for the changes. Following a flowering high civilization of Mesoamerica, a **Hell Period** was predicted in the calendars to begin in 1519—the year Cortes landed in Mexico—and conclude in 1987. This agrees with some of the Hopi people's predictions of the timing of historical cycles.

North America

To Native Americans the moon was a spirit, a being who controlled the light. Native American tribes of the North Central plains and woodlands counted their years as **winters** with the new year at the time of the change from a summer to winter. Most tribes did not recognize four seasons. Some tribes had names for all twelve Moons; others named only moons of the summer season. The moons were named according to significant observances in nature and their names varied from one tribe to another, and often from year to year so they were not absolute.

The following listing begins with the Moon containing the new year in late fall drawn from several traditions, including the Teton Sioux, Oglala Sioux, Cheyenne, Kowa, Omaha.

Moons of the Hoop of the Year

MOON OF THE CHANGING SEASON   FALLING LEAF MOON

TEN COLDS MOON
(libra)

WAIT UNTIL I COME MOON   MOON OF STORMS

MAD MOON   MOON WHEN THE DEER SHED ANTLERS
(scorpio)

LONG NIGHT MOON   MOON OF POPPING TREES

BIG WINTER MOON   SWEATHOUSE MOON
(saggitarius)

HUNGER MOON
(aquarius)

MOON OF FROST IN THE TIPI   MOON OF LITTLE WINTER

SNOW MOON
(capricorn)

CROW MOON   SORE EYE MOON   MOON OF THE

SNOWBLIND
(pisces)

MOON OF THE RED GRASS APPEARING   GREEN GRASS

MOON   PLANTING MOON
(aries)

WAIT UNTIL I COME MOON   MOON WHEN THE PONIES

SHED   PLANTING MOON
(taurus)

ROSE MOON   MOON OF MAKING FAT
(gemini)

THUNDER MOON
(cancer)

MOON WHEN THE CHERRIES TURN BLACK
(leo)

HUNTING MOON   MOON WHEN DEER PAW THE EARTH
(virgo)

In 1965, two years after he had written an article with the same title for **Nature** magazine, Gerald S. Hawkins published a book entitled STONEHENGE DE-CODED. Despite the fact that some stones had fallen, moved out of position or been lost entirely, he postulated some new ideas about Stonehenge: that the sun-moon alignments were created to make a calendar, particularly useful to tell the time for planting crops and that this helped to maintain priestly power by enabling the priest to announce the spectacular risings and settings of the sun and the moon, especially the midsummer sunrise over the heelstone through the great trilithon. Interesting to us moon-worshippers is the fact that he found that the fifty-six Aubrey holes which encircle the monument could serve as a device to predict eclipses of the sun and moon.

Fred Hoyle, an astronomer at Cambridge, enlarged on Hawkins' thesis in an article published in **Nature**, July, 1966, and again in his forthcoming book from W. H. Freeman Co. In both he shows that by the addition of six indicator stones, two of which would represent lunar nodes which are the points at which the moon's orbit intersects the plane of the earth's equator, the accuracy could be considerably improved. These nodes are conceptual not visible. Hoyle speculates that this system was invented by a society with religious beliefs associated with the sun and moon: if the sun and moon are dieties and if whenever eclipses occur the visible gods are eliminated, then evidently the more powerful god is invisible. Hoyle speculates that this is the origin of the concept of an invisible all-powerful god.

On eclipse, the Moon, and very occasionally the Sun, die. Both are then miraculously reborn, which people believed was a sign of their own cycle of death and rebirth. Hoyle makes some interesting observations about lunar as opposed to solar calendars. At Stonehenge Three, even after centuries of remodeling, there was a strong connection with the Sun and the seasons of the year, but the dominance of the Sun year seems to be challenged elsewhere. In other places a different way of following the nineteen year eclipse cycle was used. The eclipse cycle can be followed either by counting nineteen eclipse years or 233 lunations. A people who adopted the second way would be likely to believe in the dominance of the Moon Goddess. The time of 29.5 days from full moon to full moon would seem to them the crucial period in the universe, and attempts would be made to compute the seasons of the year in a lunar calendar. This has come down to us in modern times as the division of the year into months, and in the method still used for fixing the dates of most festivals.

No doubt the old method did not die without a struggle. It probably was this conflict which drove the builders of Stonehenge One from their homes in the Near East and caused them to seek refuge in the British Isles.

There have been many educated guesses about who these builders were. The monument was far more advanced in concept and construction than anything in Western Europe. It has been estimated that the 400 year long concerted effort to build Stonehenge One, Two and Three required 1.5 million days of exceedingly hard labor. How were the sparsely-fed, poorly housed, and completely illiterate people of Southern England persuaded to work so strenuously for so many generations? They were evidently inspired by the same sort of religious fervor that built the great cathedrals of Europe centuries later.

In June 1953, R. J. C. Atkinson, a noted specialist on Stonehenge, found several axe-heads and a hilted dagger carved on one of the stones. Since then thirty other such symbols have been discovered. Their design points to a Mycenean-Minoan origin.

By 3000 B.C. Stone Age people had observed the sky for over 10,000 years. It is reasonable to suppose that, not only the present astronomical details, but certain more subtle variations of the Moon's path in the sky were discovered during this great interval of time, and were well known to the first builders of Stonehenge.

After reading an impressive number of books on Stonehenge, aside from the astronomical detail, I came up with some conclusions of my own.

Since archaeologists have not **as yet** turned up any evidence of an advanced civilization living in Britain at the time of Stonehenge One (it was built in three stages), obviously there was outside help. There has been talk of artisans being sent for from the Mediterranean countries who were further along culturally, and there is evidence of their presence, or at least the presence of their tools. But it seems to me, that in order to **summon** this sort of help, the sending culture would have to be impressive in terms of either wealth or culture, and the British peoples at that time have left no evidence of being either. Therefore, staying with the idea that the British could not have done it alone, and that help from a further advanced civilization seems probable, is it not possible that one of those civilizations, which were then almost entirely matriarchal, sent missionaries? Perhaps they were even invited to do so through some of the early traders who must have heard of and even traded some of the mineral riches of this northern kingdom. We do have indications of very early trade taking place.

If I were to throw all caution, academic and otherwise, to the winds, I might even suggest that the culture which came to Britain with such sophisticated engineering techniques and such advanced knowledge of astronomical matters, might have been some of the survivors of the Atlantean holocaust. Having arrived on the shores of Britain with only the most meager of personal luggage and none of the resources they were formerly used to, might they not have built such a temple, using the stone and the labor at hand? It would be natural that such advanced people would become the priestly caste of their more backward hosts.

In America today there is a full-sized replica of Stonehenge near Maryhill, Washington on the Columbia River, 100 miles east of Portland, Oregon. It was built in the twenties as a war memorial.

o   o   o

A LUNAR ECLIPSE

An eclipse of the moon or the sun was experienced in many ancient cultures as a negative omen of war, of famine, communal disaster or anger of the gods. Great value was placed on those who could predict eclipses so that people could prepare and sacrifice to the deities to appease them. This is one of the conjectured motivations for people's dedication to the complex construction of Stonehenge. Eclipses are also a reminder of our dependence on the lights of the moon and sun and in this aspect serve to replenish our respect. Although today eclipses are explained in scientific terms, people still gather in awe to see them.

During the lunar eclipse in May, 1975, i happened to be, thanks to the goddess, staying on a small island in the Bahama Keys, a white sand jewel in the fabulously blue Carribean Sea. Countless conch shells lined the beaches. The weather was consistently bright and clear and the lagoons like liquid crystal. With a friend on the night of the eclipse, i went out to one of the few high cliff promontories over the shore. The starry phosphorous had been out again at the beach, but here on the cliff, everything looked black except the moon and its silver brick path on the water. We sat down in the beautiful darkness of an environment minus neon and waited for the shape of the full moon to begin to alter.

The hot night air had an edge of moisture in it. The rim of the sea to my left was lined with orange from the glow of Nassau city lights far away. I could hear thunder and see lightening on the horizon to my right. The weather on my left seemed to stay clear. To the percussion of lightning and thunder, the shadow of the earth started to cross over the face of the moon. The bright disc was slowly extinguished, it seemed, by a dark one, until the whole moon was obscured and the path of light on the ocean had disappeared. Somehow the disappearance of this yellow road and the disappearance of the silver at the end of it drew me. I wanted to get closer to see the moon better, or find it inside the sea. The event seemed to want me to go deeper into the darkness as the moon had. I got up from the large flat rock i was sitting on and walked toward the edge of the cliff, moving closer to the waves. Reaching the edge i looked for a long time, at the movement of the waves between the rocks, and out at the silky black sea. The waves among the rocks had an alluring rhythm and the rest of the blackness looked like the most inviting down comforter i'd ever wanted to float into. I wanted to rest, and be covered and initiated. Joining the porpoises seemed possible. I wondered what they were doing during this eclipse. The waves which i knew to be far, looked close, maybe only a step or a dive away. My friend was calling me to come back, not to go so close to the edge of the cliff. I retreated a little to sit down on a small rock, as the light started to return, as the moon passed out of the earth's shadow. It was a very reassuring and beautiful sight. I'd known all along she wouldn't stay away (would she?). When the full moon was visible and bright again, the silver plated water path reestablished itself. The storm miraculously stopped. I felt i could have stayed out there forever. But it was very late; we were tired and the mosquitoes' territorial attitude was winning out.

Early the next morning when i went out to run along the cream-colored sunrise beach, it was the most paradisical dawn i've ever seen, pink and lavender with a big lace circle full moon. She'd had a good time wherever she'd gone, and come back refreshed.

My friend and i talked about what we'd felt during the eclipse. When i'd gotten back to my room, i'd discovered i had a large cut on my foot from exploring the jagged rocks. At the time i hadn't noticed. We explained our responses with descriptions of the magnetism generated by so much moving water and by atmospheric pressure changes.

Somehow these did not describe what happened.

NOW

Also Available as a 23" X 27" Poster

ASPECTS		SIGNS	
☌ 0°	⚼ 135°	♈ Aries	♎ Libra
⚻ 30°	⚻ 150°	♉ Taurus	♏ Scorpio
⚺ 45°	☍ 180°	♊ Gemini	♐ Sagittarius
⚹ 60°		♋ Cancer	♑ Capricorn
☐ 90°		♌ Leo	♒ Aquarius
△ 120°		♍ Virgo	♓ Pisces

SOLAR-LUNAR CALENDAR

Hallie Iglehart

The human sense of experience seems to be inseparable from our sense of time. I thought about the dating we now use and its implied acceptance of the birthday of the male-son-messiah as the "beginning of time." I resolved it for myself by deciding it was a crucial demarcation to recall because it marks a change we shouldn't forget. And now A.D. translates for me as After the Death of communal non-hierarchial living.

Hallie and i worked on a simple calendar which combines this modern recognition in the form of our currently-used solar time demarcation, with re-instatement of some of the demarcations of lunar time cycles. It seems to me the combination works well and one could easily integrate lunar cycles into existing solar calendars as clarifying rather than confusing additions to our current cycle-keeping.

Like most of the calendars that have existed, the following one is based on the cycles of the Moon and the Earth and the Sun. It includes months and days that we are familiar with, so that we can begin to integrate our linear concept of time based on numbers and dates, with a cyclical one.

The ways in which different peoples think of time reflect wide cultural differences. The Thais, and some Native Americans, have little concept of the past, present or future—all time is now. The idea of a year is a fairly new practice—some cultures lived by each day, others by each Moon or season. The Polynesians and Micronesians name their days by the shape and position of the Moon. The Greeks, like many others, had no week—this is hard to conceive of in a society like ours where life is compartmentalized into nine-to-five weekdays, with a weekend for "recreation." Many ancient cultures thought of the day as beginning at sunset —they had an entirely different attitude toward night-time than we do; it was a time of meetings and gatherings. Still other societies recognized night-time and day-time as two separate, and whole, periods of time. Many others, today, rest in the afternoon, so that their periods of activity are in the morning and evening.

Our concept of time and the way in which we live our lives have a profound effect on one another. My hope is that by creating a lunar calendar with the Pagan seasonal celebrations to refer to, we can begin more and more to recognize, live by, and celebrate the cycles of nature—and feel them moving within our selves. As we observe the rhythms of the moon, the earth and the sun, we also become sensitive to our inner cycles—our biorhythms, our menstrual cycles, the rhythms of each morning, afternoon and night.

We become aware of the life-force of the more subtle rhythms going on within our bodies: the circulation of our blood, the creation and death of cells, our digestion. The rhythm of our breathing is the easiest for us to feel as our breath moves in and out, in and out, our chests and bellies grow larger and smaller like the moon in the sky each month.

Recognizing cycles means that we are more responsible for our lives for we know more about our own rhythms. We are able to make the best use of our time and energy. We know when we are most suited to work, to create, to rest, and to play; we are freed from a rigid, unnatural structure imposed from the outside.

The cycles of the Moon and the Earth and the Sun are the most visible of nature. We see the Moon change size in the sky every month—a beautiful and fascinating miracle. We watch the Earth change throughout the year, and we feel the changes in the weather. The Sun joins us and leaves us each day, grows farther away and then closer throughout the year.

These reminders of the rhythms of life are sources of great celebration —every day, every month, every year, we can celebrate the disappearance and return, the death and rebirth, of the Moon, the Stars, the Sun, and the green growth of the Earth. We celebrate with them the complex cycles within our selves of our many beings.

Because we are all so varied, each one of us could make up our own calendar—there is no correct calendar. I chose to start the year at the Spring Equinox, because it felt the most right to me. A friend starts hers at the Winter Solstice. Another friend says she has little concept of years, now that she lives in the country. She feels time in seasons. You can make up your own calendar, according to your own perception of the universe and your own rhythms. Perhaps this one will be a starting off place.

Living by the Moon, the Earth and the Sun

Each month begins with the dark of the New Moon. The year begins at the Spring Equinox. The week begins with Moonday. Any days left over at the end of the year (leap days) are free time. You can do whatever you want in them. No rules! All times of this calendar are Pacific Standard Time. For Mountain Standard Time, add one hour. For Central Standard Time, add two hours. For Eastern Standard Time, add three hours. For Daylight Saving Time, add one hour. Although I prefer observation, I have included the times since most of us still like some exact calculations. The Moon stays in each astrological sign roughly two and a half days.

I have named the months after goddesses who for me have a particular relation to that time. Kore (March) is the symbol of the return of spring from the underworld. The birthday of Isis was in April. Sappha is connected for me with May festivals. Hera is the Greek Juno. Cybele (July) is connected with summer nights. Selene (August) is the goddess of the moon. Demeter (September) is the goddess of the Harvest. Artemis (October) is the goddess of the hunt. Hecate of November is the goddess of night and relates to Scorpio. Minerva (December) is goddess of wisdom. Inanna (January) was one of the first mythical people to go to the underworld and return. Februa is the goddess mother of Mars.

Moon Viewing: New Moon

When the Moon is completely dark, she rises and sets with the sun for several days and disappears from our sight. On the fourth day, watch for her crescent in the western sky just after sunset.

Waxing Moon

As she waxes, she rises approximately fifty-one minutes later each day. For instance, one week after the dark of the Moon, she will rise in the east about when the sun is highest. You can watch her climbing in the eastern sky in the afternoon.

Full Moon

When full, she rises in the east just as the sun sets in the west.

Waning Moon

When waning, she rises approximately fifty-one minutes later each night. A week after the Full Moon, she rises in the very middle of the night. If you wake up from your dreams, she will be there, surprising you, and guiding you through your night's journeys.

The Gibbous moon is the name for when she shows more than fifty percent and crescent is the name for showing less than half.

Moon Celebrating

There is a lot to celebrate when we live tuned with the Moon, Sun and Earth. Mother Nature wants us to enjoy life, so she gives us many opportunities!

The Moon Cycle

Each cycle of the Moon is divided into four smaller cycles: the New Moon, the Waxing Moon, the Full Moon, and the Waning Moon. Each lasts roughly seven days, but there are no rigid moments where one ends and the next begins. They are not sudden shifts; and our own energy flows the same way.

The New Moon

Our month, our moon, begins with the New Moon, or dark of the Moon, a time of rebirth. For the three or four days preceding the disappearance of the Moon, we also start to withdraw from visible activity. We can welcome this opportunity to rest and be quiet and feel the deepest, darkest movements of our inner selves. In this stillness, we can allow the seeds for the coming weeks to be planted in us. At the appearance of the first crescent and for several days after, we celebrate the promise of rebirth and begin to feel our own energy moving outward.

The New Moon is the time when women usually menstruate—a magical bleeding without wound when we experience vividly the power of our bodies' cycles and our own creative sources.

The Waxing Moon

As the Moon waxes we start acting upon the revelations and inspirations of the New Moon. We celebrate her growth and our own.

The Full Moon

In most societies, the Moon was considered full for several days before and after the astrological, astronomical Full Moon. When she is full, we see and feel the culmination of the energy-seeds planted in us at the New Moon. They may continue to grow, of course, for many moons or years.

The Waning Moon

The Waning Moon is a time for harvesting, to look at what has been going on in the previous weeks, and assimilate what we have done and learned.

Pagan Festivals

The Pagan religion centers around the life-force of Nature, most visible in the cycles of the Moon, Earth and Sun. It is one of the oldest cosmologies, and more recent religions such as Judaism, Buddhism, Christianity and Mohammedanism which recognize only one power, took over multiple Pagan holidays in an attempt to win converts. Since the Pagan traditions with which I am most familiar are those of Europe, I have used some of the European names. The festivals properly began at the preceding sunset, which is when ancient peoples began their day. The Pagan calendar celebrates the New Moon and the Full Moon every month. It also marks the relationship of the Earth to the Sun, by celebrating the Solstices and Equinoxes, called the quarter days, and the cross quarter days (which fall in between), and notes the changes in weather.

Spring Equinox—The New Year

Around March 20 each year, also known as Easter, the day and night are of equal length. The Spring Equinox is the time of celebrating rebirth, the coming of Spring and new growth. In particular, we celebrate the reunion of Kore, or Persephone, the Greek Goddess of Spring, with her mother Demeter, the Goddess of the Harvest. Kore stays underground all winter long and Demeter forbids the Earth to produce until her daughter returns to her. April 1 was the date of the festival of Greek Aphrodite (hence name) and the Roman Venus feast. Eoster is the Saxon fertility goddess.

May Day—May 1

The beginning of good weather, and a time of flowers and fertility. Sacred to the Goddess Tuatha De Danaan, the fairy queen Brigid, and to the poet Sappha. Called in Gaelic **Beltane**, it is celebrated with a Maypole and general happiness. The Greek Goddess **Maia** and her six sisters were mountain goddesses of spring. May 1 was in the middle of a five day festival of Flora, goddess of flowers.

Summer Solstice—Around June 20

The longest day of the year, we celebrate the outbreathing of the earth, manifested by the goddess Rhea. Our lives are outer-directed; it is a time for experiencing.

Lammas—August 1

The time of hot weather, and the beginning of the harvest. Sacred to the goddess of the moon, Artemis. We begin to understand the meaning of our summer's activity. Also known as **Lughnasad** in Gaelic.

Autumnal Equinox—Around September 21

Again, the day and night are of equal length. We celebrate the earth's harvest, and the fruits of our own activity. This festival is also known as **Samhain**, and is sacred to the Goddess Demeter, mother of Kore, and Goddess of the Harvest.

Hallomas—October 31

The beginning of the cold weather and a time of increasing starlight and moonlight. Hallomas is dedicated to the Greek goddess of night, Hecate. It is celebrated as a time of lengthening nights, and the positive aspects of darkness. It is a time of divination, and for communicating with psychic worlds. Our outer-directed activity has quieted down, and we begin to turn inward.

Winter Solstice—Around December 21

Early Anglo-Saxons celebrated the winter solstice for one week (from December 25) by feasting, also known as Yule. This is the shortest day of the year, and the longest night. We celebrate the rebirth of the Sun Goddess—June Lucina of Rome, Atthar of Arabia, and Amaterasu of Japan. The Winter Solstice corresponds to the dark of the Moon—it is a time when we turn inward to comprehend and synthesize the outer-directed activities of the summer. This festival also recognizes the Sumerian goddess Inanna.

Candlemas—February 2

We celebrate the growth of the Sun's light, and the lengthening of the days. It is sacred to the Celtic Goddess Brigid, known also as Cerridwen, and a festival for young children. It is a time for initiations.

January and February were invented in 713 B.C. Before, many cultures did not name or count time between December and the Vernal Equinox.

Februum is a Roman word meaning purification, atonement. It is a month of cleansing for the new year, made shorter because this was considered unlucky.

The Vernal Equinox is usually considered to be March 25. This date of the pagan calendar and the pagan winter solstice was "integrated" into the Christian calendar by Abbott Dionysius Exiguus in 532 A.D. who proclaimed March 25 Christ's conception and December 25 his birth! The winter solstice is also a festival of lights.

o   o   o

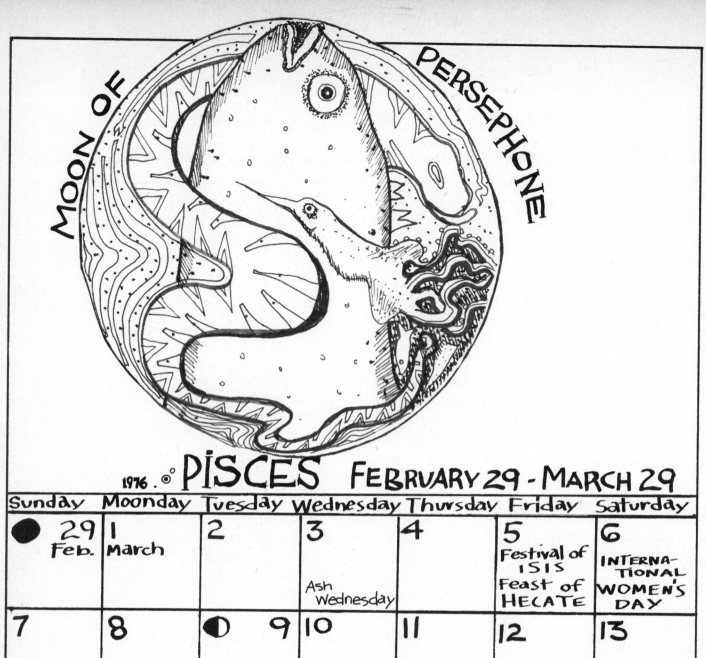

MOON OF   PERSEPHONE

1976 .°° PISCES   FEBRUARY 29 - MARCH 29

Sunday	Moonday	Tuesday	Wednesday	Thursday	Friday	Saturday
● 29 Feb.	1 March	2	3 Ash Wednesday	4	5 Festival of ISIS Feast of HECATE	6 INTERNA-TIONAL WOMEN'S DAY
7	8	◑ 9	10	11 Feast of Artemis	12	13
14	15	○ 16	17 Feast of ISHTAR	18 To March 19	19	20 Vernal Equinox LUNAR NEW YEAR
21	◑ 22	23	24	25 Feast of CYBELE	26	27
28	29				changes	

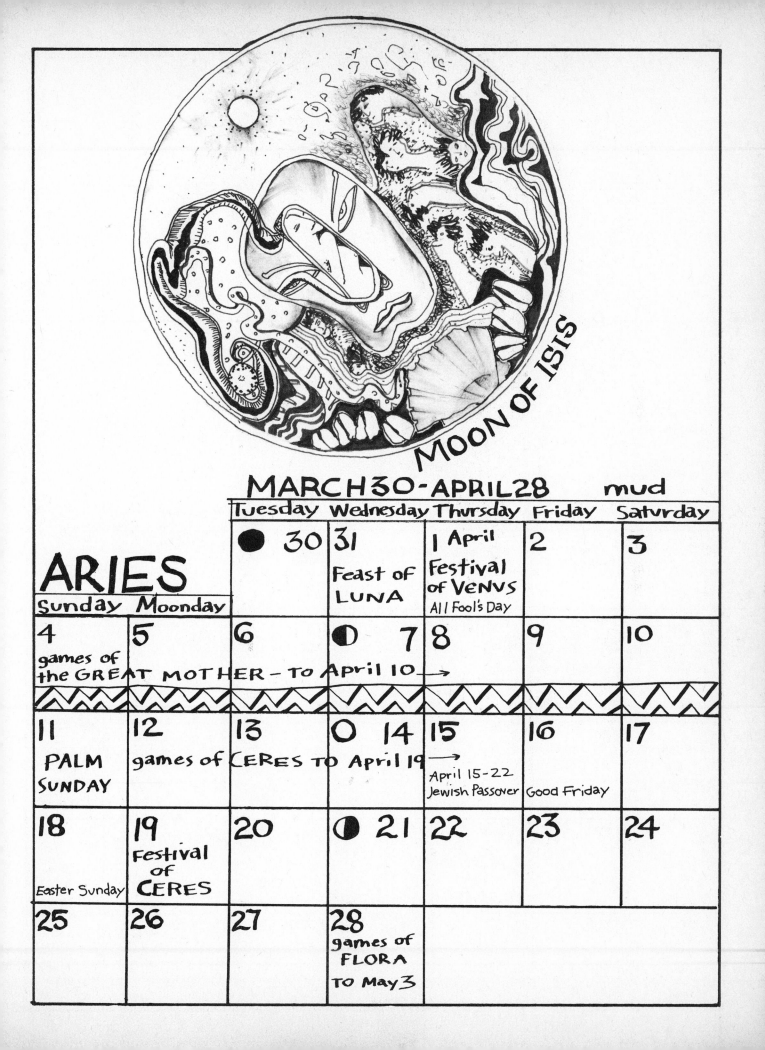

MOON OF ISIS

MARCH 30 - APRIL 28   mud

Sunday	Moonday	Tuesday	Wednesday	Thursday	Friday	Saturday
ARIES		● 30	31 Feast of LUNA	1 April Festival of VENUS All Fool's Day	2	3
4 games of the GREAT MOTHER – TO APRIL 10 →	5	6	◑ 7	8	9	10
11 PALM SUNDAY	12 games of	13 CERES TO April 19	O 14	15 → April 15-22 Jewish Passover	16 Good Friday	17
18 Easter Sunday	19 Festival of CERES	20	◑ 21	22	23	24
25	26	27	28 games of FLORA TO May 3			

MOON OF SAPPHA

TAURUS APRIL 29 - MAY 27

Sunday	Moonday	Tuesday	Wednesday	Thursday	Friday	Saturday
				● 29 Games of FLORA TO MAY 3	30	1 MAY DAY
2	3 Feast of HECATE	4	5	6	◑ 7	8
9 Feast of ARTEMIS	10	11	12	○ 13 LUNAR ECLIPSE	14	15
16	17	18 Feast of SELENE	19	◑ 20	21	22
23	24	25	26	27	flowers	

MOON OF HERA

roses

GEMINI   MAY 28 - JUNE 26

sunday	Moonday	Tuesday	Wednesday	Thursday	Friday	Saturday
					28	● 29 Pregnancy Festival
30	31 Memorial Day	1 JUNE	2	3	4	◖ 5
6	7	8	9 Festival of VESTA	10	11 Feast of Mother Morning	○ 12
13	14	15	16	17	18	◐ 19
20 Festival of Athena Father's Day	21 Day of HEATHER Summer Solstice	22	23	24	25	26

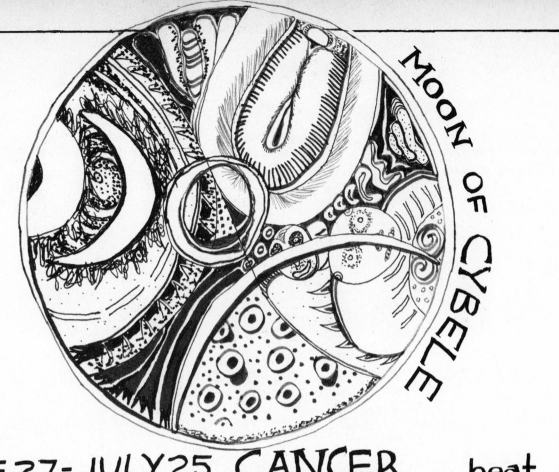

MOON OF CYBELE

JUNE 27-JULY 25 CANCER heat

sunday	Moonday	Tuesday	Wednesday	Thursday	Friday	Saturday
● 27	28	29	30	1 July Feast of HECATE	2	3
◑ 4 Independence Day	5	6 HOLLY DAY	7 Feast of ARTEMIS	8	9	10
○ 11	12	13 Festival of DEMETER	14	15	16	17
18 Feast of TAMMUZ	◐ 19	20	21 FOREST SPIRIT Festival	22	23	24
25						

MOON OF SELENE

LEO JULY 26 - AUGUST 24

Moonday	Tuesday	Wednesday	Thursday	Friday	Saturday
26	● 27	28	29	30	31

Sunday					
1 August	◐ 2	3	4	5	6	7
8	○ 9	10	11	12	13 Festival of DIANA	14 Feast of SELENE
15	16	17	◑ 18	19 Festival of VENUS	20	21
22	23	24		+thunder		

MARI

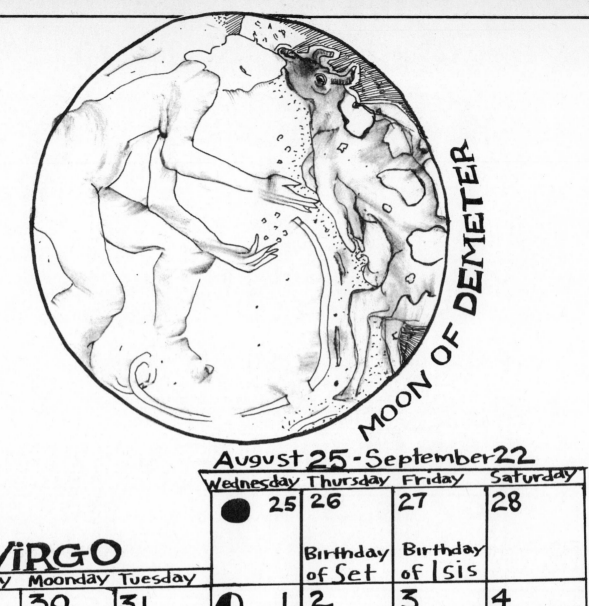

MOON OF DEMETER

August 25 - September 22

VIRGO

Sunday	Moonday	Tuesday	Wednesday	Thursday	Friday	Saturday
			● 25	26	27	28
				Birthday of Set	Birthday of Isis	
29	30	31	◑ 1 September	2	3	4 feast of Artemis
		IVY Day				
5	6	7	○ 8 Chinese Harvest Festival	9	10	11
	Labor Day					
12	13	14	15	◐ 16	17	18
19	20	21	22 Autumnal Equinox	harvest		

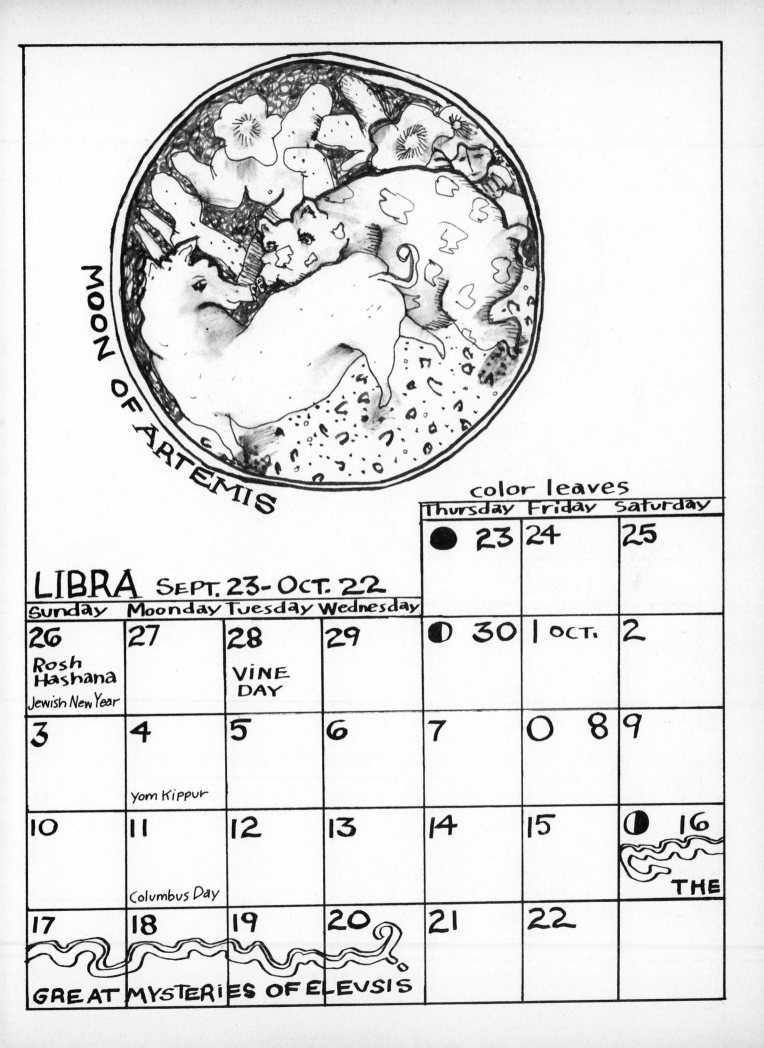

MOON OF ARTEMIS

color leaves

LIBRA SEPT. 23 - OCT. 22

Sunday	Moonday	Tuesday	Wednesday	Thursday	Friday	Saturday
				● 23	24	25
26 Rosh Hashana Jewish New Year	27	28 VINE DAY	29	◑ 30	1 OCT.	2
3	4 Yom Kippur	5	6	7	○ 8	9
10	11 Columbus Day	12	13	14	15	◐ 16 THE
17	18	19	20	21	22	

GREAT MYSTERIES OF ELEUSIS

MOON OF HECATE

SCORPIO October 23 - November 20

winds
saturday
● 23

Sunday	Moonday	Tuesday	Wednesday	Thursday	Friday	Saturday
24	25	26 Reed Day	27	28	29 ◑ Festival of Osiris till Nov 12	30
31 All Hallow's Eve	1 November Feast of Persephone All Saints Day	2 Election Day	3	4	5	○ 6
7 Feast of	8 ISIS and	9 DEMETER	10	11	12	13
◑ 14	15	16	17	18	19	20

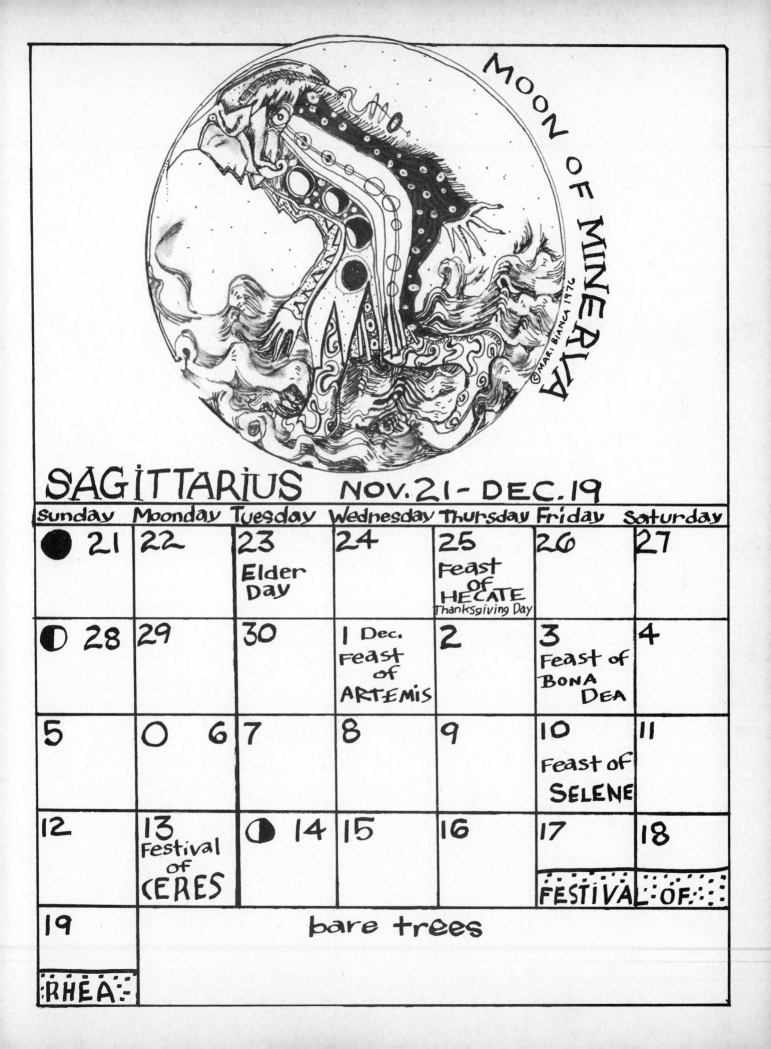

MOON OF MINERVA

©MARI BIANCA 1976

SAGITTARIUS NOV. 21- DEC. 19

Sunday	Moonday	Tuesday	Wednesday	Thursday	Friday	Saturday
● 21	22	23 Elder Day	24	25 Feast of HECATE Thanksgiving Day	26	27
◐ 28	29	30	1 Dec. Feast of ARTEMIS	2	3 Feast of BONA Dea	4
5	○ 6	7	8	9	10 Feast of SELENE	11
12	13 Festival of CERES	◑ 14	15	16	17 FESTIVAL OF	18
19 RHEA	bare trees					

MOON OF INANNA

CAPRICORN DEC. 20 - JAN. 18, 1977

Sunday	Moonday	Tuesday	Wednesday	Thursday	Friday	Saturday
	● 20 Mother's Night	21 WINTER SOLSTICE Day of 1ST mistletoe	22 Day of BIRCH	23	24	25 Christmas Day Feast of HECATE
26 MAO TSE-TUNG'S birthday	27	◑ 28	29	30	31 Feast of ARTEMIS	1 JAN. U.S. current New Year's Day
2	3	4	○ 5	6 Festival of Isis birth of OSIRIS	7	8
9 Feast of SELENE	10	11 Festival of CARMENTA	◐ 12	13	14 Mohammedan New Year	15
16	17	18	Snow and rain			

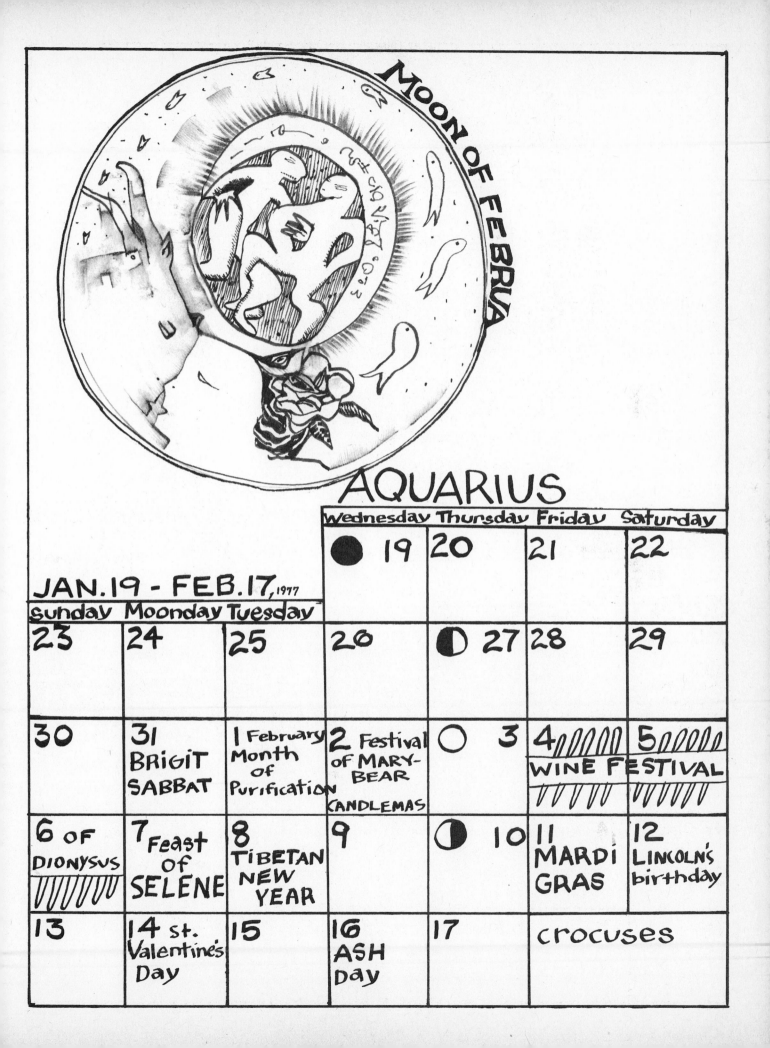

MOON OF FEBRUA

AQUARIUS

JAN. 19 - FEB. 17, 1977

sunday	Moonday	Tuesday	Wednesday	Thursday	Friday	Saturday
			● 19	20	21	22
23	24	25	26	◑ 27	28	29
30	31 BRIGIT SABBAT	1 February Month of Purification	2 Festival of MARY-BEAR CANDLEMAS	○ 3	4 WINE FESTIVAL	5
6 OF DIONYSUS	7 Feast of SELENE	8 TIBETAN NEW YEAR	9	◐ 10	11 MARDI GRAS	12 LINCOLN'S birthday
13	14 st. Valentine's Day	15	16 ASH Day	17	crocuses	

BODY TIDES

Our body cycles are the most basic aspect of our existence; and our sense of rhythm seems to define the core of our sensations. The moon is a major regulator of seasonal cycles and also of individual body rhythms.

Being in or out of sync with the rhythms of the moon seems to determine to a large degree a person's health and balance. Ancient civilizations took this into account by measuring their calendar time in lunar cycles as well as more specific daily activities. It was known that certain things (from waging wars to getting pregnant to planting crops to scheduling operations) were more successful and congruent at certain hours of the day or night and at certain points in the season. Respect for this knowledge went out of vogue as the eras of mechanization progressed and we have become more interested in surmounting natural rhythms than in moving with them. Currently, as we are recognizing the extreme imbalance caused by going against these rhythms, scientists in many fields are researching seasonal and body rhythms in order to learn how to synchronize our activities with them once again.

Light, electricity and magnetism seem to be the basic determiners of our cycles. Farther back than these forces in the process has not been "explained." But one subtle form of electricity, the L-field, has recently been "discovered." Its existence was not known before because there were no modern instruments subtle enough to measure it until the invention of the vacuum-tube voltmeter. The vacuum-tube voltmeter measures L-field voltages, fluctuations in which indicate changes in body patterns and functions. Following these patterns and marking **irregularities one can detect very early signs of disease or imbalance in a body part,** or the very early phases of a normal body process such as ovulation, or subtle energy exchanges such as the flow of electricity between one's two index fingers. An L-field is a pure voltage potential, not an alternating electrical current, with patterns which are basic functional structures of an organism.

High moods correspond to L-field high voltage and low moods with low voltages. The voltages of L-fields change with drugs, sleep and hypnosis. L-field voltage changes with wounds and returns to normal as the wound heals. Some people have normally high L-field voltage and others low. An L-field voltage can be created between the left and right hands. One conclusion of these studies is that wherever there is life, there are electrical properties.

Dr. Harold Saxton Burr has done much research into the patterns of L-fields. He found L-fields in people as well as in plants, seeds, eggs and moulds. L-fields vary with patterns of light and dark, with sunspots and magnetic storms and with phases of the moon.

Since L-fields are one of the most subtle patterns we have been able to measure, they seem to be the most basic rhythmic pattern of a living organism; that they are changed by magnetism, electricity, lights and the moon should give us clues to the most basic regulators of life cycles.

Circadian Rhythms

Circa dies means around the day. Circadian rhythm refers to the twenty- four hour alteration of light and darkness we call our day. There are twenty-four hour rhythms for every living thing, and more specifically for every organ and chemical system in our bodies.

People's bodies can maintain these rhythms even when taken away from their normal daily stimuli. The characteristic circadian rhythms of sleep and activity, or urine constituent, of temperature and performance persist even when people—volunteers in experiments—have lived for as long as six months in deep caves or simulated space capsules. But changing one's synchronization to these patterns, as in the activities of jet travellers, also causes stress on one's system in short periods. If the de-synchroniza- tion is continued over long periods of time, the person becomes ill or psychologically disturbed. Tests with students show that their life span shortens with only a simple inversion of their light/dark cycle once a week.

Understanding the general pattern of the human time structure as well as the idiosyncracies of an individual's time pattern is an essential healing tool. Every body function has a rhythmic cycle, and its ups and downs indicate critical highs and lows in its process. Each day a person's body temperature rises and falls about 1½ to 2 degrees, reaching its peak around afternoon or evening—a time of peak performance on tasks requiring close attention or muscle coordination. The body utilizes protein differently depending on the time of day; proteins seem to be better utilized early in the day. There are 24-hour rhythms in liver enzymes, in the division of cells and in all the chemical cycles of the body. For this reason the time one takes a medicine or administers any sort of cure is extremely important. Alcohol, barbituates, anesthesias, apmhetamine doses, x-rays, shock and virus can prove fatal at one point in the circadian rhythm or merely an annoyance at another. Hormones are more effective if taken early in the day. There are many illnesses that are seasonal, and births and deaths cluster at night or early morning. The impression of a trauma seems to be more fearsome in the morning than later in the day.

Every activity has its prime time on the daily cycle. It seems that each person can learn more efficiently at certain times of day, and that men and women have conspicous repetitive monthly cycles of moon change, as well as vulnerability to bacterial infection, physical alterations and stamina.

Light seems to be one of the most critical rhythm regulators. Light, in particular phases of a plant's cycle, will inhibit or stimulate growth. Light cycles regulate mating and migration patterns of animals and birds. They trigger human hormones as well as affect cell maturation in the pineal glands of newborn infants.

For all these reasons, the calendar is an important diagnostic and preventative medicine tool; with the confusion on our bodies caused by electric daylight and our modern un-synchronized living patterns with natural light, we need to develop our sensitivities of perception to our inner rhythms. The natural rising and falling of energy, the patterns of our attention spans, our moods, weight, sexuality, activity and productiveness need to become familiar to us in order to learn to live on a more effective bio-schedule and to protect our moods and health.

Balance

Imbalance is a physical sensation that one's inner workings are not functioning well with outer processes. Balance of energy states is suggested by the cycles of the moon. It would be good to set up one's activitites to coincide with some of the lunar phases. For example, one should preferably use the dark of the moon for introspection, meditation, quiet. The full moon is the best climate for far-reaching psychic activity, for scope and for creative spurts. The times in between are best for preparatory activity.

Certainty of the cyclical rhythm gives me relaxed faith that if i am feeling down or too inward for my tastes, i know it is only preparation for an outer period. When i am ecstatic or speedy and suddenly go down or in, i am not shocked because it is a natural cycle. No state is the best or the one in which one should always be. The need is balance.

Chinese, Japanese and Indian civilizations have traditionally conceived of time as a non-linear circular process (versus the western linear finite concept). These cycles are related to the cycles of season and light patterns. The following diagram is a chart used in acupuncture noting the hours in the day during which treatment is appropriate for particular organs or systems. A body part should be stimulated (by clockwise rotating inward spirals of the acupuncture needle or finger pressure) at the time designated to it on the chart. Sedation (blunt surface counter-clockwise outward message on a point) should be administered at its opposite hour on the clock. An ache is said to indicate the need for stimulation; a pain needs sedation.

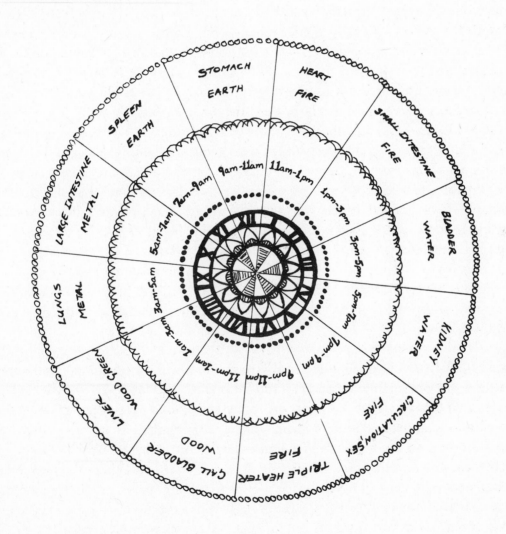

If you're really motivated, you can learn to measure your body rhythms by western medical means over a period of one or two months. The following series of measurements should be taken six times a day at approximately the same time of day. The first measurement is taken before you get out of bed; the last just before retiring. Avoid smoking, drinking hot or cold beverages, eating and exercising for at least thirty minutes prior to each session. Record any of these on your chart if they occur just before measurement, as well as extreme moods.

1) Oral Temperature. Use an accurate Ovulindex thermometer. Record time, date, and phase of moon. Shake thermometer below 96° and place it far back under your tongue. Leave it in your mouth at least seven minutes, meanwhile taking other measurements.

2) Energy: Rate your emotional mood and your physical vigor. Mood: Depressed—1; Slightly depressed—2; A little less cheerful than usual—3; Usual mood—4; Slightly more up than usual—5; Quite happy—6; Elated—7. Physical vigor: Inactive and tired—1; Slightly tired—2; Less active than usual—3; Usual state—4; More active than usual—5; Very active—6; Lively—7.

3) Pulse: Count your heartbeats at chest or outer edge of wrist for one minute timed with a stopwatch or two minutes with a second hand.

4) Coordination: Invent a game for yourself which tests some aspect of your coordination which you can use as a gauge—such as games requiring hand-to-eye coordination or any action where you do two seemingly opposite actions at once. Always give yourself the same 25 seconds to complete it.

5) Time Perception: Start the stopwatch and see if you can estimate when one minute is up by counting to yourself. Record actual time you stop watch.

6) Record the time all these games took you and your oral temperature which is ready now. Keep the chart so you can use it for comparative cycle readings over a period of time.

If you're not really motivated to do all that, you can send for a computer 6-month prediction chart of your bio-rhythms. Send a check for $10.00, with your time and place of birth and current address to: U.C., Berkeley, Lawrence Hall of Science, Berkeley, California. You can also get similar computer charts from machines in many Greyhound Bus Stations for fifty cents.

Biorhythms are based on three cycles which are chartable from the day you were born. The monthly emotional cycle of 28 days corresponds to the hormonal cycle. The mental cycle of 33 days corresponds to the number of original pyramidal brain cells from which the others multiply. The physical monthly cycle of 23 days corresponds to the sunspot cycles of 23 years. You will notice on your chart that they curve between being apart and in opposition, moving toward or away from each other, or meeting and synchronizing for those blissful harmonious days!

PHOSPHOROS HECATE — BRINGER OF LIGHT   JUNO

LUCETIA — CELESTIAL LIGHT   SAMHAIN OF THE HEARTH —

OF THE WINTER FIRES   ISIS — NET OF THE LAMPS, OF

THE PERPETUAL FIRE OF EGYPT   ASSINIBOIN, WHICH WAS

HOT AND GAVE OFF ITS OWN LIGHT   PASIPHAE, SHE WHO

SHINES FOR ALL   OUPIS THE LIGHT BEARER   THE

REFLECTOR, THE MIRROR OF THE ESSENCE, THE ETERNAL

FLAME, TORCH, HEARTH, OVEN   THAMMUZ, SHEPHERD OF

THE STARS   OUPIS THE LIGHT BEARER   PELE THE FIRE

IN THE NIGHT

LIGHT

To ancient peoples the light of the moon was its fertilizing power. Moonlight falling on a sleeping woman would generate new life in her or an actual child. The light of the moon was encouraged by lights on earth: torches, candles, fires were burned in honor of the moon as fertilizing magic. Hecate's torches were carried around freshly sown fields, long ago in Greece, to promote their fertility.

The ancient festival of candles for a moon goddess is now celebrated on the same date, February second, for the Virgin Mary. This is also the day in Brazil when the Festival of the Sea, in honor of Iemanja, is celebrated, especially in Bahia. It is the festival of Candlemas, corresponding to the Celtic Holy Day of St. Brigit, the Christianized form of ancient **Brigentis**, a triune moon Goddess whose worship at one time was widespread. On February first in the Catholic Church the new fire was blessed.

A perpetual fire was kept burning at Tara, seat of the ancient Irish kings. On midsummer eve the fire was extinguished, then rekindled the following day on the Feast of Beltane, originally a moon festival. On taboo days sacred fires were usually extinguished, signifying that the deity was in the underworld.

A mimetic effect is thought to take place. If a woman does not want a child she takes precautions against pregnancy by avoiding exposure to moonlight; the waxing moon is patroness of all things that grow.

A feast of lamps was also celebrated at Sais, Egypt, in honor of Isis-Net. In a chapel beneath the temple, lamps were carried in procession around the coffin of Osiris, for it was by the power of the moon's light that Isis could rekindle life.

The hearth is a form of domestic sun, a symbol of the home, of the conjunction of the masculine principle (fire) with the feminine (the receptacle) and, consequently, of love. Heat is a representation which bears a symbolic relation to maturation, biological or spiritual. The epithet **Phósphoros** is applied to Hecate by several sources. She is called the bringer of light. The torch she carries is called in the Homeric Hymn, Light.

The moon, thought in Malekula to be a stone, is lit up only at night by the god of light, who uses the sun as an agent. They have a saying: The inner light transforms incest, Stone and the spirit of the ancestors.

Light is becoming recognized by modern science as a critical health factor and a healing agent. In the American Society for Photobiology, research interests of the members cover fourteen specialty subgroups: bioluminescence, chronobiology, environmental photobiology, medicine, photochemistry, photomorphogenesis, photomovement, photoreception, photosensitization, photosynthesis, phototechnology, spectroscopy, ultraviolet radiation effects and vision. In an article published by the Society's president, he says that light is probably the most important single element of our environment, yet it has been largely ignored by the scientific community—perhaps because of its ubiquity. Hundreds of diseases and conditions of imbalance have been found to be caused by lack of light or by exposure to improper proportions of certain rays in the light spectrum. We all need the proper exposure to full-spectrum natural light to be in good health. Most prescribed drugs are photosynthesizers and when activated by light can produce side effects that are harmful and disturbing to our bodies.

It is becoming more obvious that the predominance of artificial light in our culture is responsible for many modern illnesses. We must consider types and sources of artificial light, their intensities and spectral characteristics, and the chemical, physiological and psychological effects of the lighting environment on people—not from the standpoint of illumination but from that of specific photobiological consequences of its use. The psychological effects of light, particularly of colored light, are well known—but not well understood. These effects may bear a relationship to biological processes in the brain induced by light, which affect psychic behavior. Light intensity as well as wavelength specificity alter productivity and mood. Tests show that, in an infant, sensory overload by prolonged exposure to highly intense illumination may produce undesirable effects on development. John Ott in Florida has done important research in this field.

Light has a number of important effects on circadian clocks. The ability to distinguish time of day without reference to external light is found in plants and animals of all sizes and levels of complexity. This was discovered by studying rhythmic changes in activity or other physiological functions which can continue in constant light and temperature, a science now called chronobiology. Light keeps bio-timing cycles synchronous with environmental day and night and adjusts them to long or short days, stops or starts them under certain conditions. Light is

Galaxy

Words and music by Malvina Reynolds

You don't care about me, Way out there, Ga-
lax-y. I don't care what the sa-ges said in the
Middle Ag-es, You don't care about me.

You are beauti-ful at night and that's right, I'm a
quari-us and Pi-ces are light years gone, I'm a
bright bit of dust and the stars are no more, And my
child of the warmth of the Sun, Like the bug and the
soul was-n't set by a star.   It
panther and I flour-ish that way,   With the
grew like a flower in the earth of the
whale and the falcon and the jay and the
Tribes, It's a flower that I prize Like the
bee, I re-joice in your sight, but I
in-dep-pen-dent stars in the skies.
fol-low my own light, Ga-lax-y.

2. A-

perceived by structures other than the eyes in all classes of non-mammalian vertebrates; while the photoreceptive structures involved have not been precisely localized or identified, it is clear that in some cases they are located in the brain not the eyes.

Ultra violet light has been found to create special conditions in humans, animals and plants. Flower colors frequently involve patterns of differential UV light reflectance, appreciated by insect pollinators but not by the unaided human eye. The wings of butterflies also contain patches of high UV reflectance which flag prospective mates. People exposed to imbalances of ultra violet light can contract or be cured of certain diseases. Studies done on restaurants which use black-lighting show that the waiters and waitresses are markedly happier on their jobs, tending to remain long term employees.

The moon is selective about which rays of the sun it reflects, according to length of the light wave. The moon reflects a very high percentage of ultra violet rays. This connects for me with the folk custom of planting or harvesting at certain times of the moon. Obviously moonlight cycles are critical determiners of plant growth and health; perhaps it is particularly ultra violet which triggers their cycles. It is reasonable to imagine that people too need certain quotas of ultra violet, and in certain cycles. Thus moonlight deprivation would cause serious health imbalances and psychic diseases. Our modern society is **moonlight deprived**, due to fear of nighttime activity in the cities and to the presence of artificial light.

The pineal gland, located in the center of the forehead about an inch into the head, has been discovered to be an important light receptor in the human body. Mystically this is the **Third Eye**, attributed with spiritual visionary power and said to be the center of cosmic perspective. Biologically the pineal gland transmits messages of its light reception to the pituitary gland which stimulates growth hormones—thus making us in our growth mechanisms sorts of "human plants."

Every color of light in the spectrum has specific body effects. Full-spectrum light is white, contains all the colors and is needed in certain amounts for physical and psychological health. The resulting balance of correct exposure to natural full-spectrum light is named in spiritual doctrines, **Knowing the Pure White Light.**

The amount of time that mammals are exposed to light varies with two cycles: the twenty-four hour cycle of day and night, the annual cycle of changing day length. These light cycles appear to be associated with rhythmic changes in biological functions. Physical activity, sleep, food consumption, water intake, body temperature and the rates at which glands secrete hormones all vary with periods that approximate twenty-four hours. In most mammals, light exerts its effects indirectly through photoreceptors in the eye. The best-characterized indirect effect of light on any process other than vision is probably the inhibition of melatonin synthesis by the pineal organ of mammals. Melatonin seems to be the major pineal hormone. It inhibits ovulation and modifies the secretion of other hormones from such organs as the pituitary, the gonads and the adrenals, probably by acting on neuroendocrine control centers in the brain.

Light and color healing are ancient practices. In acupuncture, a certain color denoting health is attributed to each body organ. If the organ does not radiate that aura it is out of balance. Meditating on the organ in its proper color can bring back its balance.

You can help increase your modern exposure to full spectrum natural light by using full spectrum lenses in your glasses (Armorlite is the only brand i know of which lets through the full spectrum). Many of our eye and body diseases are caused by the interference of glasses and contact lenses with full spectrum reception. You can also use full-spectrum light bulbs (only brand i know is Duro-test Vita-Lite), and full-spectrum window glass. You can also expose yourself to more direct moonlight.

BREATHING

Finding Your Natural Rhythm

To a great degree our breathing regulates our circulatory rhythm. Magdalene Proskauer, a therapist practicing in San Francisco, has developed a series of breath exercises aimed at helping one find one's natural body rhythm. She starts by telling her students to relax into a deep body breath, as one breathes when asleep. Neurologically this promotes part of the nervous system usually only dominant during sleep or meditation. The student gradually learns to activate unconscious visions, emotions, visceral movements and dreams while awake. One also becomes more conscious during sleep-dreaming states so that one can remember and sometimes alter them.

There are different Proskauer exercises for each part of the body, but the same three-part breath is used in all of them. The cycle is geared to eventually allow your own natural rhythm, so your body's pace takes over.

Be in a quiet, softly-lit room with a carpet or pad on the floor. Take off your shoes. Lie down on the floor on your back. Relax, arms at your sides and let your feet fall out. Let your eyes be closed.

Tune in to how you are lying on the floor; notice any parts of your body which feel a bit tense or do not seem to be fully resting.

Now focus inside your body; notice where the breathing is in your body and where you feel movement in your muscles because of your breathing. Any place you feel tense, you can try imagining you can breathe into that tight place, as

270

though you could exhale through it. Imagine that the breath relaxes the sore muscle a little. (Breathing into a body part is something you can do anywhere, anytime you feel tense or nervous. No one knows that you are doing it, and it is remarkably relaxing. The process can also change the quality of your actions if you do it in time with the tensing and relaxing of your movement.)

As you are lying on the floor now tune in to your abdominal muscles. If your clothing is tight at the waist, loosen it. Let the muscles of your stomach relax and let your breath sink lower into your body. Place your hand palm-down at the lowest place on your body where you can feel your breathing. Let your hand rest there awhile until you begin to feel the rise and fall of your body under your palm from your breathing. Let your hand and arm relax at your side again. If you see any pictures of yourself or other images during the breathing exercise, remember them and write them or draw them in a journal.

Relax your jaw and open your mouth a little so that you can exhale through your mouth. You don't need to breathe heavily. Stay with relaxed breathing. Inhale through your nose; exhale through your mouth; and pause at the end of the exhalation before you breathe in again.

This pause is the key to the effectiveness of the breathing. Many things happen with your body during the pause. One is that you are still exhaling though you may feel as though nothing is going on. Deepening the exhalation naturally is important for getting stale air out of your lungs so that there is more room for fresh air on the inhalation. Most of us don't exhale deeply enough. Often if you have the sensation that you can't take in enough air, that you'd like to inhale more deeply, it's because you haven't exhaled fully. Lengthening your exhalation helps. (This is usually the breathing difficulty in asthma.)

Fully explore the pause. How does it feel to you? Are you nervous that you won't breathe in again, unless you control it? Think of how you breathe when you are asleep. Think of the breathing of animals when they are resting. Their breath is long and rolling. They don't think to tell themselves when to breathe next. You can learn to trust your breath; it will always come in again!

Allow the pause to be whatever length it wants. It may feel quite long. Stay with the pause until your body wants to breathe in again by itself. Inhale through your nose; exhale through your mouth; then wait, like standing on the beach, and waiting for another wave to come in. Try to find a place where you are neither forcing the pause, nor making yourself breathe.

This breath pattern in itself is deeply relaxing and opens up a peaceful, centered space. You can try it at night if you have difficulty going to sleep, or anytime you feel tense and can take a few minutes to relax and center yourself. It is a gentle but powerful exercise. It brings you more into yourself. It can bring you back to your own rhythm after being distracted by outside influences.

IEMANJA OF THE SEA   ATL THE WATER MOON   CITATL

MORGANA, LADY OF THE LAKE   EURYNONE MERMAID OF ARCADIA

ISIS, GODDESS OF MOISTURE   ATAENSIC OF THE WATERS

ATHENA, THE ALL-DEWY ONE   BRIZO, WHO GUARDS THE SHIPS

APHRODITE, RISEN FROM THE SEA-FOAM   APHRODITE OF THE

SCALLOP AND THE PERIWINKLE   VACH FROM THE OCEAN

SARASVATI, OF THE RIVERS OF PURIFYING WATER

GODDESS OF STORMS

WATER

Since the human body is 98%, water and since our blood has a chemical make-up very similar to sea water, it is logical that we have significant body changes which synchronize with the ocean tides and are generated mainly by the same force, the gravitational pull of the moon.

As the earth rotates, the moon's gravitational pull produces high tides of the seas, the earth's crust, and the earth's atmosphere—every 12.5 hours, with low tides in between. The sun's gravitational force contributes to tides also. The activity and rest rhythm of seashore animals is synchronized with the six-hour alternation of high and low tides, and it seems likely that this cycle is also functional for humans. The hormones in the body which control water retention are aldosterone, adrenal steroids and urinary ketosteroids, which go through cycle level changes in our bodies.

The Chinese say traditionally that water flows more in the winter.

Earth Tides

The moon is 239,000 miles away from the earth. As the moon comes, so come the rising tides; as the moon goes, so go the rising tides. The tides rise fifty minutes and thirty seconds later each day, and the moon arrives fifty minutes and thirty seconds later each day. Tides are the highest during the times of the new and full moon because when the moon and sun are in the same line with the earth, both are pulling together which produces very high tides. These tides are called the Spring Tides, but they occur twice a month.

When the sun and the moon pull at right angles to the earth, at the time of the quarter moon, it produces Neap Tides at their lowest, because then the sun and moon are pulling opposite each other.

274

The highest of the Spring Tides occur about twice a year in the time of the New Moon when the sun and moon are in line with earth and the moon has swung to an orbital point closest to earth. At these times the gravitational pull is the greatest and tides on earth the highest. When the moon is overhead, the earth itself rises as much as twenty inches in some places.

Generally there are two high tides and two low tides daily, about six hours apart. This is due to the twenty four hour rotation of the earth as it exposes its oceans to the moon's pull. When the moon is overhead, the tide is high. The moon moves eastward; the tide follows. When the earth rotates so that the moon is "gone," there is low tide.

When the moon is not in the sky and there is a high tide rising, the moon still accounts for it as it is exerting a greater pull on the earth than it does on the seas. In other words, on our side of the earth, the moon is literally pulling earth away from ocean. Thus the ocean waters tend to heap up into high tides; these high tides are not as great as the ones when the moon is overhead. The sun's influence on the earth's tides is about one third that of the moon's.

Weather

The atmosphere that surrounds our planet is influenced by the moon in ways which affect our weather. The same gravitational force that acts on tides draws and reshapes the atmosphere at the passage of the moon.

The moon's position in relation to the sun affects the earth's daily magnetic index. Arrenius was the first known to record the notable effect of the moon on the northern lights and the formation of thunderstorms. Maximum influence takes place when the moon passes through its lowest point in the Zodiac. Arrenius and later Shuster established that a considerably greater number of thunderstorms occur during the waxing of the moon than during the waning.

Colored moons are thought to be the visual effect of different particles in our atmosphere. Blue moons are caused by smoke or moisture. Haloes around the moon are caused by ice crystals.

When dates of excessive rainfall are plotted in terms of the angular difference between the moon and sun, there is a pronounced departure from normal expectancy. There is a tendency for extreme precipitation in North America to be recorded near the middle of the first and third weeks of the synoidcal month, especially on the third to fifth days after the new and full moon. Second and fourth quarters of the lunation cycle are correspondingly deficient in heavy precipitation, the low point falling about three days previous to the date of the alignment of the earth-moon-sun system. One possible clue was found when the IMP-1 satellite reported that the solar wind previously thought to be impossible to deflect, was stopped and deflected when the moon was in a certain position to the sun. Energy-charged particles issuing from the sun hit the earth at a different angle and in a different fashion from what previously accepted theory predicted. Thus lunar phases regulate the amount of meteoric dust that falls continuously into our atmosphere. Meteoric dust has the effect of condensing the water in clouds in the form of vapor and so can cause rains.

Water Purification

In its reflection of the sun's rays, the moon selects a higher percentage of ultra violet rays than others. Ultra violet light is used medicinally as an effective healing agent for many aspects of plant and human life. It also is responsible for a great percentage of the natural process of water purification which occurs as stream water moves over rocks and the ocean currents churn up water constantly exposing new layers to the light of sun and moon.

Ultra violet can also be used commercially. Ultra violet simply and instantly sterilizes water with pure light and is virtually 100%, effective in removing virus and bacteria as well as being odorless and tasteless. It is more effective than chlorine and other toxic chemicals commonly in use and leaves no germicidal or chemical residue. Economically, 100,000 gallons of water can be purified for about five cents.

Blood

Ages ago when people slept under the stars and were open to the regularity of the moon's light cycle, all women menstruated at the same phase of the moon. This must have been a time of powerful community among all women, a time of cohesiveness of women's consciousness.

An outdated Chinese acupuncture maxim about women's periods is that those women who menstruate at the new moon are yin in the "correct" balance; those who menstruate during the full moon are "too yang." Those in between are in transition.

There appears to be a close connection between the moon and bleeding. When bloodletting was a customary form of medical treatment, it was always done when the moon was waning, because it was believed that it was too dangerous to do when the light was increasing and the tide beginning to flood. Doctors then believed the moon controlled blood flow in the way it controlled tides. In Florida a survey of over a thousand bleeding crises among patients showed 82%, of them occurred when the moon was full. Dr. Edson Andrews of Tallahassee stated the data has been so conclusive and convincing that it threatened to turn him into a witch doctor who operates on dark nights only.

DIANA OF THE WILLOWS, OF THE OAKS, OF THE GROVES

HELEN-DENDRITUS, GODDESS OF NATURE   FALLING LEAF

MOON   MOON OF RED GRASS APPEARING   THE

GREEN GRASS MOON   PLANTING MOON   ROSE MOON

OF SPRING   MERRY MISTRESS OF THE GREENWOOD

THE OLIVE, THE PALM, THE LOTUS, JASMINE, MISTLETOE

KHONS THE HERBAL HEALER   MOTHER NATURE

SOMA   HARVEST MOON   HUNTER'S MOON

MOON WHEN THE CHERRIES TURN BLACK   MOON OF

MAKING FAT   RICE MOON   SELENAI CAKES FOR

ARTEMIS   KAMANU CAKES FOR ISHTAR   HONEY,

DATES, FISH, OLIVES   NET OF THE HUNT   HUNGER

MOON OF WINTER   GAUS THE GIVER OF AMBROSIA

MILK   CERES OF THE WHEAT   HECATE, QUEEN OF

THE DUST AND MISTRESS OF THE FIELD   THE GREEN ONE

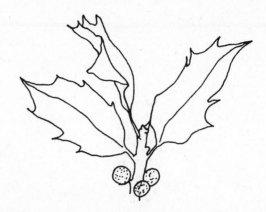

PLANTS

Harold Saxton Burr, a medical doctor and anatomist, found, in charting the life fields of trees on the Yale campus for over two decades, that recordings related not only to the lunar cycle and to sunspots which flare up at regular intervals, but revealed cycles recurring every three and six months that were beyond his explanation. His conclusions confirm practices of generations of gardeners who plant according to the phases of the moon. In Paris, a scientist named Kervran said that powerful energies are at work in the germination process of seeds, which synthesize enzymes, probably transmuting matter within them. His experiments convinced him that lunar forces are extremely important in germination, though botanists have long asserted that only warmth and water are required.

Certain plants will only germinate in the springtime no matter what amounts of heat and water are administered to them during other parts of the year. There are varieties of wheat said to germinate only as the days lengthen, but, when days are artificially lengthened, the wheat does not always germinate.

When planting by the moon it is important to consider both the phase and sign of the moon. The moon is in a sign if it is in it by noon. Which phase is best for planting depends on the kind of growth desired. During increasing light one should plant annuals which will bear above-ground crops.

The waning moon is the best time for planting biennials, perennials, bulb and root-crop plants. For transplanting follow the same pattern. Pruning and harvesting should be done in the waning moon. Water signs are the most fertile, thus, the best times to plant. The water signs are Scorpio and Pisces, with Cancer being the best. Capricorn, Taurus, and Libra are the next-best planting signs. Earth signs Taurus and Capricorn are very good for root crops. Capricorn growth can withstand drought. Libra is the time to plant for beauty and fragrance. Aries, Gemini, Leo, Virgo, Sagittarius, and Aquarius are periods for destroying weeds and insects. Harvesting in the barren signs keeps the harvest fresher. A sign's influence is greatly intensified when moon and sun are in the same sign. The first days the moon is in a sign are more influential than later days.

HEY! DIDDLE, DIDDLE!

Hey! diddle, diddle!
The cat and the fiddle,
The cow jumped over the moon;
The little dog laughed
To see such sport,
And the dish ran away with the
  spoon.

EUROPA THE COW   IO THE WHITE MOON COW
PASIPHAE, MOTHER OF THE HOLY HORNED BULL CHILD
ASTARTE OF THE TWO HORNS   GAUS THE HOLY COW
OF INDIA   THE DOVE   THE THREE DOVES
ISIS-NEPHTHYS, THE HOLY BIRD   BRIGIT OF THE WHITE
SWANS   KHENSU, EGYPTIAN BIRD GOD OF THE MOON
THE PEACOCK PRINCESS   THE BLUE BIRD   PANAGIA-
ARKOUDIOTISSA THE BEAR MOTHER

ANIMALS

The regular movements of the sun and moon are responsible for atmospheric cycles that help to synchronize mating of sea animals and the time structure of mammals. The swarming, spawning and mating of sea creatures is related to the rhythm of the tides which grows stronger when the sun and moon are in opposition or conjunction.

A biologist, Dr, Frank Brown, first became interested in lunar cycles through the swarming of schools of Bermuda shrimp which occurs at monthly intervals. He found that other researchers at the turn of the century had discovered lunar rhythms and written up findings. Their theses had been ignored because at that time, anyone who mentioned the moon was considered a lunatic, not a respectable scientist. In collaboration with Drs. Franklin Barnwell and Margaret Webb of Northwestern, Brown did a series of experiments with the Fiddler Crab. This crab is found all over the world in tidal marshes and blends with its surroundings by darkening its skin every 24 hours at sunrise. Its activities follow the tides synchronous with the lunar day, while its skin darkening follows a solar cycle. In the laboratory the peak daily activity will slowly shift from times of tides on their home beach to local times when the moon is in its upper and lower transit, possibly guided by some cues from atmospheric tides.

Female Fireworms in Bermuda, one day a month flash brilliantly exactly timed to signal male fireworms that they are about to discharge their eggs into the water. Spawning is pin-pointed to a time of year, a phase of the moon, and a specific time of day.

In Southern California when the Grunion run, they spawn on flood tides of the nights after the Spring full moons. Local residents flood to the beaches to wait. At an unknown signal, the females rush to the beaches to lay eggs and the males rush right after them to fertilize the eggs after which they return to the sea. The people waiting rush to catch the silvery fish in their nets.

Hausenchild, a German biologist, conducted experiments on sea worms which indicated that moonlight itself, rather than atmospheric changes influenced the lower forms of life.

Other animals are equally affected by the moon and by light. By turning light on and off, scientists are able to turn on and off the hormonal mechanisms controlling reproduction of rodents. When rats were maintained under constant light they went into constant estrus. Rats in constant darkness will not ovulate if given two hours of light during the critical period of ovulation. In hamsters also, interesting sensitivities to light were shown. When deprived of light, the extraordinarily fertile male hamster developed gonadal atrophy. In total darkness, the gonads shrink to one quarter of the normal size and significantly reduce the animal's fertility.

Cats, lazy by day, find the onset of darkness stimulating, and then begin to play. The cockroach is a nocturnal creature also. Turn on a light at night in an old building and the roaches scurry for cover. Yet even in the darkest buildings, one can turn on the light before noon and rarely see one.

In the Sauer's study of the celestial navigation of birds, they began their studies with the warbler songbird. These birds throughout Europe raise their young and during mid-summer feed on elderberries and blackberries. On an appointed night in August, the entire resident population of one species will disappear southward for the winter. They fly to various parts of Africa. Each bird finds its own way to its destination: the warblers do not follow the leader or make the journey as a group, and young birds making their first migrations reach their goal as surely as experienced travelers. These warblers, like most small birds, feed by day and migrate by night, when they are safer from predators and the air is generally more stable.

In migrating, it was found that the birds were affected by moonlight, as well as by bright shooting stars. When clouds become too dense, the birds flutter aimlessly for awhile and then go off to sleep. In a planetarium, if the warblers sensed the "stars" as corresponding to real stars, guided only by images projected on an artificial sky, a bird that had never been outside a cage pointed in the direction for a flight to the headwaters of the Nile.

What do cows say to each other at night?

N-O-O-M

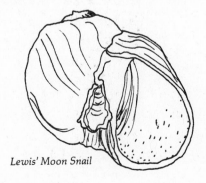

Lewis' Moon Snail

THE OWL AND THE PUSSY-CAT

THE Owl and the Pussy-Cat went to sea
    In a beautiful pea-green boat:
They took some honey, and plenty of money
    Wrapped up in a five-pound note.
The Owl looked up to the stars above,
    And sang to a small guitar,
    "O lovely Pussy, O Pussy, my love,
What a beautiful Pussy you are,
        You are,
        You are!
What a beautiful Pussy you are!"

...They dined on mince and slices of quince,
    Which they ate with a runcible spoon;
And hand in hand, on the edge of the sand
    They danced by the light of the moon,
        The moon,
        The moon,
They danced by the light of the moon.

"Where on earth have you been?"
asked Mother Mouse. "I have been
looking for you."

"I have been all the way to the moon,"
said Arthur in excitement. "It *is* big, and
round, and yellow. It *is* made of cheese.
And it is very delicious!"

Mother Mouse smiled. "Funny little
mouse!" she said kindly.

The Cat and The Moon

The cat went here and there
And the moon spun round like a top,
And the nearest kin of the moon,
The creeping cat looked up.
Black Minnaloushe stared at the moon,
For, wander and wail as he would,
The pure cold light in the sky
Troubled his animal blood.
Minnaloushe runs in the grass
Lifting his delicate feet.
Do you dance, Minnaloushe, do you dance?
When two close kindred meet,
What better than call a dance?
Maybe the moon may learn,
Tired of that courtly fashion,
A new dance turn.
Minnaloushe creeps through the grass
From moonlit place to place,
The sacred moon overhead
Has taken a new phase.
Does Minnaloushe know that his pupils
Will pass from change to change,
And that from round to crescent,
From crescent to round they range?
Minnaloushe creeps through the grass
Alone, important and wise,
And lifts to the changing moon
His changing eyes.

—W. B. Yeats
"The Wild Swans at Coole," 1919

You are the white line
        of road in the moonlight
Drawing me into the trees.

CALLIOPE OF THE BEAUTIFUL FACE   ERATE THE

BELOVED   TRIVIA, GODDESS OF ENCHANTMENT   AY

OF THE BEAUTIFUL FACE   OUPIS THE FAIR-FACED

BRIGIT OF THE GOLDEN HAIR   BRIZO THE ENCHANTRESS

BRIDE   APHRODISIA THE DIVINE   DIVINIA   THE

MUSE   MOTHER OF THE VEDAS, GODDESS OF ALL

CREATIVE ARTS   UNKATAHE GODDESS AGAINST DISEASE

SARASVATI OF THE HEALING WATERS   ISHTAR,

PROSTITUTE COMPASSIONATE   ALL ACCEPTING ONE

AU CLAIR DE LA LUNE

WILL IT BE MOON LOVE

FLY ME TO THE MOON

SHINE ON HARVEST MOON

MOONLIGHT BECOMES YOU

MOONLIGHT SONATA

BLUE MOON

THERE'S A NEW MOON OVER MY SHOULDER

PAPER MOON

IN THE LIGHT OF THE SILVERY MOON

GIVE ME THE GIRL, GIVE ME THE MOONLIGHT

ALABAMA MOON

I SEE THE MOON AND THE MOON SEES ME

UNDER THE SUN, MOON AND STARS

MOON SHADOW

EVERYONE'S GONE TO THE MOON

WHEN THE MOON COMES OVER THE MOUNTAIN

NO MOON AT ALL

IT MUST HAVE BEEN MOONGLOW

In Dedication

All saints revile her, and all sober men
Ruled by the God Apollo's golden mean—
In scorn of which I sailed to find her
In distant regions likeliest to hold her
Whom I desired above all things to know,
Sister of the mirage and echo.

It was a virtue not to stay,
To go my headstrong and heroic way
Seeking her out at the volcano's head,
Among pack ice, or where the track had faded
Beyond the cavern of the seven sleepers:
Whose broad high brow was white as any leper's,
Whose eyes were blue, with rowan-berry lips,
With hair curled honey-coloured to white hips.

Green sap of Spring in the young wood a-stir
Will celebrate the Mountain Mother,
And every song-bird shout awhile for her;
But I am gifted, even in November
Rawest of seasons, with so huge a sense
Of her nakedly worn magnificence
I forget cruelty and past betrayal,
Careless of where the next bright bolt may fall.

—Robert Graves
from The White Goddess[19]

LOVE, BEAUTY, HEALING

The aspects of the goddess symbolic of love, beauty and healing are closely related, and the secrets of one open the mysteries of the other. Respect for her cycles is thought to lead to fertility, balance and love. Union with the goddess is the source of the fruitfulness of all the earth, and runic fertility magic is the origin of art. It is only with her that one creates; through her cycle is the source.

Cosmic rhythms were the original basis for healing in all cultures. The ancient Greek name for seasonal and daily cyclical treatments was metasyncrasis. In the 1700's THE DISCOURSE CONCERNING THE ACTION OF THE SUN AND MOON ON ANIMAL BODIES by Dr. Richard Mead describes knowledge of these cycles which Northern European Medicine had retained. As late as 1887, Whilhelm Fliess published his formula for the application of biological rhythms. He noted a 23 day physical cycle as well as a 28 day emotional-hormonal cycle in all people. (In the 1930's the 33 day creativity-mental cycle was "discovered.") Sigmund Freud read Fleiss' book on biorhythms and followed his theories and practice. When Fleiss' drug treatments were condemned, his biocycle theories were thrown out too. By now we have been largely alienated from our cycles by the un-naturalness of industrial living and by the separation of women from active roles in our process of love, beauty and healing.

The presiding medical system has tried to separate the caring (female-muse-maid- assistants) from the curing (male-all-powerful-doctor-gods). Class discrimination in healing professions is severe because of the expense of medical and psychological training. Nurses can use their numbers and importance to change this diseased system. The sexism in the healing professions damages everyone because misconceptions about sex roles lead to mistreatment of our bodies. Psychotherapy, a patriarchal invention, is based on theories that categorize the soul and define heterosexuality as the only healthy sensual expression. We need to rediscover our natural body rhythms and heal by them. We must replace unnatural medicine with wholistic practical healing.

292

Body Tides

An 80% water and 20% mineral proportion is about the same in the elements of the earth's surface as in human beings. Our body fluids respond to the lunar tide cycles especially those of the new and full moon, and may result in neuromuscular irritability or excitement, depending on the individual. There are many smaller body cycles which correspond to lunar cycles. Skin erruptions and swellings intensify with the waxing of the moon and improve with its waning. Our epidermus is on a monthly cycle shedding constantly, taking about 29 days to renew itself completely.

SHING MOO, PERFECT INTELLIGENCE   ISIS MAAT, ANCIENT WISDOM

SOPHIA, DIVINE WISDOM   THE HOLY GHOST, DOVE OF WISDOM

In ancient cultures the same source was thought to be the origin of all fertility, and all creativity came from the Original Egg Mother. Thus the moon mother was thought to be responsible for rich harvests, birth and works of art. She was the Great Midwife.

Robert Graves' book, THE WHITE GODDESS is a treatise on the moon as poetic muse. He says that the real gage of poets' vision is the accuracy of their portrayal of the goddess and her dominion. The reason good poetry is tested by its success in causing all kinds of visceral reactions, from standing one's hairs on end to shivers and swoons, is that a true poem invokes the Great Goddess, the awesome principle of regeneration.

To create any kind of great art it is necessary to follow her patterns and to respect her place in our lives. Modern poetry, Graves says, has failed to do this and is, thus, not true or great poetry. Only the White Goddess can illuminate our unconscious and reveal the mysteries.

the moon falls asleep
in the movies
goes there to sleep
'bang, bang' goes the movies
'yammer, yammer' goes the movies
the moon, the moon
won't nothing wake the moon
but the quiet
of people leaving.

the moon weeps
dreams
and galoshes
and spit
and cats, the size of dimes
asleep
in your pocket.

loud as backyard cats the moon
knits her hair over her eyes
with mourning
pours water on her feet
brays
changes color & month
gives up coffee & late night
hours
takes a lover
loves her

the moon lives in detroit
continually
not even by car no place else
such an experience
of the world
she wouldn't have
no other

the cat walks the leather fence
of its dreams singing songs
its tongue is sweet
as grape jelly and its hooves
are wet and silver. it sings. and the sky
stands on one foot, listening. and the moon licks
her fingers and the cat
licks its toes. it sings. and the bright green stars
breathe through its whiskers.
and the snake-round moon squats
on the porch railing close
to its tail. the cat sings
its dreams, its turquoise and lapis
dreams.

the moon runs naked through
the trees yelling, "touch me! touch me!
touch me!"

—Faye Kicknosway

294

Moon Opera

Written in 1937-38, after CARMINA BURANA, Carl Orff's DER MOND (on Philips Records) is a mythical form of morality play. Set in old Bavaria, the triple realms of Heaven, Earth, and Underworld are traversed through moonlight, taverns, rogues, fairy tales and night folk. The fatalistic theme that everything must have its place and order, otherwise meaningless turmoil will arise is acted out by the poeple stealing the moon and taking it under the earth to divide. Following the old mystery play division of the stage into three areas of simultaneous action, we encounter earth and dead folk and the shepherd of the stars. The moon proves to be dangerous in the hands of the people; they misuse it, so the shepherd carries it off to the unattainable heavens. The opera was first performed in the old National Theater in Munich, February 5, 1939—seven months before the outbreak of the Second World War. The mythical Hades proved too real to make the play popular. The second production was 1947 in Nuremberg. The final version was done in 1970.

A rough translation of the song from the German:
Chorus of the Dead:
What is that/ What is that sort of light?/ That's the moon/ We've brought it here/ to pass away the terrible long night/ Its light didn't leave us in peace/ so we climbed out of our narrow chests/ and hung it up there/ We're glad that it draws you into this light which it makes/ That's the moon/ and its power/ But so that it isn't alone/ hanging sadly in its own light/ let us all make whoopee/ & have a load of fun/ This is the way our plan goes/now, dear corpses, listen to us!/ We don't want to stay lying in our coffins/ We want to enjoy ourselves again/ we want to booze, feast/ and if possible/ commit adultery/ To carry on so until in the end/ even the moonlight stops shining. That will certainly be time enough if we're sleeping for all eternity/ Today is the call: Resurrection!

The Star Shepherd:
Your wine is good, the moon shines bright,
I shan't go away from my place.
I haven't been so happy for a long time/here i shall stay/it pleases me so/ the moon shines bright, the wine is good/ it runs like fire through my blood/ i feel so much at home here/ i'd like to take my boots off
Chorus of the Dead:
Fill up! fill up! Everyone fill up!/ just like life it must be/ till even the moon stops shining/ then all our fun is at an end.

o   o   o

I did nothing whatever, except moon about the house and gardens.

—J. K. Jerome, IDLE THOUGHTS, 1889

I might as well wish for the moon as hope to get her.

—William Thackery, 1861

o   o   o

Moon

i took with me to bed last night
the moon
thigh touching thigh
his luminous cheek on mine
lips unmoving
our faces conversed
in the dark
the mist of his breath
in my dreaming ear
my fingers asleep on his neck
his cold hair covered my eyes
while the body made round mine
a liquid fortress
a sheep cried in the night
a racoon stirred
and several times i woke
to make sure he was really there
but some time in the night
a disappearing love
he drew the quilt around me
and transient
stole away

—Nina Winter, August 1973

Moon Song

© words and music
Ruth Mountaingrove 1972

Lovingly

A maj.

1. Would that we were both en-chant-ed, would that we were both en-chanted would that we were both to-geth-er

Would that we were both to-geth-er, would that we were both in pas-sion, both in pas-sion, both in pas-sion

2.

Now we both wait for each other
Now we both wait for each other
Surely the moon will change her
Surely the moon will change her
Would that we were both enchanted
both enchanted
both enchanted

3. You are in your turning
You are in your turning
I am in my circle (my circle)
I am in my circle (my circle)
Would that we were both together
both together
both together

4. Sometimes my heart aches to see us
Sometimes my heart aches to see us
Caught in our single circlings
Caught in our single circlings
Would that we were both in passion
both in passion
both in passion

5.
Goddess, oh open the door
Goddess, oh open the door
Call my love to lie by me
Call my love to lie by me
Surely the moon will change her
will change her
will change her ..

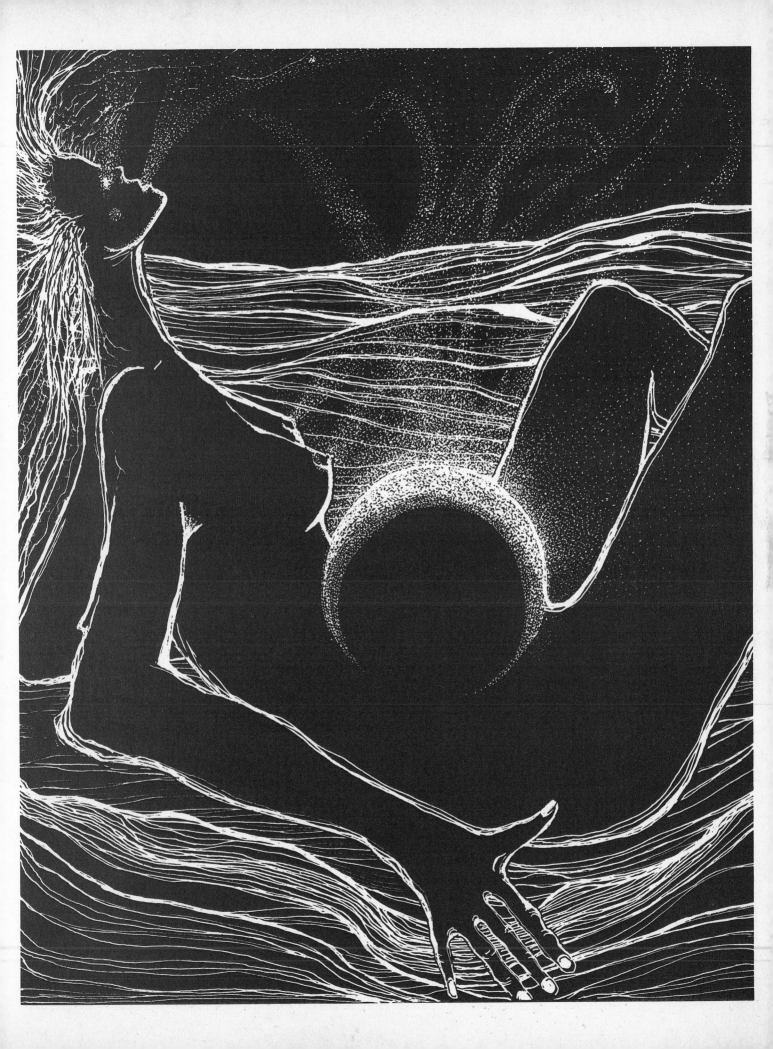

LUNACEPTION

Louise Lacey is a woman, like many other women, who recently decided to quit taking The Pill. Her doctor admitted that he thought the lumps he'd found in her breasts were due to the oral contraception he'd prescribed, and that they would probably increase as long as she kept taking it. Lacy's book, LUNACEPTION, is the story of how she quit the pill, how she dealt with the body changes which resulted, how her lumps disappeared and how she found a new (an ancient?) method of birth control which does not disturb our bodies' chemistry. In fact, it seems to bring one's system naturally into perfect balance.

Lacey discovered through her anthropological research that in ancient cultures menstruating women (the original women's groups?) segregated themselves from the rest of the community at the dark of the moon. It appeared that all women were fertile and had their periods at the same time and this communal menstruation period was correlated with the phases of the moon. Lacey also researched studies of the effect of light cycles on animals. She remembered that farmers leave lights on in chicken coops at night to improve the egg production. She even found a medical study in which doctors instructed supposedly infertile women to leave a light on in their bedrooms on the 14th, 15th, and 16th nights of the month, counting the first day of their periods as day one. After a few months most of the women's periods regularized and they became pregnant as they had wanted.

She discovered that light stimulation of the pre-optic region (that is, the pineal gland, the legendary third eye) causes ovulation. She asked herself, **What kind of light must have evolutionarily affected the human woman's body three nights out of the month?** The answer that came with an **inspirational bolt of lightning** was **the full moon.** She asked herself why the medical establishment would not want women to re-establish their natural lunar rhythms:

I could think of several reasons why no such study might have been made:

300

Reason One—The Marxist Approach. The drug companies are making literally billions on versions of The Pill and other purchasable contraceptives, and would have scant interest in a method that didn't require a consumer purchase.

Reason Two—The Generalist Approach. Almost everyone in science is intensely over-specialized, and few do much synthesis. Medical researchers may know that hospitals receive many more cases of imminent birth at the full moon, but they pass it off because they don't know about the farmer and his chickens, or the anthropologists' unclean women, or the findings of the marine biologists, etc. And each specialist tends to be dubious of the value of other specialties.

Reason Three—The Social Cynic Approach. Americans are so conditioned to putting faith in technology and despising our bodily processes that women wouldn't go to the trouble of getting their bodies back into step with Nature. They want a prescription, something in a bottle or a dispenser.

Whatever view I might subscribe to, it seemed clear to me that the established order was not interested in reestablishing women into their natural rhythm with the moon. If the idea were to be tested at all, it would have to be tested by the women themselves.

Lacey went on to experiment with and develop an understanding of the temperature changes of the female hormonal cycle and how they coordinate with the night light cycle. In LUNACEPTION (Coward, McCann, Geohegan) she describes the method in detail. Here is a summary.

Doing It

Using a graph on which you will record your temperature you will chart your menstrual and ovulation cycles. By sleeping with the light on three nights a month, you will entrain your ovulation to a regular rhythm. You can and should continue to use any method of birth control EXCEPT The Pill or variations thereof until you have established your rhythm to your own satisfaction.

You will need:

1. A chart (instructions for making one below);
2. A pen or thin felt-tipped marker;
3. A good-quality oral thermometer. Don't buy the cheapest, regardless of guarantees;
4. Some form of insulation from light in your bedroom;
5. A nightlight, lamp, hall, or closet light;
6. Conscientious attention to this routine for five minutes a day on a regular basis.

Making The Chart:

Buy plain quarter-inch-ruled (1/4 inch) graph paper where stationary supplies are sold. Nine sheets of 8⅜ x 11 inch paper will, when laid end to end the long way, give you more than a year's worth of information.

Start with one sheet and add as needed. With the graph paper positioned so that the long direction runs from left to right, write or type in up and down the left hand side a list of temperatures, by tenths, starting near the bottom with about 97.5 and on up to 100.0.

Across the top, one to a square, list the dates starting with the date you begin using the chart. If you are now using The Pill, wait until the end of your current menstrual cycle to stop taking The Pill and to start using the chart. Otherwise you may start any time.

Decide on a time of day when you will take your temperature. The important thing is to do it the **same time every day.** A few minutes either way won't matter, but you should do it within fifteen minutes of the same time, every day, seven days a week. So while it may be convenient to take your temperature when you get up each morning, because you get up the same time each day to go to work, if you are in the habit of sleeping in on the weekends that idea won't work. The most effective way to establish a routine is to tie it in with some other daily routine, like meal preparation, make-up removal, etc.

Always keep your chart, pen and thermometer together.

Preparing Your Bedroom

I believe that technology is responsible for the fact that many women's ovulation cycles are not regular. Street light, building lights, automobile lights, hall lights, television . . . the list of light "additives" is enormous in any urban community. It is nearly impossible for an urban woman today to sleep in the dark unless she makes special provisions to do so. One way or another, you must find a way to make your bedroom dark. You may have to buy a shade, rehang your drapes, or put a towel along the crack at the bottom of your hall door. See what you can work out. The object is to sleep in the dark except as indicated below.

Using The Chart

Each day at the same time take your temperature. Do not smoke, eat, drink or brush your teeth for ten minutes before hand. Leave the thermometer in your mouth, under your tongue, for at least four minutes. If you have a cold or other infection, your temperature will not be normal. This is one reason why you need to chart your temperature for many months. If you do not know how to read a thermometer, ask your druggist to show you how when you buy it. A good quality thermometer (not the cheapest) is necessary because cheap ones are frequently not accurate and will not give you reliable information.

Make a dot on the graph in the column below the date, exactly opposite the temperature the thermometer shows. Draw a line from yesterday's dot to today's.

Using The Light

Establish a light source of low power in your bedroom. It may be a 15-watt nightlight plugged into a socket near your bed, a 40-watt bulb in the closet, or a dim hall light. It should not be bright, but should be perceptible through closed eyelids. Counting the first day of your period as Day 1, count forward 13 more days, to Day 14, and mark that day on your chart. On the night of Day 14, sleep with your light on. Do the same on the nights of Day 15 and Day 16. Then return to sleeping in a dark room.

Reading The Chart

The purpose of the chart is to give you a visual image of the changes your body temperature goes through during a menstrual month. All women normally go through these changes; women on The Pill or women who have had a complete hysterectomy or who are past menopause do not. The temperature changes are related to hormonal changes of level during the menstrual month. As ovulation occurs as a result of the secretion of a group of hormones, it is possible to get a rough picture of what is happening inside your body by charting your temperature. The picture is rough because your temperature is affected by other things than just your hormonal balance. You may have a cold, etc., which would warp the general trend of your picture.

Generally speaking, the chart will show something like the following:

From the beginning of your period until the night before you first sleep with the light on, the temperature will remain about the same, around a few tenths of a degree. Then there will be a slight fall, followed the next day by a steep rise. Sometimes the rise will be by as much as a whole degree or more. The temperature will then stay high, varying as much as half a degree up and down, until the next period starts, when it will abruptly fall back to the original place.

The midmonth dip-followed-by-a-steep-rise fingers ovulation. The medical people call this period a phase shift. While a phase shift covers a period of 48 hours, ovulation takes only a few moments, and the fertility of the egg only lasts for about eight hours. As you cannot know which eight of the 48 are fertile, you should abstain for the whole period. Also, sperm have been known to live for 48 hours inside a woman's body; if they are there and waiting for the moment of ovulation . . . This is why you should abstain from sexual relations for a full five days, two days before you use the light, and the three days you use it.

You can use your chart to indicate not only the days when you are menstruating, and the days when you sleep with the light on, but also many other things. You can mark the days you make love, the days you feel particularly like making love, and the days when you have no interest in sex at all. If you mark your chart conscientiously you will find many patterns you never suspected.

Miscellaneous Exhortations and Sidelights

If you are just coming off The Pill, you may ovulate more than once a month for several months. While the lighting regimen should bring you back to normal fairly quickly, it is important for you to use another efficient form of contraception, such as a diaphragm, until you are sure your body is back to normal. In any event, **anyone** trying the Lunaception method should do the same until she can see a consistently recognizable pattern in her cycles.

According to Masters and Johnson, some women sometimes ovulate when they have an orgasm. You can find out if you are one of those exceptional women by keeping a close watch on your temperature chart. If you are, you will need more protection than the light regimen can give you.

You can also use your chart to measure other cycles, too. You will find you have rhythms of physical activity, self-image, mood, coping ability and even in the subject matter of your thought.

If you are alert to it, you can notice changes in your vaginal discharge and nasal mucus at ovulation.

Sleeping in the dark during menstruation may make your periods shorter and heavier. This has happened with nearly all the test women in my test group.

Hallucinogenic drugs with an anti-seritonin effect—LSD and mescaline —have been known to cause ovulation when taken during the mid-quarter of the month. Lunaception users should avoid them from day 10-17.[20]

THE GREAT MIDWIFE   EGG MOTHER   NKOSUANO THE

MOON-EGG OF GHANA   DRUIDIC EGG OF THE WORLD

GAUS THE GIVER OF AMBROSIA   NEITH, MOTHER WHO

GAVE BIRTH BEFORE BIRTH WAS, WHO BORE THE SON,

BIRTHGIVER   HOLDA THE EARTH MOTHER   SHAKTI

THE PRIMEVAL   ASTARTE THE WOMB   DIANA, THE

OPENER OF THE WOMB   ISHTAR THE MOTHER OF ALL

MAGNA MATER   MOTHER EARTH

BIRTH

The universal Goddess as Birth Giver is among the oldest of the great divinities known to the myths of the world represented everywhere in shrines dedicated to local mother goddesses. Countless images have been found from the Neolithic period and much earlier. The moon is so closely linked to birth that in many societies it was called the great midwife.

Statistics on the hours of human births suggest that most normal births occur at a particular phase of the circadian 24 hour cycle; 60%, begin at night, regardless of the season, peaking around 3 A.M. Midwives have always complained about the hours they are forced to keep by babies that insist on being born before breakfast. Labor pains begin twice as often at midnight as at noon. Hospital births show a significant trend for maximum births occurring after a full moon and minimum births at a new moon. Other studies show a connection between birth and tides. The majority of stillbirths or neonates with fatal complications are born in the afternoon. Most girls' menstrual periods begin between 4 and 6 A.M., next between 8 A.M. and noon, and least in afternoon or evening.

Studies on animals which simply changed the amount of daylight exposure from 12 to 14 hours created cannibalism, or in the females prevented ovulation. Much of modern woman's menstrual blues and infertility must be due to the irregularity of artificial light cycles. The male animals' hormone cycles also were upset by light cycle changes; many developed gonadal atrophy and shrinkage. The relationship of the moon's phases to the time of development is also shown to affect the foetus position.

The mystery of giving birth—that is, the woman's discovery that she is a life force—amounts to a religious experience untranslatable in terms of masculine experience. In ancient Denmark, women met together in the house of new mothers and sang and shouted while they made a manikin of straw called the Ox. Two women danced with it, making lewd gestures, shouting Sing for the Ox. Then another woman began to sing in a deep, coarse voice having a dialogue with the Ox with ritualistic meaning.

In Europe in the north of Schleswig, the village women used to run wild to the house of a new mother dancing and shouting. If they met with any men they snatched their hats off and filled them with dung; if they came across a cart, they broke it in pieces and set the horse at liberty. When assembled at the house of new birth, there was a frantic race through the village. Women ran together shouting and crying out in celebration. They went into houses, took all the food and drink they wanted, and if there were any men present they compelled them to dance.

Giving birth was considered the second significant step in female initiation after menstruation. Hospital births under the supervision of males today symbolizes the subversion of female power and the attempt to eliminate the succession of female mysteries.

This is a photo from a painting by Erika Asher of her daughter, Keja Ho. It is part of a series of stages in Keja's journey to the moon.

. . .there was a sudden roaring through furious darkness, and the Queen of the Night
stood before them. She was dressed in heliotrope—the dark blue of her realms—hung with
starry spangles, and on her brow, a jewel cut the shape of a crescent moon.

ALLATU OF THE UNDERWORLD   KILILI WHO LEANS OUT

OF THE DARKNESS   QUEEN OF THE DARK SKY

GODDESS OF THE TERRORS OF THE NIGHT   GODDESS OF

DREAMS AND OMENS   SOMA GIVER OF VISIONS

HILDE OF THE MILKY WAY   KALI-DURGA OF THE DARK

LILITH THE DARK MOON   LEUCIPPE THE NIGHT MARE

ST. LUAN OF THE NIGHT   TRIVIA GODDESS OF

NIGHT TRAVEL   QUEEN OF GHOSTS

'In dreams begin responsibility.

—Old Play

Bedtime

The Man in the Moon looked out of the moon,
    Looked out of the moon and said,
"Tis time for all children on the earth
    To think about getting to bed!"

                                        —Mother Goose

Ivan's Song Between the Graves

One day I was walking down by the beach
But the rays of the sun fell on my face
I walked until I found the beach deserted
And there I rested
But the cold of the night awoke me
I will walk to the end of my life
And the moon and the night were shining like silver
I will walk till the end of my life.

                            —From Los Ninos Abandonados[22]

The Dream-Ship

When all the world is fast asleep,
    Along the midnight skies—
As though it were a wondering cloud—
    The ghostly Dream-Ship flies. . .

And all the angels, silver-crowned,
    Pilot and helmsman are,
But the angel with the wreath of rue
    She tosseth the dreams afar.

The dreams they fall on rich and poor,
    They fall on young and old;
And some are dreams of poverty
    And some are dreams of gold. . .

                                    —Eugene Field, 1902

SLEEP

Our bodies are on hour and a half sleepy cycles. If you know your rhythms you can calculate all kinds of useful things such as when to plan to go to sleep or wake up, what hour not to take a class, what hours you will be most alert. To figure out your individual sleepy cycles, notice the distinct times of day—for perhaps three days—when you seem to get tired. Do you always fall asleep in Biology class at 4:15? Do you usually go to sleep at night by 11? Do you wish your job started at any other time besides 8 A.M.? When you have pinned down several distinct sleepy times, simply begin counting in hour and a half intervals from that time. If you begin with your 4:15 slump you should expect to be drowsy every following hour and a half.

Knowing this cycle can be useful if you think you have trouble falling asleep; you can be sure to only go to bed on a sleepy cycle. Many so-called insomniacs are people who go to bed on their waking cycles (in between their sleepy cycles) and lie around for the next hour-and-a-half thinking about what difficulty they have sleeping. If they'd tune in to their sleepy cycles and only go to bed on cycle, they'd probably go easily to sleep.

This knowledge is also good for those of us who find early morning rising painful. Never set your alarm for one of your sleepy cycles. Always set it a half hour or so before so that you are in a waking cycle. If 7:30 is a sleepy time for you, you may find getting up 40 minutes **earlier** will be more comfortable. If possible never schedule a speech or an appointment with a client on your more intense sleepy cycles.

The world also seems to divide up into **larks**, early risers, and **owls**, those of us who wake up when everyone else is asleep. When possible i give in to my owl tendencies. I love the nighttime for working and think best when the moon is out and the city is still. When free to follow my ideal schedule, i eat dinner at four in the afternoon, sleep from six to eight and then work through the night until three or four in the morning; then more sleep until 9 A.M. I would imagine that if left to follow our instincts rather than industrial time clocks, we would sleep shorter intervals several times a day, like cats, rather than in long chunks.

The moon is the goddess of Time and bestows somnambulism. Sleep is the rejuvenator of our bodies and psyches. One of the most effective sleep potions is hot milk and honey.

DREAM

Practices of so-called primitive cultures are often aimed at balancing the subconscious life of the community with the conscious. The dream practices of the Senoi people are among the most developed. Each morning they tell their dreams to one another and, as dreams are considered messages from the spirits, they act on them during the day. If an individual encounter is dreamed, that person tries to carry it out. If a new method of raising crops is dreamed it is tried by the whole tribe. If a dream feels unfinished, one returns to it the coming night. Monsters in dreams are considered power figures with whom it is essential to make peace. One is encouraged to re-dream a conflict in order to this time turn and face the monster and talk with it about what it wants, grapple with it, offer it a gift or share food with it. In many cultures the moon is considered the homeland of dream creatures and night spirits.

Telling one's dreams out loud, painting them or writing them down are powerful ways of increasing your dream memory capacity and of integrating unconscious attitudes with daylight activities. For a long time, i have kept a sporadically written dream journal and drawn pictures of some of the visions i've had while doing breathing exercises or other body work. The ones which follow are some i remembered, after reading moon mythology. They stood out as particularly filled with lunar symbology. Dreams are the stories of our relationship to the Moon Goddess . . .

314

Dream, February 1971

I am a white sorceress living in the woods. There are cabins, and lots of people around. It is the time of a community festival. I am wearing a long white filmy dress, tattered and covered with blood. I have blonde hair and think i am very beautiful. I go to a church where a very powerful black witch lives; she is lying on the floor of the vestibule of the church. She has a head, but no body, just a black cape spread out on the floor. I go onto a glassed-in porch where there is a brown guinea pig squeaking in pain. I am very frightened. It is giving birth to an egg-shaped tumor from inside it and is very frightened. I wake up before it dies as i am afraid to see it die.

Dream, 11/1/71

I am in a field full of snow. I am sitting inside a brown car which belongs to a man i know. We are snow-bound in it together. Everything is silent and white and cold. Snow is piling up around us on top of snow. Inside the car feels like a neutral warm vacuum. Everything around me looks beautiful. The quality of cold steadily piling up is disconcerting. I am in the driver's seat. Outside on the windshield sits a human-sized raven who scrapes the snow off the windshield as it accumulates. I do not want to be seen inside the car, but the bird keeps on opening up the space. It begins pecking at the glass, making small holes. Suddenly a bolt of light rockets out of the pierced windshield, depositing a baby of many colors—i feel as though i am the face of the baby as well as the mother of the face. The bird eats half of the face as though it is paper. No blood. But the face rejuvenates itself, until the persistent bird succeeds in consuming all of it. I feel sorry it's all gone. The egg is transformed into a vagina containing a brown male eye, which disturbs me so i push it out. This motion gives birth to bushels of green peacock feathers. I feel empty and good.

Friday, 6/22/72, Dream

In the twilight i go down a green hill and walk under a wooden house which has a tall crawl space. I look around and see that between the pillars holding up the house is a single driftwood bar. There are also huge spiderwebs of different colors: gray, grey, white, rust—i don't see any spiders but i'm frightened that they are hiding in the corners. I walk along trying to decide which place to risk getting tangled in to break through. Finally i come to one section where only half the way is blocked and the rest is open, and i walk out.

Dream, 3/24/74

I decide to go to a Tai Chi class to practice jumping. When i get there my teacher, Li-ta is just ending the class by showing the students a mustard can. He says to look closely at it. It is yellow with red writing; from far away i can see a circle on it which has an inverted triangle inside. Up close it is clear that the picture is an Egyptian female goddess with lots of symbols around her. Li-ta says that her name is The Fantastic.

Winter, 1975, Dream

I am living on the moon. It is silvery blue and black and cold. I leave the house i'm visiting for a walk. As i am standing talking with someone, out from behind the mountain comes a gigantic moose which charges toward me and immediately bites off my right hand. I am furious and terrified. The moose talks and threatens me. I make some kind of pact with it that i'll do such-and-such so that it won't chomp off more of me.

Saturday morning Dream, June 14, 1975

Caught on a telephone wire there is a cracked black antique carved Chinese trunk with five layers of successively smaller boxes. Like a notice in a newspaper, inside the innermost box, is a note which says that cats can write messages like spiders with filament from their rectums on clouds. An example is given of a cat who could write all nine clouds.

☆　　　☆　　　☆

The following illustrations are from my journals of visions i had while doing body meditations in Magda Proskaver's breathing class...

The oversized mother ship
✫ is whirling me further & further
away from the earth. All is darkness &
silly stars who whirl in their own alone
madness. I don't want to be dragged
out ✫ of reach. I don't want to be
attached by a cord to a mind-eating
machine; but fear of drifting abandonned and motorless in space panics
& dedays. I realize I want to cut the cord anyhow & with
that decision, the realization & picture that I can create my
own balance from inside myself. I chop the mother
machine space cord. She whirls alone into abyss. I give
forth & allow my own embryo to balance my flight,
float, peacefulness & wholeness, non-threat, back to earth,
the green, solid, sun.

Magda, (navel), 1971
Spring

8/1 meditation - on top of my head dancing around the hole it came up out of: an animal with my face, rabbit ears + white fur + a huge beautiful tail of peacock feathers, fox fur + polar bear fur, with which it's sweeping off the top of my head + dancing + swaying + stomping...

... which turns into a horse & Knight riding around the hole, followed by a steam train engine, which turns into a covered wagon pulled by horses, + then into a beautiful brown race horse, with purple + white costume, racing other horses, I'm riding + am horse too, I win, part of the race I'm a skeleton horse + rider, I say "it just happens" + quit trying + I win, a garland of roses.

my center is an egg.
my left shoulder sways & bears
a swan; the right moves through
the heavy air — Pegasus, its feet stomp & reach.
Magda — (navel & shoulder) 1971   spring

German   — der Mond

Yiddish   — לבֿנה (Levone)   ראש חודש   New Moon

Dutch   — maan

Danish   — mane

Romanian   — luna

Portuguese   — a lua

Greek   — σελήνη

Irish   — Gealach, luan

Welsh   — Ileuad

Russian   — луна́ (luna)

Polish   — Ksiezyc

Turkish   — Ay

Hawaiian   — Mahina

Eskimo   — Tatkret

Swahili   — Mwezi

Serbo-Croation   — mjesec

Italian   — la luna

French   — la lune

Japanese   — Ótsukisama (reverent), tsuki (everyday)

Chinese   — Yuet

Spanish   — la luna

Egypt   — pooh

Persian   — mâh

Sanskrit   — Gaus

Bahasa Indonesian — bulan

Korean   — 달 (tal)

Pygmy Africa   — Pe

THE POLITICS
OF
FEMINIST SPIRITUALITY

THE MOON IS MY SHEPHERDESS
I SHALL NOT WANT

Bring no more vain oblations; incense is an abomination unto me; the new moons and sabbaths, the calling of assemblies, I cannot away with; it is iniquity, even the solemn meeting. Your new moons and your appointed feasts my soul hateth; they are trouble unto me; I am weary to bear them . . . Come now, and let us reason together, saith the Lord.

Isaiah, I, 13:18

Rebellion is as the sin of witchcraft.

Samuel, I, 15:23

Annie and I came into Portland searching for knowledge. We went to the metaphysical bookstores looking for a book to turn us on, open our minds to higher vibrations. We spent hours reading words; his words, his god, his religion. In the last bookstore, my head started spinning around. Whirling out into the world, I reached the car knowing deep in my heart that I would not find my womanspirit in any of these pages of male complexities. I knew my knowledge was going to have to come from within, from my own spiritual experiences. From being in tune with my own cycles of birth, death and rebirth, with the cycles of nature and those of the moon, with the female principle, the womb of life. My spirituality will come from beating drums, dancing, making bird calls and howling, humming and singing with my sisters under the moonlight. It will come silently in a grove of trees or upon a rock by the sea. It comes to us in our circles and from our own souls.

—Shanti[23]

I have often wondered whether there is not something wrong in our religious systems in that the same ritual, the same doctrines, the same aspirations are held to be sufficient both for men and women . . . the ancients were wiser than we in this, for they had Aphrodite and Hera and many another form of the Mighty Mother who bestowed on women their peculiar graces and powers.

—A.E.

Laurens Van der Post on German and Japanese countries using the same mythological dominant during World War II:

The parallels were not only close but often so refined in detail that the sun, for instance, which is the image of the light of reason in man and walks tall as a god in most highly differentiated mythologies, was for the Japanese the same feminine phenomenon it was for the Germans, while the infinitely renewing and renewable moon that swings the sea of change and symbolizes all that is eternally feminine in the spirit of man, by some ominous perversity of the aboriginal urgings of both Germans and Japanese, was rendered into a fixed and immutable masculine . . . We had noticed that as the moon filled out and the nearer it came to the achievement of its own, incomparable Javanese fullness, the more it seemed to swing a sea of unreason in the minds of the Japanese, drawing it like a great neap tide high up on the foreshore of their imagination. And as the moon began to decline, a kind of dark insecurity often seemed to overcome our captors and they themselves would be compelled to inflict the worst and most indiscriminate of their beatings and the most horrific of their cruelties on us.[24]

Traditionally, spirituality has had to do with loving, and politics has had to do with power. We have seen them as unrelated because we have experienced our personal lives and relationships as separate from our work and institutional involvements.

—Riddle, Quest, Spring 1975[25]

What is the relationship between spirituality, as we have defined it, and politics? Politics, by its very nature, is partisan; spirituality affirms the interrelatedness of all things. An awareness of this inter-relatedness must inform our sense of revolutionary urgency, as expressed in political ideologies, strategies and lifestyles. Our spirituality —the awareness of oneness and openness to new sources of power—should help us deal with the inevitable tensions between goals and process, compromise and ideology, survival and revolutionary integrity. It is the recognition of this intimate relationship between spirituality and politics that makes the women's movement different from other movements.

—Davis & Weaver, Quest, Spring 1975[25]

THE POLITICS OF FEMINIST SPIRITUALITY

Integration of self-change with institutional change is a revolutionary practice in our society. Segmentation is the basis of patriarchal socialism or capitalism —separation of women and men, of theory and practice, of learning and working, of experience and belief, or production and product, of means and ends, of mind and body, of race, of age, of "class" and, interestingly enough, of religion and government.

The integration and recognition of the relationship between all these processes is the basis for the sanity and power of feminism. Any activities, theories or organizations which connect parts of our lives are usually considered 'dangerous to the establishment; pointing out the relationship between sexism, racism and capitalist production is a crime against existing institutions because the state perpetuates belief in their unrelatedness. Making these connections gives us power because the institutions cease to be abstractions, becoming understandable and then changeable factors in our lives.

Feminism is vitally concerned with the development of political-personal theory, but it never remains a politic of idealism because it is simultaneously concerned with the application and testing of our theories. It is (hopefully) reality in constant evolution, theory as the articulation of our own experience. Feminism is concerned with the reintegration of all these segmented parts and, therefore, the creation of a way of life ecological to the whole person. Thus, feminism is committed to the eventual replacement of patriarchy and capitalism with more coherent forms as a necessity for social and personal survival. It is a collective, non-hierarchical, nonsegmented, experience-based, ecological, evolutionary process—and as such it is **revolutionary** because these aspirations contradict the processes of patriarchal capitalism.

This is why the idea of women's religion is so anathematic to our current system. Not to worship the male principle would mean to turn away from

326

everything this system deifies, and on which it has succeeded. These are the reasons witchcraft was (and is) a crime punishable by oppression and death, a crime against the state.

Witchcraft, a religion of the people, based on moon worship and fertility magic, was a spiritual movement which revered women and the lunar creative power; it was based on the interconnectedness of all things, the understanding of the necessity of and nonhierarchical respect for all elements of the life process. The dark of the moon, the period and principle of meditation, "death" and visions, was equally revered with the brightness and outward focus of the full moon principle. Legalization and compartmentalization of lunar fertility rites was considered impossible, as this would mean destruction of the religion's life force. So witchcraft, with its reverence for the naturalness of the human race as well as our spiritual connection to every world aspect, became the focus of all the might and destruction the incoming patriarchal religions could muster.

Witchcraft as a way of life was forced to become a secret cult. As early as pre-Greek cultures we have records of Thessalonian sorcerers who debased witchcraft. Later Greek classical literature is full of references to the matriarchal-patriarchal struggle. In a pronouncement of the General Council of the Church in the 9th Century, there is a section on evidence against women who held allegiance to Diana-Hecate and who professed to ride to their meetings on certain beasts. The Church Council of Treves 1310 condemned any woman who claimed to ride with Herodiana.

The struggle raged on for centuries, and matriarchal knowledge became more and more suppressed. There are voluminous records, even up to the Salem trials in the early United States, which tell of the fate of women who dare to worship their own power. In a 300 year period over 300,000 witch practitioners were put to death for adhering to their religion, and for defying the establishment of patriarchy.

Witchcraft, the religion of integration, had to be discredited and eliminated before the "success" of patriarchy could be insured. It took a long time to do, and it is a process which went on in every culture.

It stands to reason, with so many centuries of brutal religious persecution, that women today should have a deep fear of conceptualizing our own spirituality. Women who try are severely penalized. Rev. Carter Heyward in New England is persecuted and harrassed for her ordainment as a female Episcopal priest in 1974. Z. Budapest is put on trial in Los Angeles for her activities as a Hungarian witch in 1975.

Because of all this, it is essential that we **do** create our own spiritual practices. Our spiritual beliefs define what we respect, what we love—and what we ultimately perceive as our highest values. For a feminist, or for any woman, to perpetuate a patriarchal religion and to worship a male god is for her to deify her oppression.

The rituals presented in this section are by different women attempting the creation and renaissance of female spirituality, that is, of the ultimate holiness of life-sacredness of women and the female creative process. Within a world which for centuries has tried to brand women as 'unclean,' as 'devils' or as the immoral corruptor of man,' this healing process is a vital one.

Female spirituality is not a carbon copy of male religion, just as matriarchy is not the flipside of patriarchy. Female spirituality is based on different active principles than what male religion has come to promote.

It is my belief that **reforming** patriarchal religions, such as Hinduism, Judaism or Christianity, is not possible, just as reforming capitalism is not possible. The very institutions are contradictory to feminism. Women need to once again create new theory and practices for ourselves in order to reunite the spiritual element with the social-political.

At the same time, just as with feminist change within a capitalist society, i recognize that complete change is not always instantly possible. So i have included rituals by women whose work i would consider reformist not revolutionary, but which in any case represent an important revelatory step away from patriarchal allegiance and toward thinking for ourselves.

It does seem to me though that it may be possible to create women's religions within this culture even before the rest of the institutions have caught up with them, and to use these spiritual groups as vital centers for creating radically different ways of living. Women's spiritual groups can become birth centers for social change.

Ancient patriarchal secret societies and tribes began to take power by force and claim superiority over female religions when women were in the first stages of realizing (probably due to the new knowledge of the process of fertilization gained when people started breeding animals) that sperm was related to procreation. The world-wide belief that children were born from the union of the moon and her female earthly representatives came under question, and matriarchal supremacy suffered a critical shock. Patriarchal tribes capitalized on the period of social adjustment by asserting sperm-phallic creativity over female birth.

The social turmoil must have been enormous and must have undermined all the traditions, organizations and whole cultures based on goddess worship. Female fertility became debased instead of revered and most critically women lost their belief in the miraculousness of their natural processes. It was a ripe atmosphere for military coup.

By now we have had time to absorb this information, to understand that our validity does not need to be tied to unassisted human birth and to learn that male god-supremacy-phallic-dominance is definitely not a superior or healthy alternative.

The task of our age is to pool this inherited knowledge and, through re-establishing our collective female consciousness, to develop a way of life which doesn't need hierarchy at its base and which returns us to our efforts to live out the knowledge that we are all one. This evolution is dependent on our willingness to be unconventional, to free our imaginations and our bodies from our cultural restrictions and to unite at a deep level with other women.

The rituals which follow are not endings but beginnings of this process. They are attempts to bring spirituality, that is our connection with the creation of our own destiny, back into the practice of the people.

o   o   o

The women say that they have found a very large number of terms to designate the vulva. They say they have kept several for their amusement. The majority have lost their meaning. If they refer to objects, these are objects now fallen into disuse, or else it is a matter of symbolic, geographical names. Not one of the women is found to be capable of deciphering them. On the other hand the comparisons present no problems. For example when the labia minora are compared to violets, or else the general appearance of the vulvas to sea-urchins or starfish. Periphrases such as genitals with double openings are cited in the feminaries. The texts also say that the vulvas resemble volutes, whorled shells. They are an eye embedded in eyelids that moves shines moistens. They are a mouth with its lips its tongue its pink palate. As well as rings and circles the feminaries give as symbols of the vulva triangles cut by a bisector ovals ellipses. Triangles have been designated in every alphabet by one or two letters. The ovals or ellipses may by stylized in the form of lozenges, or else in the shape of crescent moons, that is, ovals divided in two. These are the same symbols as the oval rings, settings surrounding stones of every colour. According to the feminaries rings are contemporaneous with such expressions as jewels treasures gems to designate the vulva.

o   o   o

They say that at the point they have reached they must examine the principle that has guided them. They say it is not for them to exhaust their strength in symbols. They say henceforward what they are is not subject to compromise. They say they must now stop exalting the vulva. They say that they must break the last bond that binds them to a dead culture. They say that any symbol that exalts the fragmented body is transient, must disappear. Thus it was formerly. They, the women, the integrity of the body their first principle, advance marching together into another world.

> You say there are no words to describe this time, you say it does not exist. But remember. Make an effort to remember. Or, failing that, invent.
>
> —Monique Wittig[26]

LET US PAINT OUR FACES WHITE & DANCE TO THE MOON
LET US WEAR BLACK ROBES & DANCE TO THE MOON
SO THAT WE CAN FEEL THE WHITENESS OF THE MOON'S FACE
AND THE BLACKNESS OF THE SKY SURROUNDING HER

WE SING TO THE MOON
WE RAISE OUR HANDS TO THE MOON
WE RAISE OUR WHITE FACES TO THE MOONLIGHT
WE MOVE OUR BLACK ROBES IN THE NIGHT LIGHT

WE DANCE ON THE NIGHT WHEN THE MOON IS FULL
BECAUSE WE KNOW HER MOVEMENT IN OUR BODIES
AND IN THE BODIES OF PLANTS AND OF ANIMALS
AND IN THE BODY OF THEIR MOTHER THE BLACK SEA

WE SING TO THE BLACK NIGHT & THE LIGHT OF THE MOON
WE DANCE IN A CIRCLE LIKE THE CIRCLE OF HER CYCLES
WE CLASP ARMS WITH THE SISTERS OF OUR CYCLES
WE SING TO THE MOON OUR SISTER
WE SING TO THE MOON OUR MOTHER
WE SING TO THE MOON OUR NIGHT LOVER
AND WE SING FOR THE LOVE OF EACH OTHER

Photo: Imogen Cunningham

ANN, IMOGEN, THE MUSE AND THE COAT

When a woman named Ann Lansing from Boulder, Colorado, came to the Alyssum Feminist Center drop-in group and described her work as a seamstress, i thought the goddess had sent her! Her favorite jobs were making costumes, and i had wanted to try—from the inspiration of Leonor Fini—making my version of a moon goddess robe. In ten days of talking over our fantasies (Ann's were silver and aqua, while mine were black and pearls), drawing designs together, and Ann sewing night and day, we came up with the vision-come-true: a black velvet hooded coat with aqua satin crescents around the skirt and a white calla lily climbing up the back. Ann's work was inspired; now i put on the coat when i want inspiration to bring more manifestations of the goddess into my life.

That week my friend Freude, whom you can count on for fantastic brainstorms about serious business, suggested that a photographer she knew in San Francisco, Imogen Cunningham, would be the person to translate the coat into a photo. When i phoned Imogen, her assistant, Tom Eckstrom, told me to have official word sent from Random House describing the terms of the project. A week later, i drove to San Francisco with the coat and some photos of the moon, and walked into Imogen's garden in front of her white frame house. I saw Imogen under a tree with her photographer's cloth over her head, and Tom, setting up an old 4 × 5 camera with a soft focus lens she hadn't used since the twenties.

We had several sittings together before we came up with a print on which we all agreed. During these afternoons, i came to like and respect Imogen and Tom a great deal and to admire their subtle working relationship. Imogen, without knowing a thing about my work beforehand, tuned in very quickly to the spirit of the project and accomplished something rare: the combination of someone else's ideas with your own art. In 1976 at ninety-three she was vital and dedicated to her work. She was completing a book of her photographs after ninety (U. of Washington Press), as well as a book on old age (which in her words in "hell").

I particularly appreciated her ideas on school ("Get out!"), on psychology ("People think too much about themselves . . ."), and on religion. When i mentioned that i anticipated some disapproval of the content of my book because it expressed several currently unorthodox views she asked, "Like what?" I said, "I come out in favor of paganism." And she said, "Well, I should hope so!"

RITUALS OF INITIATION AND TRANSFORMATION

Spirituality in my experience, and what i would call feminist spirituality, is the process of integraton, of connection. A spiritual moment is the sensory experience of the fusing of several aspects of normally segmented reality. This process has an infinite number of aspects, rather than hierarchical layers.

Feminist spirituality, unlike most patriarchal systems today, is not focused on transcending everyday life but on recognizing the power in it. It is also not focused on "transcending the self or the ego," but on integrating one's ego-self with the collective self. Women have been denied selves too long. (It is men whose current spiritual work could be the loss of their dominant egos.) Nor is the focus of feminist spirituality "stilling the mind." (This also could be a current male priority!) Women's focus is integrating our thinking with our senses so that our practice is whole, peaceful and sane.

More definition of my semantics and my understanding of feminist semantics seems necessary here.

Matriarchy and Matrilineal

There are many possible definitions of the terms matriarchy and matrilineal. They could be used to describe societies in which women have more social power than men, in which the female mode is dominant, in which female persons are dominant, in which older women are dominant. They could only refer to the custom of recognizing the family succession through the female line. They could refer to the worship of female deities. They could refer to an Amazon lesbian separatist state. Or just to a culture in which the power was more equally divided between women and men than it is now.

333

In this book when i use of the term matrilineal, i am referring to only the custom of family name and legitimacy being determined by the female members. When i use the term matriarchal, it means a broader cultural condition to me in which women determine the policies, are the most powerful members of the group in which the female mode presides, but also in which people are generally more equal in rights than now so that it is not necessarily a situation of oppression of males.

It seems critical not to repeat the patriarchal mistakes of hierarchy, segmentation and oppression. That non-oppression is such an effort i consider a measure of the corruption by the current mode of all our would-be revolutionary consciousness.

Feminism

Feminist is one of the harder terms to define because it is an evolving process, and every woman has her own version; however, there are some definitive universal premises. One premise of feminism is that the root oppression of all oppressions is sexism. Non-recognition of this is why almost all non-feminist revolutionary attempts crumble and why feminist politics is based on the continuous and immediate integration of personal and social functioning. Feminism purports that each person must understand the core of their own nature and sexuality first in order to maintain integrity and health and, therefore, that we as women need to honor our love for women and remember that we are our primary source for understanding and creativity in the famale mode. Feminism is based on love of women and hatred of patriarchal oppressive systems (rather than of male persons, as sensationalized slanted media would have us believe). Collectivity and creativity are basic modes of feminist action.

Gynandry, Androgyny, Pansexual

Androgyny refers to the concept of a mode in which the sexual differentiation is more equally balanced. It seems a good term to apply to men interested in this balance. My dislike of using it when referring to women is that the word (Greek, aner masculine; gyne feminine) still incorporates a sexual supremacy, with the male part coming first, implying a male base of larger proportion, with a pinch of the feminine thrown in.

Gynandry is a term coined to speak to this issue and perhaps it is good to apply to balanced women as the gyne comes first implying a female predominance. Yet it still incorporates a sexual hierarchy. That we can't even invent nonhierarchical words seems an indication of the sexism inherent in our language structure.

Pansexual is a term some people use to refer to people or attitudes not specifically female or male. But this term doesn't appeal to me because it sounds neuter, implies loss rather than wholeness, and denies our sexual roots.

For now i perfer gynandry when looking for an adjective to describe women's balanced states. **Gynergy** refers to the woman power-spirit building up today in woman-identified women.

Hermaphrodite

Womanscience

Instead of littering and unbalancing the moon, womanscience seeks to study her principles through the many mediums she offers naturally: light cycles, biorhythms, tides, weather changes, the activity of animals and plants. Womanscience assumes that the moon belongs to herself, that she is an inviolable essential part of the cosmos, that she is speaking to us in her own language, that our job is to listen with all our senses and to act on her lessons, that she is our ally, our friend. Some of the forms of womanscience, or the study and practice of the teachings of the moon, are magic, witchcraft, goddess religions, ancient astrology, early agriculture and feminism. A crucial problem with most current religions is that women have been methodically eliminated from sacred practice and the female principle has been denigrated as immoral and heretical. Slander campaigns are familiar methods of political oppression, and like the Black is Beautiful restorative process, we need to reaffirm our connections with feminist spirituality in our roots to counteract negative oppressive teachings.

We need to reaffirm our bodies as temples of our holy spirits. We need to let our "religions" stay open-ended, non-ossified and continuously evolving. We need to study matriarchal records and current feminist knowledge, and to integrate our knowledge with our practice. We must develop collective systems of spiritual exploration, based on the natural ecology of mother earth. We need to develop our psychic powers and our respect for non-verbal sensory as well as tangible facts. Non-monogamy and non-monotheism are part of her teachings. Our theory must come out of our own practical experience, inclusive of all peoples.

We can, using the knowledge and patterns of ancient moon rituals, create modern ones to fit our lives now, as one aid to our passage into more ecological states. It is important to only participate in these experiments with people with whom you feel safe, free and comfortable and who you trust are committed to the renaissance of the healing process.

Moon rituals are related to our understanding of healing because healing is the outcome of integration, of spirituality. Rituals of transformation are meant to mark the something-lost-and-something-gained inherent in all change. Rituals are ways of integrating the past, present and future. Many women today are doing this. A sampling of their work is included in this section as illumination of how to make this knowledge functional and current. It is also presented in the hopes that others will be inspired by these muses to create their own moments to celebrate her rhythm. The moon shows us that in order to change we must move according to our natural cycles of birth, letting go, rebirth. We must learn to live these cycles gracefully and lovingly.

Reclaiming Our Lunar Roots

When holidays come along, honor their lunar origins in your celebrations. On the first full moon of spring at Easter, remember that this is the day for the celebration of the renewal of fertility in the world. The eggs are symbols of the Egg Mother. Lilies are sacred to Diana. The three days of mourning before the rebirth of Easter symbolize the three days of the dark moon.

In mid-August the Feast of Assumption of the Virgin Mary was originally Diana's principle festival. It was a holiday for slaves and outlaws and for the reform of social oppression.

Christmas is a winter solstice celebration honoring the birth-power of the goddess. The festivities include decorating trees sacred to Diana, topping them with the star of paradise, honoring the horned animals sacred to her, singing to her fertility and giving gifts of herbs, incense and potions.

Moon festival foods are hearth-baked breads, croissants or goddess-shaped moon cakes, wine, milk and honey drinks, egg nog, fruit and seeds.

Burning a yule log is a good offering as fire honors her. Ashes and smoke symbolize wisdom and spiritual transformation.

Watch the seasonal cycles of the moon consistently from one favorite spot: a hillside, a tree, a lake, your bedroom window, your garden. In the example of the Stonehenge Celtic priestesses, construct several arches, from woven fiber or light wood, to frame the lunar equinoxes from that point. Celebrate when the moon returns to these points.

Put a bowl of water outside during your ritual or on your window ledge. At the closing of the ceremony each person dips her hands into the water which has by now absorbed moon beams and spreads it on her face.

What keeps the moon in place?

Its beams.

Celebrate Your Lunar Birthday

Our current tradition celebrates the anniversary of the sun's position on our birth. Determine which 2½ days the moon will be in the same sign as your natal moon during your sunbirth sign. Every 19 years your lunar birthday will be the same as your sun calendar birthday.

337

Moon Meditations

Stand at open windows during different phases of moon.

Moonrise

Feel the energy of it coming up.

Full

Imagine the moon inside of you (belly, head, toes, fingers, palm, chest, heart) and see if you can carry it with you, during the night, during the day.

Tuning

Allow its light to bathe and fill and cleanse you to spread inside you like waves. Make the sound of the full moon inside of you. Make the sound of each phase. Dance to its vibratory frequency.

Long Distance Healing

Send an extra dose of moon energy to someone.

Long Meditations

Keep your eyes on the moon steadily for one night's rise to set.

Imagine how your civilization would be if we followed her modes and cycles.

o   o   o

Science

What I know about the moon,
is that the moon is made of
grey dust/ green cheese/ the homes of
the dead/ the souls of the next born/ magnets
    of the tides
the swords of the amazons
the cream of the stars
spider dust/ rock/ hot air and powder
life giving cellular magnets
water pullers/ blood markers/ sirens
mermaids out of sight
the eyes of the dead
the energy of the next born
women's blood
women's faces
women's eyes
everyone's wishes
everyone's death and rebirth
layers of death and rebirth
the moon has an atmosphere of cherry
    smelling light
the moon smells good
the moon is made of warm snow
the moon smells like me
the moon is populated by invisible animals
    and people and birds
the moon is made of old seashells
the moon is a big seashell
the moon makes a sound
  can you hear it
  it sings
  she sings
  she sings songs to us
the moon sings us to sleep
the moon sings us stories which
  we think are our dreams
the moon goes swimming in the waters of the
    earth

in our dreams we go to the moon awhile
our dreams happen on the moon
the moon is in constant slow ecstasy
the moon loves playing tricks
  catch me if you can
  mother may i
  hide and seek
  charades
  trick or treat
  ball, all kinds
the moon is full of blue lagoons
the lagoons are full of blind fishes
who sing and blow bubbles
the moon is a sticky bubble
  that pops once a month
the moon is a bubble in the air
  made by the turning of the
  earth and the stars, which are
  also shiny bubbles—it pops
  every 28 days and is remade
  again by the action
of the stars in the night sky
the moon is the maker of
  the sun and stars and earth
stars pop out of its craters
the moon gives birth to
  the sun every month
the earth and sun came from the moon
  the moon gave a lot of
  its light to the sun because
  she only needed her
  electricity—
the earth used to be inside
  the moon but it got
  too hot so she
  set it out/
gave it a whirl.

WOMEN'S ARCHITECTURE

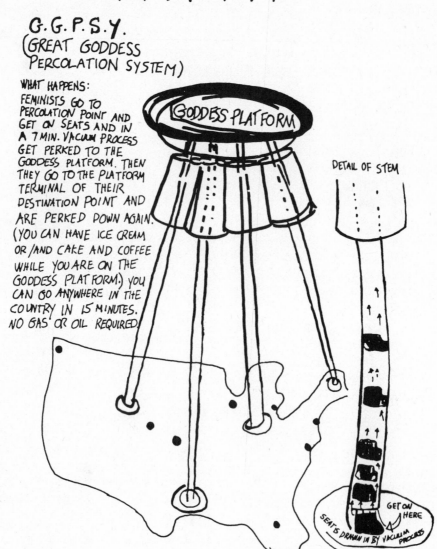

G.G.P.S.Y.
(GREAT GODDESS PERCOLATION SYSTEM)

WHAT HAPPENS:
FEMINISTS GO TO PERCOLATION POINT AND GET ON SEATS AND IN A 7 MIN. VACUUM PROCESS GET PERKED TO THE GODDESS PLATFORM. THEN THEY GO TO THE PLATFORM TERMINAL OF THEIR DESTINATION POINT AND ARE PERKED DOWN AGAIN. (YOU CAN HAVE ICE CREAM OR/AND CAKE AND COFFEE WHILE YOU ARE ON THE GODDESS PLATFORM.) YOU CAN GO ANYWHERE IN THE COUNTRY IN 15 MINUTES. NO GAS OR OIL REQUIRED.

GODDESS PLATFORM

DETAIL OF STEM

SEAT IS DRAWN IN BY VACUUM PROCESS   GET ON HERE

"In our continuing search for origins and expressions of sexism, we must develop and project our own imagery and values into environmental forms. . . . We must begin by evaluating our **manmade** environment from a feminist perspective. Our physical environment, whether it is buildings, communities or cities, reflects the nature of our institutions and the priorities of the decision makers. . . . We feel that this process will increase our awareness of the powerful nexus between fantasy and reality. In this way our dreams and visions can become tools for the creation of actual change."

Noel Phyllis Birkby and Leslie Kanes Weisman[28]

MEMOIRS OF A RITUALIST

Maggy Anthony

At the sound of a drum pounding slowly, and two long notes blown on a conch shell, the procession moved across the street to the beach. Some thirty or forty people carrying candles and carnations in red and white, made up the parade. Leading them was myself, the drummer, and the young man who blew into the conch shells. The sun had set several minutes before, and as we reached the beach we looked out over the ocean before us. In the darkness of the night, only the Moon's light indicated where the sea left off and the night sky began.

I made a short salutation with both arms upraised to the Moon. Then I bent down and dug a crater in the sand and put a lighted candle in it. I added my white and red carnations and murmured my intention. All along the beach, the other people of the procession did the same. Soon the beach was a pock-marked, silvery lunar landscape. Once more I raised my arms to the Moon and started to walk into the water. As I walked, the wetness crept further and further up my purple velvet dress, but my rapport with the Moon and Sea was too great for me to break away. Suddenly, the whole scene was illuminated as if by brilliant sunlight, with giant kleig lights. The media men had jumped into the sea to record the whole event for the television cameras. I turned and fled up the beach into a cloak that a friend had awaiting me. We jumped into the car and sped off.

Thus went one of the first rituals I ever planned and performed. I had been called in by the owners of a dance hall that fronted the beach because they felt there was some sort of "bad luck'" pursuing them. Not only had business dropped off, but some pigeons that had been the property of a stage magician they had hired to entertain had been found with their throats cut. Then the magician himself, freaked by the loss of his birds in such a grisly manner, had leapt off the retaining wall at the beach and badly fractured both legs. They had told a friend of mine of all this and the friend had suggested that since I was so interested in ritual and ancient religions that I might know of something to help them. When they called me and told me their problem, the first thing that came to my mind was the sea that they faced. I asked them if they had ever held any sort of blessing ceremony by the sea or had paid any attention to it. When they replied that they barely gave it any thought, I suggested that that might be the trouble. They asked me if I would perform such a ritual. I had never done such a thing for others before, as I am a great believer in creative ritual to be done by individuals for themselves. But they professed that they knew nothing of such matters and wouldn't know even where to begin. So I took on the job of inventing a ritual for them and conducting it. Their responsibility was to make sure that all the people present had candles, matches, and carnations.

As I began to plan the ritual, I felt that two different things had to be done in this case. First, I felt that the hall itself should be "cleaned" out. (This event took place pre-"Exorcist," so the word did not occur to me.) For this, I adapted an American Indian ritual of staking out the four directions within the hall and making a small tribute in the form of a verbal recognition of the forces of each of the directions. Then I burned some laurel leaves, which have a nice clean smell. I lit a candle for the guardian spirit of the hall, a candle for anything that might be troubling the hall and a candle for the new life of the hall. This finished, I gave the signal for the procession to the sea, across the wide highway. The rituals at the sea, which I have already described, were largely borrowed from an Umbanda ritual to the Sea and Moon Goddess of Brazil, **Iemanja**, with some improvisation by myself. The media were largely unexpected because I assumed they had taken all the photographs they had wanted at the hall. I was greatly shocked when the cameraman with the kleig lights showed up in the sea ahead of me, so suddenly. I fled, because I had been deeply involved in my dialogue with the Moon and Sea and felt the camera as an intrusion. However, later examination of the height that the water had reached on my robe, pointed out the possibility that I might have been swept out to sea by the undertow if the lights had not intervened. I do not know how to swim.

Since that time, I have planned and carried out many rituals both for myself and others. When I do it for others, it is largely to show them how to go about doing it for themselves. And in doing the ritual, I always remember a pertinent scene from the movie, "Little Big Man" with Dustin Hoffman and Chief Dan George. It is the last scene in the film. The old Chief has gone up to the top of the mountain to wait for death. He feels it is his time. Hoffman is watching him, feeling sad as the people in the audience felt. The old Chief lies down in full regalia, closes his eyes and waits for Death to come to him. Suddenly, the rain

342

begins to fall. First it is just a few drops on the old man's face, then more and more, and finally it rains hard. The Chief opens his eyes and gets up slowly. He turns to Hoffman and says, "Sometimes the magic works and sometimes it doesn't," and walks off.

It is like that with ritual. You can do all the planning in the world, but unless that unknown element enters in (what some people call magic, other, archetype) all efforts are in vain and the ritual remains as empty as most modern church ritual. I know of no way to positively guarantee that occurrence but there are many things one can do to help. First of all, it is absolutely essential to never use the same ritual so often that it becomes possible for those participating to give it lip service without thinking about it. Constant small alterations aid this. Secondly, it is important that mental preparations take place before the ritual, possibly aided by physical rules. Some ancient examples of this are things like a short fast (no dinner or food after lunch), meditation beforehand, and a ritual which effectively throws off the cares of the daylight world just left behind. Other things such as the wearing of clothes not worn for any other purpose, and the location of the ritual if possible in a place used for no other purpose. In these days of crowding and "multi-purpose" rooms, this is often difficult. But if the ritual must take place indoors, one can do things like use an altar that does not serve another purpose during the day. Or select an old cabinet that shuts up when not in use and looks like any other piece of furniture, but when opened, reveals its true purpose of shrine and meditation focus. You can see that the underlying theme of all these preparations is to make things as special as possible; to take the hint of the everyday away from them, so that we are prepared by the sight of them for something unusual to occur, something other. Of course, when rituals can be held outdoors, especially at night, we are all such urban people that the locale itself is magic enough. To see the ocean at night, far from all thoughts of getting a tan, or romping in the water to get out of the heat, is to experience nature in Her very primal, self-contained form.

I once gave a ritual in the marshes in a town called Mill Valley in California. We were surrounded by lights from houses, but just the effect of standing in the sand, barefoot, the full moon shining on us and the marsh water lapping gently near us, proved very moving and peaceful. All participating said later that after a few moments of concentrating on the ritual, the surrounding town was forgotten and we became a small group apart from daily cares of the community.

Perhaps the greatest aid to successful ritual is that all parts of it come from the innermost part of the people participating. It is all right to use rituals of other cultures as a basis or part of your own, but if you do not improvise yours along with it, or modify with something from your own psyche, you are apt to feel a little foolish as you stand there, a 20th Century American of mixed heritage, trying to duplicate a ritual from a culture far removed in time and space. Ritual comes from deep within the psyche of all people, and, therefore, must have ingredients from your own unconscious mind to trigger the experiences you wish. One of the best places to discover such material is in dreams. You will find that once you set your mind to seriously thinking about ritual, you will start dreaming and fantasizing it. Also, as you start performing a ritual, things you didn't plan come to mind spontaneously. Allow them! Use them! When they come up spontaneously, they are bound to be meaningful and what Jung called, "synchronistic."

For instance, in a tarot class I once taught, my associate, Stephen Kathriner, and I planned to let people in the class have the experience of the Empress trump by having them make an image in mud of the Great Mother. We had the lights of my dining room turned out and only a candle glimmering. All furniture was removed and the bare floor was spread with paper to cut down on the messiness. As each person came to the front door, her coat was taken, and she was led in silence to the dining room and told to sit on the floor. Drum music was playing very low on the phonograph. When all the class members were present, Stephen started to intone an original prayer for blessing. Then I came in with two buckets of mud and set them down before him. Next, I took pomegranate seeds for the young Goddess, grain for the Mother Goddess and ashes for the Moon, and mixed them one by one into the mud. Suddenly, the feeling came to break away from the ritual we had planned and I marked the forehead of everyone there with mud from the mixture, blessing them in the name of the Mother, and told them to grab some mud for themselves and make the image of the One who gave life to all things. At the moment this happened, there was a silence and a feeling as if something had seized the group and made them draw a deep intake of breath in unison. Then they all plunged their hands into the mud, pushing each other aside at times in their zeal for the material. All hands plunged deeply: cared-for hands, unkept hands, white hands, brown hands, hands with polished nails, hands with bare nails with gleaming white moons on them. In the darkness, they made these images with their hearts and the deepest wellsprings from which life comes. After something like fifteen minutes of furious activity, they subsided, one by one, with the fruits of their labor in front of them. At this point, Stephen suggested that we all take our images in procession to the living room and place them on the hearth to begin to dry. He handed around glasses, produced a bottle of honey mead wine and filled everyone's glass. Again, unplanned, a feeling came to me. I took a big gulp of the wine and spewed it out of my mouth all over the statues that sat on the hearth.

The gesture surprised me as much as it surprised everyone else, but again, it triggered a reaction in all present and made the occasion a little more special. Later, I remembered that I had seen the mediums in the Unbanda cult do this to people and learned that it was a blessing. So my psyche had provided the proper gesture at the psychologically right time. Because I had learned to let the spontaneous occur, the whole ritual was enriched. I am certain of one thing: the people in that class never forgot the archetype of the Great Mother.

When getting into rituals for the Moon specifically, it is well to sit down with a piece of paper and pencil and write whatever associations you have to the image, **Moon**. Then read the list and associate to the words on it. For instance, if you have written the word, **silver**, your association to silver might be light, or candle. You could then concretize this image by using silver candles in your ritual. If you think of a specific Goddess in regard to the Moon, like Isis, you might find yourself associating the word **winged** to Her. You might then feel that you not only would like something of Isis in the ritual but something to do with wings, or feathers, or flight. As each of these images comes to mind, you will have other associations to them and then it takes only a bit of imagination to begin planning your ritual. If you are still stuck, this is the point to try using your dreams to aid the process of imaging. Start with an image associated to what you want to do, then sit in a state of passive receptivity with your eyes closed, until things begin to happen to that original image. For the Moon ritual, you might start by getting a visual image of the Moon in a night sky. Then you might see some trees appear beneath it. As you wait, you see a figure, draped in white, with the face covered below the eyes, walk out from the midst of the trees. It is you! You look closer and see that you have a bundle of wood in your arms. You see yourself set the wood down and lift your arms to the Moon. You hear yourself ask the Moon to come down in Spirit and enter the wood. You then build a small fire and once more ask the Moon to descend. Then you feel the power descending and you ask for Her blessing for yourself and the others present. Suddenly you notice that there are others present too. They group around you as you call the Moon to enter the fire. One by one the people come forward and take a piece of flaming wood from the fire, holding it like a torch. They go back into the circle, until, as the last one is done, you and the fire are encircled by torch bearers. And so it goes. Let your image move forward until it seems to run out of juice. Stop the process and write it down while it is still in your mind. With practice, you can create entire rituals this way, good ones because they issue from the deep recesses of your psyche.

Another aid to imaging is your reading. A good ritualist is helped immensely if she is well-read in mythology, fairy tales, primitive religion, anthropology and folklore. When you most need it, some of the material will filter through to consciousness from the storehouse of the dreaming mind.

A good preparation for ritual making also, is the continual day-by-day attention that you give the sacred in your life, whatever form it takes. A small table with a favorite image, painting, or fetish on it on which you keep a candle burning, or regularly burn incense. Keeping flowers is a good example of what I mean. By paying regular attention to something, you invest it with life; in turn, it becomes part of the life of your mind. Burning a candle, or having fresh flowers in a special place, demands attention. In giving attention, you begin to get a feeling for ritual. Many years ago I was fortunate to have a house large enough so that I could have my own meditation room. I called it that not because I used the room for that purpose, but because I did not know what else to call it. It was a room of my own, in which I could get away from the routine chores of caring for the house and my children and where I could "get my head together" at the end of the day, undisturbed. I painted it the color that I wanted it, furnished it the way I liked and put all the objects that were especially meaningful to me in it. When it was complete, I found that I used it only at the end of the day, once the children were in bed. Even then, I didn't feel as though I could enter the room in my everyday clothes, so I showered and dressed in a caftan before entering. I found that all I wanted to do in there was to sit on the sofa I had brought in and think quietly and undisturbed for two or three hours. I always burned a candle and incense and occasionally, I would lay out the tarot cards for myself. After a few weeks, without planning it, I had set up an entire ritual for entering that space and had become very protective of it. It was kept locked all day and no one entered without an invitation. A friend who came in at my invitation one night after I had spent several months of evenings in it, said that it made him uncomfortable. When I asked why, he said that the room was so highly charged with my personality that it was like plunging into my soul and he had trouble speaking lightly in there. All this had taken place, I believe, because I had marked out the space as sacred and in doing so had naturally evolved rituals concerning it.

The key words in evolving rituals are **spontaneity** and **sacredness**. For, unless you delineate the sacred and then allow spontaneous responses to come forth into action, ritual will not occur. If the **Divine** or the **Other** is to enter, a place must be made ready in the psyche.

SEA RITUAL

Dion Fortune

Violet Firth was a Freudian analyst who became absorbed in Jungian psychology when few others recognized its interest in the 1920's and 30's. Under her new name, Dion Fortune (which comes from a motto meaning, God not luck), she wrote several novels and books on magic and became one of the most famous woman occultists in the Western world. She was also a member of the original Order of the Golden Dawn with Arthur Machen, Aleister Crowley and William Butler Yeats.
The following sections are from her book MOON MAGIC (Samuel Weiser Press, 1956).

Then Morgan rose, and her cloak of dark gauze floated out from her shoulders like wings and the silver robe shone through it. She struck a bell beside her and its soft note filled the room with humming overtones that died slowly away. She raised her hand: "Be ye far from us, O ye profane, for we are about to invoke the descent of the power of Isis. Enter Her temple with clean hands and a pure heart, lest ye defile the source of life."

"The temple of Isis is built of black marble and hung with silver, and She Herself sitteth veiled in the innermost. She is all Goddesses that men's hearts have worshipped, for they are not many things, but one thing under many forms.

"Those who adore the Isis of Nature adore Her as Hathor with the horns upon Her brow; but those who adore the Celestial Isis know Her as Levanah, the Moon. She is also the Great Deep whence life arose. She is all ancient and forgotten things wherein our roots are cast. Upon the earth She is ever-fecund: in heaven She is ever Virgin. She is Mistress of the Tides that ebb and flow and never cease. In these things are the keys of Her mystery, known only to the initiated."

Morgan struck the bell again; its vibrations sank to silence once more, and we sat in silence for awhile. It seemed to me that we were on a low rocky outlet surrounded on all sides by the sea, and upon it was the black and silver temple of Isis, through whose arched portico we looked out on the water.

Then Morgan rose again, and lifted her arms to the moon as the women of ancient times had done before her.

"O thou most holy and adorable Isis, who in the heavens art Supernal Mother, and upon the earth Our Lady of Nature, and changing Moon, ruling the tides of flux and reflux upon the earth and in the hearts of men. Thee, we adore thee, we adore in the symbol of the Moon in Her splendour, ever-changing. And in the symbol of the deep sea that reflects Her. And in the symbol of the opening of the gates of life.

"We see Thee crowned in silver in the heavens, and clad in green upon the earth, and in thy robe of many colours at the gates. O heavenly silver that answerest to the celestial gold! O green that risest from the grey! O rainbow glory of living!

The soft-bell tones sounded again, and taking her note from the bell, Morgan began to sing, the song of which the snatches had plagued me for weeks past:

> "O thou that wast before the earth was formed—
>   Ea, Binah, Ge.
>
> O tideless, soundless, boundless, bitter sea,
> I am thy priestess, answer unto me.
>
> O arching sky above and earth beneath,
> Giver of life and bringer-in of death,
>   Persephone, Astarte, Ashtoreth,
> I am thy priestess, answer unto me.
>
> O golden Aphrodite, come to me!
> Flower of the foam, rise from the bitter sea.
> The hour of the full moon tide draws near,
> Hear the invoking words, hear and appear—
>   Isis unveiled, and Ea, Binah, Ge!
> I am thy priestess, answer unto me!"

"Be ye far from us, O ye profane, for the unveiling of the Goddess is at hand. Look not upon Her with impure eyes lest ye see your own damnation.

"The ignorant and impure man gazeth upon the face of Nature, and it is to him darkness of darkness. But the initiated and illuminated man gazeth thereon and seeth the features of God. Be ye far from us O profane while we adore God made manifest in Nature."

The voice fell silent again, and the sea outside answered with a slow wash on the rocks that was like the beating of muffled cymbals.

Then Morgan slowly rose, all her silver draperies a-shimmer, and stood upright in the rigidity of Egypt; she raised her hands from the bent elbows until the palms faced me, and there was power coming form these palms. I saw that her face had changed, and was almost negroid about the mouth, though the still, calm Nordic breadth of brow remained. Then a voice spoke that was not Morgan's voice, curiously inhuman and metallic.

"I am the Veiled Isis of the shahows of the sanctuary. I am She that moveth as a shadow behind the tides of death and birth. I am She that cometh forth by night, and not man seeth my face. I am older than time and forgotten of the gods. No man may look upon my face and live, for in the hour he parteth my veil, he dieth.

"There are two deaths by which men die, the greater and the lesser. The death of the body and the death of initiation. And of these two the death of the body is the lesser. The man who looks upon the face of the Goddess dies, for the Goddess takes him. They that die thus go by the path of the well-head that is by the white cypress. He that would die to the birth, let him look upon the face of the Goddess in this mystery. Be ye far from us O ye profane, for one goes forth by the path that leads to the well-head beside the white cypress."

Morgan began to sing:

"The inner earth, where lead the pathways three.
Who drinks the waters of that hidden well
Shall see the things whereof he dare not tell—
Shall tread the shadowy path that leads to me
　　Diana of the Ways and Hecate,
　　Selene of the Moon, Persephone."

It seemed to me as if death were calling to me out of the great deep, and my life ebbed away from me like a man bleeding to death. If ever a man died, I died then; but I heard the voice of the Priest of the Moon, speaking to me through the gathering shadows:

"The daughter of the Great Mother is Persephone, Queen of Hades, ruler of the kingdoms of sleep and death. Under the form of the Dark Queen men also worship Her who is the One. Likewise She is Aphrodite. And herein is a great mystery, for it is decreed that none shall understand the one without the other.

In death men go to Her across the shadowy river, for She is the keeper of their souls until the dawn. But there is also a death in life, and this likewise leadeth on to rebirth. Why fear ye the Dark Queen, O men? She is the Renewer. From sleep we rise refreshed; from Death we arise reborn; by the embraces of Persephone are men made powerful.

For there is a turning within of the soul whereby men come to Persephone; they sink back into the womb of time; they become as the unborn. By the embraces of Persephone are men made powerful.

For there is a turning within of the soul whereby men come to Persephone; they sink back into the womb of time; they become as the Unborn; they enter into the kingdom where She rules as Queen; they are made negative and await the coming of Life.

And the Queen of Hades cometh unto them as a bridegroom, and they are made fertile for life and go forth rejoicing, for the touch of the Queen of the kingdoms of sleep hath made them potent."

I knew that the time had now come that I had foreseen from the first, when my life should be poured out on the altar to give the Goddess power; but I had thought of that sacrifice as a bloody rite, violent and terrible, but this was a slow ebbing away of strength and a sinking down into nothingness that was only terrible because it was the end. I felt sleep rising over me like a tide as the sea rose over the rocks outside, taking back again that which belonged to it, lent for an hour to the air. I was returning to the nothingness whence I had come, and life was ending as it had begun, in sleep.

I remembered the words of one of the wise, "Or ever the silver cord is loosened or the golden bowl is broken—" I felt the golden bowl of my soul lifted up and poured out on the altar, the cubical moon altar; but it must have been that the silver thread was not loosed, for I still lived, though I came as near to death as a man might and yet return.

With the eyes of vision I saw the stars moving in the heavenly spaces and tides in the earth soul following them as the earthly seas follow the moon. Then through my vision I heard the voice of the Priest of the Moon again.

"Our Lady is also the Moon, called of some Selene, of others Luna, but by the wise Levenah, for therein is contained the number of Her name. She is the ruler of the tides of flux and reflux. The waters of the Great Sea answer unto Her, likewise the tides of all earthly seas, and She ruleth the nature of Woman.

But there is likewise in the souls of men, a flowing and an ebbing of the tides of life, which no one knows save the wise; and over these tides the Great Goddess presides under Her aspect of the Moon. She comes from the sea as the evening star and the magnetic waters of the earth rise in flood. She sinks as Persephone in the western ocean and the waters flow back into the inner earth and become still in that great lake of darkness wherein the moon and the stars are reflected. Whoso is still as the dark underworld lake of Persephone sees the tides of the Unseen moving therein, and knoweth all things. Therefore is Luna known as the Giver of Visions.

The voice ceased and I thought it was the end. Then I saw that in the utter

350

darkness light moved like a tide, and knew that even death has a manner of life of its own. It seemed to me that I looked out over the dark lake of the Underworld to where Persephone, who was Morgan, sat on Her throne and awaited my coming. I remembered that in my sea cave vision I had been required to swear that I would go to my death without struggling, for the sacrifice must be consummated by the unreserved surrender—and I willed to cross the dark water and come to Her.

I found myself in the strange, highpowered boat called Millions of Years wherein Osiris voyages, and I was Osiris. Beside me were the Gods that travelled with me, that were also my other selves. Horus, hawk of the morning, was look-out in the bow, and Toom, god of the gathering dusk, sat silent in the stern; and at my feet the Kephra Bettle, symbol of the sun at midnight, held in his paws the emblem of time that is past. And so we travelled the dark waters of the lake of the Underworld to come to the Queen of the Dead, my magical bride. And as we drew towards Her the light increased till it was the light of the room and at the far end I saw Morgan sitting. And as I looked, I saw Her begin to change from silver into gold, and a glowing aura of all the colours of the rainbow sprang out around Her. Her sleeping eyes opened into an amazing animation of life, and she glowed with the life of the glorious dawn. Then the tide that flowed from me to her, turned and flowed back from Her to me, and I felt my life returning to me, but different, for it had been made one with the life of the Goddess.

o   o   o

. . .The high full moon in the mid-heavens shines clear;
Oh hear the invoking words, hear and appear!
Shaddai el Chai and Rhea, Binah, Ge—.

Sink down, sink down, sink deeper and deep.
Into eternal and primordial sleep.
Sink down, forget, be still and draw apart
Into the inner earth's most secret heart.
Drink of the waters of Persephone,
The secret well beside the sacred tree.

I am the secret queen, Persephone.
All tides are mine, and answer unto me.
Tides of the airs, tides of the inner earth,
The silent secret tides of death and birth—
Tides of men's souls, and dreams, and destiny—
Isis veiled and Rhea, Binah, Ge.

Isis, The Moon Goddess

I was of the cult of the Black Isis, which is very different from that of the green-robed Isis Goddess of Nature to whom the women prayed for children. They represent Her with a human face, or horned like a cow; but the Black Isis is the Veiled Isis, upon whose face none may look and live, and because I represent Her, I too went veiled and cloaked and I have never lost the habit to this day; I do not like people to look upon my face in bright light, and if I must show it, I show it masked in laughter and animation. Very few have seen my face in repose, for repose is a transparent mask.

Some equate the Black Isis with Kali, and say that She is evil; but I do not think She is, unless one counts elemental force as evil, which I do not. She is indeed the Breaker in Pieces, but then She sets free. She is also most ancient Life, and people fear the primordial as they fear nothing else. Freud knew that. She is a resevoir of tremendous and dynamic force, and when dynamic force comes welling up, that is She.

I cannot do it single-handed; someone has to see the Goddess in me, and then She manifests. I am not the Goddess, but I am the priestess of the Goddess, and She manifests through me, for all women are Isis. Not many can see the Goddess manifest, and of those that can see, not all can bear it, and then they hate me because they fear Her.

For my purpose I used the opalescent moon-colours on a base of silver; the purple that is a plum-colour, and the reds that are magenta or maroon, and the blues of sea water and the sky at night; never the strong primaries such as a man uses when he is a magus. Always the shadowy, blended colours are mine.

I like rings too, so big that I can hardly get my gloves on over them; and bracelets like fetters on my wrists. My hands are supple with ritual, and I am as bold in my nail laquers as in my lipsticks. I have used silver and gold lacquers and reds so dark that they are almost black; and iridescent lacquers that make my nails look like opals and I wear my nails long to match my tiger teeth. But I who am the eternal woman, the archetypal feminine—I do not speak to the surface of consciousness, the sophisticated mind that the novelties catch, but to the archaic and primordial that is in the soul of every man, and I will pit my charm against that of any fashionable woman. They may have lovers, but I am beloved.

For I use colour and movement and sound and light as other women use fashions, but more important than all these is scent. I value scents highly and attach great importance to them, for there is a whole psychology and theology of scents. The scents I employ are spicy and aromatic—the flower scents are not for me—no one has ever likened **me** to a flower though I have been told I am as beautiful as a leopard. Sandal and cedar and Russia Leather—these are my favorites. I also love the after-odor of burnt musk and the way it clings. Camphor I love too for its cleanliness. Of the essential oils, I use geranium, jasmine, and attar—none other. These are the psychology of scents, but of the theology there are two I esteem most highly—galbanum and frankincense—the harsh, musky, hyrcinian sweetness of galbanum that is earth of earth, and the sharp stimulus of frankincense, which is as if all the trees of Paradise were burning.

SAINTHOOD RE-EXAMINED

According to my knowledge of Christian mythology, and according to my friend Toni Maher (singer, actress, teacher; born Irish Catholic so-she-ought-to-know!), initiation into sainthood for women has so far included a requirement of sexual disfigurment or torture. Some historical examples which stand out are the cases of St. Agatha who had her breasts torn off and of St. Lucy who was sexually molested and had her eyes gouged out. The saints are usually pictured with the instruments of their torture, thus Agatha is usually shown holding pincers. Maria Goretti, a young field worker in the 1930's, was stabbed while resisting rape, and then made a saint. Catherine Tekewitha, "Lily of the Mohawks," became a Jesuit martyr among the Iroquois when she was tortured for embracing Catholocism. If this path is the price of recognition from this god, i don't choose it; however, i am interested in examining the old notions of sainthood for corruption in our philosophies of the pathways to enlightenment.

One of the striking things about the patterns of initiation in ancient religious and spiritual cults is that, in general, the male societies conceived of and practiced physical torture as the doorway to adulthood and enlightenment, while the women's societies required a meditation, study and celebration period. Among other corruptions and co-optations, it seems we have adoped the negative definition of the process of enlightenment. How many of us have had to be driven to the brink of self-destruction or physical violation before realizing the validity of woman-identified consciousness for our own health?

What are the dynamics of feminist enlightenment? What brings women to feminism. Can we pin down the crucial ingredients? Can we speed up this process?

It seems our understanding of initiation has become negative male-defined, that we have lost touch with our process of learning from gentle reminders of joy. disappointing experiences with male-identification, culminating in one major horrible incident. A horrible incident seems to mark many women's turning points. How many women do you know who suddenly understood what feminism was about after a rape, an involuntary sterilization operation, a divorce, a sexist job firing, a bout with the tortures of male-devised birth control or a "celibate" guru who wants to sleep with his students? For me the last straws were physical violations and phychological mind-rapes from a series of sexist therapists. Why don't we recognize the signals before the process gets out of hand? Do we need extremes of violation to wake us up? Why can't we get the message sooner and in a gentler way?

It seems our understanding of initiation has become negative male-defined, that we have lost touch with our process of learning from gentleness, from joy.

We are evolving. Let's build life-oriented collective pleasure principles into all our systems of social change and individual enlightenment. The message learned from joy is a different one from that of suffering. Masochism and suffering as the doorway to enlightenment is not necessary or desireable. It is not woman-oriented. It is not life-oriented.

Because we don't live within a perfect environment of integrity, we can't and shouldn't avoid suffering for our cause when no other path of success is possible; but only when there is no other way. In the areas among ourselves where we do have control, let's adopt the principle of enlightenment by pleasure.

Let's shift the focus in our culture back onto joy rather than crucifixion and persecution. What lost and new layers of vision are open to us through these avenues? Let's create initiations among our sisters and brothers through love. Let's implement feminist historical principles at every level of life to create joy-based instincts of learning.

o   o   o

NON-SAINT JOAN AND THE WITCH WITHIN

Mary Daly

Mary Daly, an ex-nun, has written several books and articles on the politics of religion. She uses the example of Joan of Arc's fate to describe the danger to women of the patriarchal system, and the persistence of goddess spirituality.

Characteristically, the church burned Joan of Arc as a heretic and, when she was safely dead, canonized her as a Christian saint. But what if Joan was really a "heretic"—a member of the Dianic cult-as the well-known scholar Margaret Murray maintains? Murray proposes that the questions asked at Joan's trial reveal her accusers' suspicions that she represented an underlying organization which they dreaded—the Old Religion, whose roots go back to a pre-agricultural period. This was an ancient religion of Western Europe which still survives underground. It had "beliefs, ritual, and organization as highly developed as that of any other cult in the world." Murray marshals historical evidence to support her thesis that Joan's accusers were aware of her connection with the ancient religion. She points to the incredible exchange of letters after her execution which reveal that Joan was no ordinary heretic:

After the execution, the judges and counsellors who had sat in judgment on Joan received letters of indemnity from the Great Council; the Chancellor of England sent letters to the Emperor, to the kings and princes of Christendom, to all the nobles and towns of France, explaining that King Henry and his Counsellors had put Joan to death through zeal for the Christian faith; and the University of Paris sent similar letters to the Pope, the Emperor, and the College of Cardinals.

Moreover, Murray's research indicates that there was widespread belief that Joan was God Incarnate. It was a belief of the Old Religion that God could appear as a woman, a man, or an animal. Such a God is found in Italy, Southern France, and the English Midlands, and is commonly called Janus or Dianus. The feminine form of the name, Diana, is found throughout Western Europe. It is the name of the female deity or leader of the so-called Witches. For this reason, the Old Religion is also referred to as the Dianic Cult. The fact that the French never lifted a finger to save Joan—difficult to explain—might be accounted for by their belief that as God Incarnate she was doomed to suffer as the sacrifice for the people.

Joan's trial, then, could be seen as part of the war between Christianity and the Old Religion, or Ritual Witchcraft—an ancient religion of Pre-Christian origins, which should not be confused with "Black Magic." Christian writers, of course, have wanted to claim Joan as a true Christian. However, Murray's contention is that these have been misled by such phenomena as Joan's "Voices," to whom Joan gave the names of saints, for "the questions showered upon her show that the judges had shrewd suspicions as to the identity of these persons," that is, that the "Voices" were human beings, persons of a different religion than Christianity. I should like to point out another item that might be significant. Joan's questioners were constantly asking whether she marked her letters with the sign "Jesus Maria" and a cross. On March 1, 1431, she gave an interesting answer: "On some letters, Yes; on others, No!" She added: "At times I used the cross to warn those who understood (what it meant) not to do what I had written in that letter." Why would a Christian symbol be chosen to bear this negative message?

The issue that Joan's accusers made of her insistence upon wearing male clothing is significant. On this the judges laid most stress. "Though Joan had recanted and been received into the Church, the moment she put on male attire she was doomed on that account only." Murray points out that the simple fact of resuming male garments was a signal for her death without further trial, and suggests that for Joan, as a member of the Dianic cult, the wearing of male attire must have been an outward sign of that faith, and the resuming of it must have meant the relapse.

It may be that future historians, prodded on by the work of scholars like Murray and burning to discover the truth about Joan and about the Old Religion rather than with zeal to entomb her within Christianity, will find more evidence that supports this interpretation of Joan's life and death. Yet even abstracting from this not yet fully explored question, it is clear that there is something deeply significant about the connection between Joan's reassuming of male attire (a "mortal sin") and her execution. Phyllis Chesler points out that Joan begins to step completely outside the realm of patriarchal culture:

> For this, she is killed in her own lifetime—and reexperienced by those women who are mad enough to wish to "step outside" but who do not wish to be crucified for doing so.

The essential reason why Joan was killed was that she signaled to some extent an escape from patriarchy.

In some ways it was an ambiguous escape. Joan's fate involved the sacrifice of The Maid. This is a proud title, for traditionally in the Old Religion The Maid was one holding a high position in the Coven. Yet, as Chesler points out, Joan's sacrifice was used for purposes of male renewal.

In the Madonna's case the renewal is achieved through classic patriarchal rape-incest; in Joan's case, first through military victories and then through patriarchal crucifixion, guilt, and expiation.

The final indignity, not stressed by Chesler, was the fact that having killed her the Church made her a saint. It should be noted that she was killed in the most horrible way—burned alive—whereas her lieutenant, Gilles de Rais, was granted the mercy of strangulation before burning.

As Antichurch, the women's revolution is an affirmation of Joan's escape from patriarchy. It says "No" to whatever there was of cooptation and ambivalence imposed upon her fate. Above all it says "No" to her imposed "sainthood" and "Yes" to her real sainthood—her transparency to the power of be-ing which made her life a sign-event, expressing the witch which burns within our own true selves. Joan's potential stature was reduced by the patriarchal imagination into that of the Virgin-Warrior who aids men to fulfill men's goals. The witch that burns within our being will have to bring out that potential stature, repudiating ambivalence and servitude, refusing the tortures and degrading honors which are their only rewards.

Mothers, Daughters, Comrades

The religions of patriarchy—especially the Judeo-Christian tradition and its hideous blossom, Freudian theory—have stolen daughters from their mothers and mothers from their daughters. Chesler reminds us that Demeter, the goddess of Life, and Persephone, her maiden daughter, were for a long time celebrated in elaborate ceremonies. "But somehow—no one really knows why—such celebrations of mothers and daughters certainly ceased." Christian women go to church and sing of themselves as sons of God. The Virgin Mary was allowed only a son, but no daughter. Mothers in our culture are cajoled into killing off the self-actualization of their daughters, and daughters learn to hate them for it, instead of seeing the real enemy. If they begin to see, the pain drives them to their paternal analysts, who help them to understand that they must hate their mothers for not having destroyed them enough to erase the pain. Still, the destruction has not been complete, and women are beginning to dream again of a time and space in which Mother and Daughter look with pride into each other's faces and know that they both have been victims and now are sisters and comrades.

By the time of Joan of Arc, within the Dianic cult the worship of the male deity seems to have superseded that of the female. Murray holds that only on rare occasions does God appear in a female form and that as a general rule the woman's position, when divine, is that of the "familiar" or substitute for the male God. Yet this ambivalence was probably a late development, and it was still possible to see in the chief woman of the cult the remnants of the Mother-Goddess and her autonomous power. The Old Religion was not "pure," but its women could still be powerful figures not yet reduced to the condition of the bovine Madonnas adored by the artists of Christianity. The New Being of Antichurch is a rising up of Mother and Daughter together, beyond the Madonna's image and beyond the ambivalent Warrior Maiden's image. The togetherness comes from nonimmersion in either role, and it comes from our desperation which has made us remember and look forward to the Golden Age. This remembering/looking-forward already colors our existence in the boundary space and time where some women are beginning really to live.[27]

As wimmin and feminist witches, we see the devil as the bondage and ignorance imposed upon wimmin by patriarchal rule. We see male gods as inventions of patriarchal wishful thinking.

The spells have been passed down from mother to daughter, surviving patriarchy. The Craft is the religion of the oppressed. There is only one rule—"Harm none, and do as thou wilt."

—Z. Budapest

You are a witch by saying aloud, "I am a witch" three times, and thinking about that. You are a witch by being female, untamed, angry, joyous and immortal.

—New York Covens

MY SALEM IN L.A.

Z. Budapest

Z. Budapest is a Hungarian feminist living in Los Angeles, California, U.S.A. She and several other women run a store there, the Feminist Wicca. In 1975 (possibly contributing to her arrest) she founded and incorporated the Dianic Sisterhood of the Wicca, to be the first person to legalize such a woman's religion in 10,000 years. She was then arrested and put on trial for divination under the auspices of a 1946 L.A. municipal code which prohibits "making predictions." Her case is a strong reminder of the importance for establishing the legality of the freedom of women to choose and practice their own religions.

There was something in the sound of the air; my witch ears listened and it said, "The time has come to legalize woman's religion." The Susan B. Anthony Coven has grown into the largest feminist Dianic Grove on the West Coast, and we have planted a Dianic sister grove in Europe, Grove Sappha.

We signed papers on January 19th incorporating the Sisterhood of the Wicca. Three weeks and a few days later in February, 1975, I was arrested by an undercover policewoman and booked under a state law that is over 100 years old. When the trial began on April 10th, the City Attorney, Judith Stein, dropped the state law charge; it included "intent to defraud," which could not be proved. They tried me under a 1946 L.A. Municipal Code which prohibits any person from making predictions—by cards, palmistry, astrology, or psychology. The exceptions: if I were a minister, priest, pastor, or reverend of a bona fide church, it would be O.K. to read the Tarot. Not once did priestess come up.

Judith Stein proved to be the type of lawyer who defends rapists against the victims. She told the jury that Hitler had an extensive occult library, winked often to the jury, and played cute, saying, "The type of books Z. sells in the Feminist Wicca bookstore, well, I leave that to your imagination."

The Feminist Wicca, the manifestation of growing Witchcraft amongst women, carries books on spirituality, the Goddess, herbs, astrology, etc. We sell oils, powders, incenses, candles, tools of the Craft.

Three vice squad undercover agents testified against me. Our defense was strong. Dr. Barbara Chesser testified that divination (fortunetelling) is an integral part of the Craft; that the Craft is a religion dating back sixty thousand years; and that exchange of money or goods is also connected with such services universally.

Meanwhile my people, about 300 women and pagans, were demonstrating outside. "Witch trials are women trials," "Salem 1675—L.A. 1975," "Hands Off Woman's Religion," said the signs. There was singing and dancing, candles burning to the Goddess of freedom, and a cauldron smoking with mixed herbs.

Marge Buckley, my attorney, was valiant and articulate. In her summation argument, she quoted the charge of the Goddess as her closing words. We rested our case. After four hours, the jury came back with the guilty verdict—just in time to go home at 5:00.

I am now under probation and have to deny my services to my sisters, who since have been politicized by my persecution. I also had to post $2,500. bail, unheard of in such "crimes" as reading the tarot. We are now appealing to the Supreme Court to remove laws interfering with practices of the Craft.

A week after the trial ended, I received from the State of California our papers saying that we are now incorporated as a legal church to the Goddess and women only, the Sisterhood of the Wicca. This was the real news. Such a church has not existed in 10,000 years in the western world.

When I talk to people about the trial, all ask me, "Why you?" The interesting thing is, it isn't just me. Psychics have experienced growing harassment since the Jesus freaks got hip to the existing laws against us and started making complaints. An entire convention was arrested in Chicago this year.

For the past year, the movement has been scrutinized by CIA and FBI spies; feminists are at the boiling point. Women are in jail for defending themselves against rapists; Inez Garcia and Joanne Little are fighting to protect their bodies; I am fighting to protect my soul and my religion. I see our struggles as interconnected: we are all fighting for the freedom to be. I do not face the threat of death, but the time is not long past when I would have. Nine million women were burned in Europe for upholding the same beliefs that I practice.

Why is reading the Tarot such a crime? Our religion uses the Tarot to council people and guide them spiritually. This guidance is only a small part of our pagan tradition. As an entire theology, we are competing with the Judeo-Christian tradition for followers. I feel that there is less attempt today to disguise the fact that the Judeo-Christian church and white male supremacy are interdependent entities. As in heaven, so on earth. As long as the world accepts an all powerful jealous and possessive male god in the spiritual authority as Lord, there shall be a male authority on earth. The Patriarchal religions are a mere 10,000 years old; compared with the 100,000 years of proved universal Goddess worship, the self-created male gods are Johnnies-come-lately. By owning oil wells, food chains, and lobbyists, they have attained an excellent position for oppressing women by moralizing against us.

Paganism is the only religion today that glorifies women as the expression of the female principle of the universe, from whom all life comes. Priestesshood was the oldest profession for women, not the male mythical "art" of prostitution; we invented religion. But we do need to re-connect with the most ancient teachings of paganism rather than the popularized "occult." Naturally, the feminist witch is not at all welcome in the male-dominated multi-million dollar business that constitutes the occult world of the 20th century. Witchcraft and the earth religions are life-oriented philosophies; male god religions are death-oriented: warring gods, crucifixions, deprivations, suffering for a slice of the Pie-in-the-Sky after death, sin, guilt, the devil, are all given to us by the Judeo-Christian-Buddhist-Hinduist-Confucionists.

The peasants celebrated universal events: solstices and equinoxes, full moons and new moons. Our calendar follows natural events. The peasants knew that there was no male who ever gave birth to anything, let alone the universe!

As I try to discover how to run a religion that is destined to be the fastest growing one among oppressed people, I am calling for a coalition between the politically sophisticated feminist community and the pagan community who is now beginning to fight against our common oppression. Our appeal will take two years, and we have to lose some more before we are on the upcoming tide. But win we shall. Freedom of religion, selfgoverning among the pagan traditions needs to be worked out.

This Halloween we are launching a National Halloween Offensive against the exploitation of our most sacred holyday: the Feast of the Dead and the Witches' New Year. There will be a circle around the globe of women and pagans in a candlelight procession protesting the exclusion of women from spiritual leadership and anti-witch laws on the books. The return of the Goddess is evident.

Blessed Be!

o   o   o

The following sections are from Z.'s book THE FEMINIST BOOK OF LIGHTS AND SHADOWS which can be ordered from the Feminist Wicca, 442 Lincoln Boulevard, Venice, California 90291.

Manifesto of the Susan B. Anthony Coven

We believe that Feminist witches are wimmin who search within themselves for the female principle of the universe and who relate as daughters to the Creatrix.

We believe that just as it is time to fight for the right to control our bodies, it is also time to fight for our sweet woman souls.

We believe that in order to fight and win a revolution that will stretch for generations into the future, we must find reliable ways to replenish our energies. We believe that without a secure grounding in womon's spiritual strength there will be no victory for us.

We believe that we are part of a changing universal consciousness that has long been feared and prophesized by the patriarchs.

We believe that Goddess-consciousness gave humanity a workable, long-lasting, peaceful period during which the Earth was treated as Mother and wimmin were treated as Her priestesses. This was the mythical Golden Age of Matriarchy.

We believe that wimmin lost supremacy through the aggressions of males who were exiled from the matriarchies and formed the patriarchal hordes respon-sible for the invention of rape and subjugation of wimmin.

We believe that female control of the death (male) principle yields hummin evolution.

We are committed to living life lovingly towards ourselves and our sisters. We are committed to joy, self-love, and life-affirmation.

We are committed to winning, to surviving, to struggling against patriarchal oppression.

We are committed to defending our interests and those of our sisters through the knowledge of witchcraft: to blessing, to cursing, to healing, and to binding with power rooted in woman-identified wisdom.

We are opposed to attacking the innocent.

We are equally committed to political, communal, and personal solutions. We are committed to teaching women how to organize themselves as witches and to sharing our traditions with wimmin.

We are opposed to teaching our magic and our craft to men.

Our immediate goal is to congregate with each other according to our ancient woman-made laws and remember our past, renew our powers and affirm our Goddess of the Ten-thousand Names.

Wimmin's Religion, As In Heaven, So On Earth

What people believe (faith—religion) is political because it influences their actions and because it is the vehicle by which a religion perpetuates a social system. Politics and religion are inter-dependent.

Every new social structure strives to come up with some kind of mythology of divine origin for its values and aims. The mythology is passed on for generations, and often, its validity goes unquestioned for centuries. For example, a self-created male god who has no mother is a totally unsupportable concept. It is, to say the least, not supernatural, but merely unnatural. Nothing in nature parallels, let alone substantiates such an absurdity. Everything, even a star, originates somewhere—every creature in the world has a mother force. Obviously, to deny motherhood is to deny wimmin. Patriarchal religion is built on this denial, which is its only original thought—the rest of the edifice having been ripped off stone by stone from the Old Faith of Paganism. The Christian Trinity is a word by word reversal of the Fates, the Three-fold Mother, the Three Graces. The Dove is the sacred bird of the Great Mother. The Great Mother was eventually incorporated into the new Christian religion in the form of the Virgin Mary, who is today worshipped in an "idolatrous" fashion in the Catholic Church.

Who absorbs whose culture is a crucial issue on the cultural battlefield. Those who refused to accept this accomodation and continued to practice the ancient art were persecuted.

Wimmin's spirituality is rooted in Paganism, where wimmin's values are dominant. The Goddess-worship, the core of Paganism, was once universal. Paganism is pleasure-oriented, joy and feasting prone, celebrating life with dancing and lovemaking. Working in harmony with Mother Nature, we discover and recover the All-Creatrix, the female power without whom nothing is born nor glad.

Male energy pretends to power by disclaiming the female force. Today, given the patriarchal society within which we live, witchcraft with a Feminist politic (Dianic) says clearly that the real enemy is the internalized and externalized policing tool that keeps us in fear and psychic clutter.

The craft is not only a religion; it is also a lifestyle. In the time of the Matriarchies, the craft of wimmin was common knowledge. It was rich in information on how to live on this planet, on how to love and fight and stay healthy, and especially, on how to learn to learn. The remnants of that knowledge constitute the body of what we call "witchcraft" today. The massive remainder of that knowledge is buried within ourselves, in our deep minds, in our genes. In order to reclaim it, we have to open ourselves to psychic experiences in the safety of feminist witch covens.

364

A new kind of trust is the most important contribution wimmins's spirituality has to give to the wimmin's movement. We learned we can trust our bodies when we learned we had the right to control them. We are learning we can trust our souls through learning that our right to have them is rooted in our recognition of the Goddess, of the female principle within the universe and ourselves.

It is from this source that our independence comes.

Self Blessing Ritual

This ritual should be performed before doing any magical work.

Begin after sundown. Prepare your altar with two white candles annointed with van van oil or blessing oil or your favorite ritual oil. The altar is dressed in white, the chalice is filled with half wine and half water. Sprinkle salt on the floor and stand barefoot upon it.

Light your altar candles, saying: "Blessed be thou, creature of fire." Light meditation incense or peace incense.

Dip your forefingers into the chalice; touching your forehead, say: "Bless me, Mother, for I am thy child." Dip your fingers again and touch your eyes, saying: "Bless my eyes to see your ways." Dip again and touch your nose, saying: "Bless my nose to smell your essence." Dip and touch mouth, saying: "Bless my mouth to speak of you." Dip and touch breasts, saying: "Bless my breasts, formed in strength and beauty." Dip and touch genitals, saying: "Bless my genitals that create life as you have brought forth the universe." Finally, dip and touch feet, saying: "Bless my feet that I may walk on your path."

Take a little time before extinguishing the candles. You shall experience a surge of energy and lightness of the heart. Blessed be.

Candlemas: February 2

Theme: the celebration of the waxing light. It is the high point between Winter Solstice and Vernal Equinox. The waxing light of the soul is understood here; it is a major Sabbat to initiate new witches.

The altar is set up at the North of the circle. Candle colors are pure white. The cauldron is placed in the middle with sacred herbs or weeds: rowan, apple, elder, holly, pine, cedar, juniper, poplar, dogwood.

Cast the circle as usual, admitting the eldest first, youngest last. The High Priestess purifies the circle, consecrating it with fire (incense). The four corners of the universe are invoked with the appropriate Goddess; unify to raise power.

High Priestess:

"In the olden times, the Goddess had many groves and wimmin served her freely and lived in dignity. The Goddess' presence was everywhere, and her wimmin knew her as the eternal sister. The patriarchal powers burned down her sacred groves, raped and killed her priestesses and enslaved wimmin. Her name was stricken from library books, and great darkness of ignorance descended upon womankind.

Today, there is a new dawn. We are welcoming new witches into our coven, as we strive to replant the Goddess' groves. We, the wimmin, are the grove; through us the return of the Goddess is evident. Let us give birth to each other spiritually as the Goddess brought forth the light of the world! Behold the great Goddess of the ten thousand names! Blessed be!"

o   o   o

ROSH CHODESH:
NEW MOON RITUAL OF RENEWAL

Fanchon Shur

Hanukkah is the Jewish Feast of Lights. Traditionally each month the new moon is a sign for celebration, in accordance with Israel's ancient lunar calendar.

On these new moon festival days the Hallel is sung. The specific Hallel referred to here uses the liturgy from numbers 113, 114, 116 and 117. Among the powers attributed to the god of the Hallel are the gift of fertility to childless women and the gift of light to the world. Fanchon Shur has composed a choreographic prelude to be performed with the Hallel Psalms in her effort to revive original Jewish lunar roots.

There is a yearning in our times among all people to re-kindle the awe for the wonderousness of nature. This yearning is a spiritual force emerging to help us save our very small planet.

We live by a solar calendar. We experience life in short, one day cycles. We have neglected our Jewish moon-based calendar which gives us a deeper connection with all our life cycles. Although we, like our ancestors, do not worship the moon,
we stand in awe of this creation of the ETERNAL ONE.
We notice its cycles in heaven as the clearest symbol
in nature for ALL cycles:
first and foremost for the monthly cycle of the woman,
for the tides of the great seas,
for the development of human life
in ten lunar months
and for the emotional cycles of
women and men as well.

Bonia Shur, my husband, composer, and Director of Liturgical Arts at Hebrew Union College was asked to write a HALLEL, to be sung at the New Moon. The HALLEL is designated by Psalms 113 through 118, as the ecstatic exaltation and praise to the Lord. Jewish folk tradition has kept alive the symbol of the monthly renewal of the moon as a symbol of humanity's ability to renew itself. I heard the composition grow into a 20 minute work for unison choir, male and female cantors, and orchestral ensemble. It is a personal, intimate, surging prayer, with contrasts of mood, delicacy, and depth. It is simple, and antiphonal, with responsive singing for congregation. Filled with its beauty, the words re-affirm the LORD, the MASTER, and it hungered for a feminine element. Bonia asked me to choreograph a prelude, a RITUAL of RENEWAL which would lead the congregation, through dance, into the musical HALLEL, and would tie together the feminine and masculine elements.
I created a simple dance:

The HALLEL will open with a ritualistic entrance in which Fanchon welcomes us as a congregation by offering her radiance and gathering the aliveness of our faces into her RITUAL of RENENAL.

Slowly the dancer shapes an orbiting path symbolizing the waxing and waning of the moon.

As the gravity of earth exerts its pull, so the dancer, as woman, responds, submits and descends to its center.

The transitional moment in the Ritual finds the dancer in a tight form on the floor.
The compressed life-force
bursts through her clenched fist . . .
. . . Celebration . . .
Again the dancer flows into the orbiting cycle.

Fanchon's third cycle gathers the musicians into her sensitized space,
and the mood for the HALLEL is born.

368

I have preceeded the dance with many different introductions.
For a cantorial convention in San Francisco I spoke personally,
intimately about myself as a woman and as a Jew.
When I was five years old, my mother was fifty-six
years old, and every Friday evening we went to
Synagogue, and I remember the rabbi blessing us, and
I heard the words "Lord, Him, the King," and
in my head, in the softness of my mother's bosom,
I found no comfort in the HE, or the KING, or the LORD.
I had no father,
only my mother and me;
An ache, a loneliness, an emptiness,
no He or Him . . . only a She, a HER, A WOMAN loved
me and SHE was my comfort and my strength and my salvation.
She was mother, creator, compassion and could lift
up a truck if her child were underneath.
Many years later, my life joined with a man,
an energetic, creative composer. We struggle,
we face ourselves in the mirror of our children's
growth, in the mirror of the fullness of our
individual creative vitality. We work very hard.
The liberated path is difficult for me.
And in my union with this man, I seek
(as in all aspects of my life) expression to merge
the creative energy of female and male.

    I dance this ritual to LIBERATE MYSELF WITH THE SUPPORT AND
ASSISTANCE OF YOU, THE CONGREGATION, AND TOGETHER WE ARE
CREATING A CONTEMPORARY COVENANT WITH GOD.

And the feminine shall encompass the warrior. (Jeremiah)

A cantor then reads these poetic images by Kate Hughes:

Dawn child,
my sleeping conscience,
fearless,
moving instinctively. You are hope born enfolded in the veined translucent
petals of (men's) arms, obstinate.
If I could raise you awakening
to the sea cries and to the land cries . . .
I turn the earth with my hands,
crumbling dry clods,
and plant my seed with trepidation . . .
We speak a common language in the moment of birth.
Star drops dashed on dew teared bornings,
tumble, mother earth, erode the formal ridges faulting,
Split the howling thunder warning rain on
granite avalanche and agony revealing . . .
Sculptured mornings!
QUAKE, QUAKE, THE CRACKLING SHELLS OF DAWNING!

from Layers of Life,
by Fanchon Shur

After these spoken images, I dance an unfolding and enclosing processional through the central aisle, dressed in white, silken long gown, spiraling skirt with thin green cording sewn into the spirals, spiraling through my white torso and silken sleeves, exciting one's sense of purity and freshness.

Bonia plays a xylophone, in repetitive patterns, translucent reverberating sound, delicate, pulsing, ongoing, yet restrained. After the cycling solo, the musicians move into the orbit in a floor plan of spirals, with Bonia taking the center (as conductor) of the orbit and myself joining into the grouping of musicians.

In a different presentation, a synagogue service, the Rabbi spoke to his own congregation, sharing his own feelings extracted from thoughts we had previously shared.

. . . thoughts . . . .
on the cyclical nature of our lives . . .
in the quietness, the subtlety of each moon cycle,
full of waxing and waning flow,
we recall our own emotional cycles:
loneliness,

370

searching,
encounter with Divine essence
and then loss of unity, leading again to . . .
loneliness, searching and again encounter with God . . .
or . . .
again returning to the cyclical rotations
childhood, adolescence, ripeness, death,
each lifetime,
each menstruation,
each fertilization,
we too wax and wane with the INFINITE ONE
THE SCHECHINAAH.

Tonie's ROSH CHODESH (New Moon) celebration is not a calendrical coincidence, Rather, it is a timely spiritual gift at this historical moment of Ecological
Crisis. ADAMA mother earth, given to MAN to subdue and to conquer (but never
to destroy) stands in peril. We must humble ourselves, search deeply to understand the real needs of earth, the element of the feminine within the earth and the
cosmos and re-integrate them within ourselves.
sensitivity,
kinesthetic
    In dance, we often use images of the cosmic forces, since our every motion is
governed by gravity's pull to the center of the earth, and our resilient response
releases us into our own outer spaces. No coincidence that the very moon which
affects the flow of our own blood should set one in motion.

anger,
clarity,
resolution
I come not to worship the moon, the cultic worship of an object,
but rather to worship all of nature's integrations,
effects,
designs,
majesties . . . in a new light, at a time when our earth
given to man to subdue and to conquer, is truly at the
brink of destruction . . .
for conquer we have, rape we have, . . .
I come to listen,
to revive the feminine gifts,
to weave together the feminine with the masculine

the instinctual with the rational, the
unconscious with the conscious . . .
GIVING US THE ONLY STRENGTH AVAILABLE TO US.
. . .thoughts continue . . . verbally . . .

In yet a different setting we prepare the congregation in the morning for the Ritual that same evening. Contemporary rituals, in order to create maximum involvement on a participatory level, need preparation, since most of our communities are not homogeneous bodies of people, and this format is ideal.

Bonia and I spend all morning with the congregation, preparing the actual motions in the dance with them, teaching them the chanting responses to the Hallel (in Hebrew).

I ask the congregation (dressed comfortably) to explore elements of opening-enclosing, with their own hands and arms so as to better enter my welcoming space. The HALLEL will open with a ritualistic entrance in which Fanchon welcomes us as a congregation by offering her radiance and gathering the aliveness of our faces into her RITUAL OF RENEWAL.

I enjoin the congregation to explore with me, from their seats, in diads, the cyclical changes in our life energies, as symbolized by the waxing and waning of the moon. Facing our partner, seated, we will press palm to palm, alternating strong pressure with light pressure, creating an exchange of opposite energies. We will explore our personal cycles in our spatial expression, using our own positive and negative space in relation to a partner, recalling our changing responses to the outer world (as space). Facing new partner, we shall exchange motions slowly, quickly, slowly, and heighten our sense of time in our life cycles, and shall exchange motions of bound flow and free flow, and heighten our awareness of how we respond to life cycles. We shall share as couples, in dialogue, perceptions of our own lives in their spiraling renewal, and Bonia shall take some phrases from our images and we shall chant a communal blessing offering each other our gratefulness for the privilege of experiencing life's ongoing RENEWAL.

There is an orbiting section in the dance which creates subtle shape changes in a circular spatial path about an invisible center. I will ask the congregation to experience rotation around their own center, using their head, torso, so that they can feel my spatial rotation kinesthetically. Then, they lightly hold fingers and rotate together with me. Slowly the dancer shapes an orbiting path, symbolizing the waxing and waning of the moon. As the gravity of earth exerts its pull, so the dancer, as woman, responds, submits and descends to its center . . .

We explore the energy of a closed fist; anger, contained power, spiral unfolding of each finger, cupping, releasing . . .

The transitional moment in the Ritual finds the dancer in a tight form on the floor . . .

372

The compressed life-force bursts through her clenched fist . . .

Celebration:

Again the dancer flows into the orbiting cycle. Bonia guides the congregants into chanting spontaneously, in order to free them from the traditional identification with prayer from a page in a book, so that they can empathize with the Hebrew prayer modes developed in the musical Hallel. We all create prayers together with corresponding movement to prepare us.

Fanchon's third cycle gathers the musicians into her sensitized space, and the mood for the HALLEL is born.

We respond as a community at the ending of the Hallel music, by sending sound and motion across the large room spaces, enlarging and multiplying small impulses and connecting the highly sensitized space we have created. We shall send an extended hand, or a turn of the head, or a lean from one to another, like a surge or wave, through the congregation, involving the choir, congregation, dancers.

That same evening, in the presence of the NEW MOON, the HALLEL: RITUAL OF RENEWAL begins, with a participating, prepared, anticipating congregation.

o   o   o

Through Jewish religious history the moon has served to mark all festivals and life cycles for community. Judaism, although a patriarchal faith, has fed me with great strengths and ethical values, metamorphosed by time and society and my own creative visions. Our people have given, and given the maximum, women and men, in the cause of humanity.

I fear that another twist of misplaced anti-Semitism can infuse the woman's liberation movement so as to link Judaism with patriarchy therefore with suppression.

The Nazis succeeded in linking Jews with Communism, Capitalism.

The deep seated Christian myths about the Jews have permitted twisted misplaced angers and guilts to rear up into ugly massacres, and the incredible millions of dollars today helping the terrorists with anti Israeli propaganda make me hesitate . . .

I offer my own liberated energy to my own people as they are ready to receive it and I share it with all the people in the world who are ready to accept me for what I am . . .a free, sometimes liberated, loving woman . . .and a Jew.

January 1976
Fanchon Shur
Cincinnati, Ohio

373

photos: Erika Asher

URSA MAIOR: SUMMER SOLSTICE CELEBRATION

Barbry MyOwn

Who We Are

We are a group of seven women who have been meeting weekly for three seasons to explore various forms of female spirituality. We have taken the name Ursa Maior, after the great she-bear, or big dipper, a constellation which resembles our structure in that it appears to be seven distinct stars but is actually a web of complex galaxies. Sometimes we call ourselves a coven; other times we prefer the word "circle." We know that these words are ours to demystify and define: we are what we dare to say we can be. We are a leaderless group, and we cooperate only to the extent that allows each individual full self-expression—we are not creating a theology or dogma, but acting on our feelings as we grow and change together.

We have done a lot of work together with ritual, because we know that small, repetitive acts **do** take root in our unconscious and manipulate material reality. Hence we want to be conscious of our actions and affect the material plain **positively**. After nine months, or a full gestation period together, we decided to create a ritual to share with other women. Rita, Hallie, and I prepared the following ritual which we have performed twice: once at a summer solstice for forty pagan women attending a mixed (men and women) gathering, and once for 150 women at the woman spirit festival in Oregon. We did things slightly differently each time, so the following account is a collage of both experiences. We are sharing it here in hopes that other women can use it, or parts of it, or be stimulated by it in a way which furthers their spiritual growth.

In Body and Spirit

We wanted to do a ritual about our bodies for two reasons. Politically, it is important to us to gain control of our bodies by loving them, caring for and healing them, making them strong and creating bonds of woman-love between them. Thus we need a ritual that affirms our self love, heals us, strengthens us and positively reinforces our sexuality. Spiritually, we see our bodies as divine manifestations of womanenergy. As we understand the relationships between the various parts of our bodies we begin to perceive potential patterns for relationships between separate earthly bodies and even earthly and heavenly bodies (moon, stars, planets).

As women, we have historically been associated with the "mundane" concerns of the body: we care for shit, piss, blood. Patriarchal "spirituality" has always been cerebral, sterile, divorced from such mundane concerns. The three of us felt we could not maintain the schizophrenia of drawing any more lines between "body" and "spirit," so we expanded the ritual to include a ceremony at the end integrating the energy raised by loving our bodies with the lives we live daily on the "mundane" plane.

We took this ritual to a pagan gathering, whose traditions customarily "close the circle," or return to the mundane world after ritual magick, and used the vehicle of celebrating our bodies to make the qualitative leap into celebrating the lives we live in them. Our bodies **are** the synthesis of the mundane and the spiritual: we are taking power over both aspects of ourselves.

We Are Created

We began the ritual with a birth rite. Marge and Deborah made an archway with their arms, and each woman walked through and joined the line to create half of a new arch, until a long tunnel was formed. At every pair in the tunnel, each woman was embraced, kissed, and told, "Through women you were born into this world. Through women you are born into this circle."

This ritual was conceived from childhood games like "London Bridge," which are, after all, actings-out of old mythologies. When we elevated it to a conscious ritual it gained power in our rational minds. The second time we performed it we came full circle when a girl-child participated. We all had to get down on the ground to crawl under her arms, and this returned some of our original child-connections to the birth process. We all attained a very keen physical high by holding and slowly kissing every woman present.

Next, the two lines separated into a circle, and Rita arranged an altar in the center to hold the necessary tools. Everyone placed their hands on the bellies of the women next to them, and we chanted to raise power from our second chakras. Working in Ursa Maior, most of us have found that we spend energy with all other chakras but seem to receive and generate energy most easily in our bellies.

We Raise Power

I recited a poem which is very special to me because it's the first thing I ever wrote specifically to heal with. I think there are a lot of connections between poetry and magick—the old concept of making something reality by giving a name to it—and **finally** we women are giving names to things again, because the reality that's been created under patriarchy has come from words like "kleenex," "tampax" and "zerox." Poetry is really a spell, and this poem is a heavy spell for me because I have used it successfully to cure cramps, cause periods to flow, etc. Acting with the

power raised by women who have believed and supported me in this work, I really got high and gained a new sense for words—a dance and rhythm and lilt that felt good just to say:

Belly Song

In my belly a round hole is the center of the earth.
In my belly a hole: sometimes empty; sometimes full—
This is its job: when empty to fill
When full to empty. A round hole is a sacred place
Mine to guard. I hide it jealously.
In my belly a round hole is the center of the earth.
Hey!

My belly is the earth: she grows food, she gives life.
My belly is the earth. She is mother.
My belly is a mother who refuses to birth
For why nurse one babe when there are so many?
My belly pours blood to the center of the earth
Where it changes to milky flowers. The universe
Of four-leggeds is welcome to eat these flowers.
My belly is the earth. She is a good mother.

My belly is the ocean! She ebbs, she flows.
My belly is the ocean, and I—I have swallowed
All the waters to protect them. When the two-leggeds
Who crawled out are ready to swim home . . .
Then I will let loose the tide dammed in my belly
And the world will be clean again.
Today is a good day. Today is a good day to begin.

My belly is the moon. She waxes, she wanes.
My belly is the moon—and she is beautiful!
When full she is strong!
When small she hides away in a sacred place.
I will make myself a bed of clouds and hide away
Until I can face the world again.
Today is a good day. Today is a good day to begin.

A man dies just once in his life, and barricades his grave,
And not even one flower can spring from his bones.
A woman dies with every moon, and all the universe roots
In her grave without lament. She will come back,
Bigger than life, and rise again in the evening sky . . .

My belly is a round hole and a sacred place.
Today is a good day. Today is a good day. Today is a good day.
Today is a good day to begin. Today is a good day to begin.
Today is good. To begin today is good. To begin today
is good, is good, is good . . .

We took the power raised in our bellies and danced with it as Rita taught us:
8 steps into the center, 8 steps back.
5 steps into the center, 5 steps back.
3 steps into the center, 3 steps back.
8 to the left. 8 to the right.

We repeated this 9 times: slow, faster, slowing again, accompanied by making woman noises:

waking	working noises	lovemaking noises
eating noises	fighting noises	birthing noises
playing noises	laughing noises	quiet noises

The Power Grows

Rita then read us part of a poem by Carol Erdman, which was printed in the Volume I, No. 2, Winter Solstice issue of WomanSpirit:

There is power in the blood of the women.
Long ago, when we knew our full power,
We set apart our warrior before battle;
We set apart our priestess at her task;
We set apart the women when the moon of their
   nature was full and overflowed into darkness.

There is power in the blood that transforms us.
The blood of men is pain,
The blood of men is suffering,
The blood of men is death.

There is power in the blood of the women.
There is power in the blood that transforms us.
There is power in the song of our blood.

This is the song of our blood.
This is the song of the blood in our veins;
This is the song of our blood contained;
This is the song of our blood transforming.

This is the material of our craft.
As our potter takes her clay,
As our athlete takes her muscle and sinew,
As our poet takes her words,
As our carpenter takes her wood,
As our weaver takes her yarn,
As our teacher takes her experience,
So our mother takes her blood;
With her blood she makes babies,
With her blood she makes milk.

This is the blood that promises renewal,
This is the blood that promises sustenance,
This is the blood that promises life.

. . . Hallie and I took a cup full of dark, heavy smelling woman blood and went around the circle, dipping our hands in it, painting each woman's face, saying: "This is the blood that promises renewal. This is the blood that promises sustenance. This is the blood that promises life."

Every month for ten years I have bled. I have seen, touched and tasted my blood, felt the pulling in my belly. But never has it looked so dark, smelled so strong, felt so thick. Never has it pulled my belly so insistently as when Hallie's eyes held mine and we painted each other's faces. The sky was dark, as blood. The entire meadow smelled as blood. My feet danced in the remaining blood we poured on the ground. My belly signalled me, letting me know that before the full moon set, I, again, would bleed with my sisters.

A circle of painted warrior women, we sang our song of strength:

·····SONG FOR OUR BODIES·····

Verses 1-3

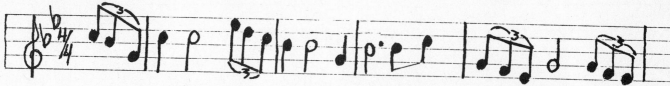

You--once had---a-----body as strong as the trees do--you

once had a --------body---as healthy as the trees do. You

once had a--body as happy as the trees do and they tried, they

tried so hard to take it from you.

2.

You once had a body as pure as the trees do.
"   "   "   "   "   as proud as the trees do.
"   "   "   "   "   as free as the trees do.
And they tried, they tried so hard to take it from you.*

3.

They made the sky dirty so the air couldn't breathe for you.
they made the earth dirty so the fields couldn't feed you.
They made the ocean dirty so the water couldn't clean you.
And they tried, they tried so hard to take it from you.

*Use any adjectives you want to--it's your body!

382

Verses 4-6..(cut time)

We are making our   the air's   breathe
sky clean   gonna   for us, we are

making our   the fields gonna feed
ground clean   are   us, we are

making the ocean the water's gonna clean
clean   us, we are

making our bodies clean
our bodies' gonna be for us!

5.

You've got a body as strong as the trees do.
  "   " " " as healthy as the trees do.
  "   " " " as happy as the trees do.
It's yours--it's all for you--It's all for you!

6.

You've got a body as proud as the trees do.
  "   " " " as pure as the trees do.
  "   " " " as free as the trees do.
It's yours--it's all for you--it's all for you!

We Become Form

The power has been raised— it is time to invoke the Goddess. We have not defined "Goddess," except in the loose terms, "woman energy." We hope to invoke a materialization of that woman energy, to love it, play with it, exalt in it. I say, the invocation:
The Women gather to invoke the Goddess.
The women gather in a circle and speak Her name.
The women call the Lady out of darkness and give to
    Her a shape they recognize.
The women gather in a circle. With their words they
    give the Lady form.

The women name the Goddess with their own names.
The women shape the Goddess with their own forms.
The women gather in a circle and give names to their own forms.
The women come out of the darkness in shapes they recognize
    and call by name.

Once the world was full of the Goddess.
Everyone spoke Her name, until those who were fearful
    called it a holy secret.
When Her names went unlearned
Her body went unformed.
The Lady went off into darkness in unrecognizable form
O! Weep for the Lady who has no form
And bring Her out of darkness!

Say: We will speak of the Goddess out loud!
(All: We will speak of the Goddess out loud!)
We are not afraid to say her name.
Say: We will call out a form for the Goddess!
(All: We will call out a form for the Goddess!)
We are not ashamed to name her form.
The women call the Lady out of the darkness a bit at a time, saying:
    "Here are Her legs, Her calf muscles, Her thighs;
    Here are buttocks, belly and breasts.
    Here are Her arms, Her neck, Her face, Her throat;
    Here is hair for Her legs, for Her labia.
    Here are the clitoris, nipples,

Here are tongue and teeth.
Here are all the parts of the Goddess.
Here stands the Lady in recognizable form."

The women say:
"We are not fearful!
We are not ashamed!
Her names are holy, but they are no secret.
Today we call the Lady into our circle with loud names.
We call Her flesh.
We say, belly, thigh, nipple, clit, womb, genital."

Today we call the Lady Woman!
Today we give the Woman form!

The materialization of the Lady is the clearest vision I have yet seen of Her: 150 women, painted with blood, holding each other, full moon in the valley. The three of us take turns in the circle, gazing into each woman's eyes, being compelled to touch a part of her body, saying,
"Here are the breasts of the Goddess, which delight her lovers.
Here is the hollow of Her throat, a quiet Voice.
Here are her ovaries, like clusters of pomegranate seeds.
Here are the eyes of the Goddess in which the world reflects . . ."
and so on. For the first time I really **feel** what it means to be part of an organism. As one woman's arms can lift mail sacks, by extension, so can mine. As one woman's feet can dance, so do mine. As one woman's body loves another, so does mine. Hallie chants:
"We see with these eyes,
We walk with these feet,
We create with these hands.
We see who we are and what is.
We walk where we need to go,
We do what needs to be done.

We see with these eyes,
We walk with these feet,
We heal with these hands.
We see who we are and what is,
We walk where we need to go,
We heal ourselves, our sisters, and the world.

We see with these eyes,
We dance with these feet,
We build with these hands.
We see ourselves, and the truth,
We dance to the tune of our bodies,
We build the worlds we want to share."

Never Ending

Hallie picks up a ball or red yarn, and says:
"As women have always woven, so we weave this yarn
    into the circle of our lives.
As women have always woven time and the fates, so
    let us weave this yarn into the
    circle of our lives.
As women have woven the seeds with the earth,
    so let us weave this yarn into the
    circle of our lives.
As women have always woven baskets and tools,
    so let us weave this yarn into the
    circle of our lives.
As women have always woven threads into clothing
  and shelter,
    so let us weave this yarn into the
    circle of our lives.
As women have always woven words into poetry,
    so let us weave this yarn into the
    circle of our lives.
As women have always woven, so we weave this yarn
with the Goddess who is here with us.
The Goddess is always with us.
As each woman weaves the yarn around the woman
next to her, let her call on the Goddess to be with
her in her daily life. Let us all answer,
"Goddess be with us."

She passes the yarn around the circle, in and out, until we are all woven
together, swaying, nurtured by the same umbilical cord, tied by the same blood
lines to the same mother, same sisters. Each woman contributes:

  "When I wait in line at the supermarket . . ."
  "When I defend myself against a rapist . . ."
  "When I work on my car . . ."
  "When I feed my children . . ."
  "When I get busted . . ."

All of us saying, "Goddess be with us. Goddess be with us . . ."

Hallie's voice is so reasonable, so calm, even though I feel her vibrating, feel a pulsing in the yarn that connects her to me. She says, "We gather here when the moon is full in her promise and
   manifestation of the growth of womanenergy on the earth.
We call on the Goddess whose body we see and feel reflected
   in our own bodies.
We call on the Goddess whose blood, like our blood, flows
   with the cycles of the universe.
We call on the Goddess whose circle is never broken,
   whose circle we are a part of wherever we go.
Today we do not break this circle but each of us carries a
   part of it with her into the world.
THE CIRCLE IS NEVER BROKEN."

Rita and I move around the circle. I will not use a knife for an athame, but I have a little pair of golden scissors shaped like a bird. We cut the yarn, tie a piece around each woman's throat, waist or wrist. We kiss . . . blessed be . . .blessed be . . . blessed be.

This is the first ritual I have ever attended where there is not a great deal of confusion about whether the circle has been properly broken before we start feasting—no one asks "May I leave the circle?" We feast, we come and go. This is not a doctrine, not a church service one must be excused from. The next time we do the ritual, there are so many women it is long, some get impatient, but we are learning. Our lives are not separated into time for work, time for ritual. It is one circle, never broken. Our lives are one ritual, lasting all night, lasting all week, lasting all year . . . we are one circle, never broken. But we are free to come . . . and go . . . and come . . . and go . . . and come . . .

From Hallie

Creating a ritual may sound awesome, but for us, we did it trusting that time and growth and our cooperative energy would take care of the birth. That trust and energy was just as much at work when we gathered on the land. Forty women, dressed in robes and feathers and flowers, cut-off jeans, women in their own naked skin, women in leather leggings and gauze and T-shirts. We were all born into our circle.

When each of us bore the mark on her face of the blood we have been taught to be ashamed of, the mark of the blood we have reclaimed, of the blood we are proud of, of the blood that we share, I looked around the circle, and saw us all with our red marks on our foreheads, saw us all with our hands clasped in a continuous cycle of energy. I felt very quietly, very surely, that we were touching souls with our foremothers in other times and other lands, women who knew the value of our moonblood. They knew, as we were remembering, how our monthly blood shows us the secrets of the rhythms of healing, of growing, of living.

And to show how little we understood the process consciously, yet how much we know with our whole selves, Linda remembered a dream she had had half a year ago, when we first started meeting, when we knew little about rituals, and had no idea where we were going: we were just a class that had been meeting for a while and enjoying each other.

I had had to come up to the ritual a day late. When I arrived even later than I was expected, with people worried about me and looking for me, I had on a beautiful, horse-head T-shirt my friend Chellis had given me for **her** birthday. I was so attached to it, loving its recollection of my own childhood with horses, and its visionary Amazon quality, that I didn't change into the long white dress I'd brought for the ritual. And now, hours later, as everyone was about to leave, Linda of our Ursa Maior group, rushed over to me:

"Hallie! I just remembered this dream I had months ago, when we were first meeting!"

What could she be so excited about? And why is she telling me about it? I wondered. But not for long.

"I dreamed," Linda said, her brown eyes glowing and her long sybil hair hanging round her, "I dreamed that we did a ritual. And the signal for the ritual to begin was the appearance of a horse's head. And now we've been waiting for you all this time, before we could do the ritual, and you arrive with a picture of a horse's head on your breast!"

The past and the future are here with us now in the present. And so are we all together. All women, all times, all places.

—Hallie Mountain Wing, 1975

388

Indian Love Letter

Lady of the crescent moon
tonight I look at the sky
You are not there
you are not mad at me, are you?
"You are angry at the people,
Yes. I know."
  they are changing
  be not too hard
If you were taken
  to the mission school,
not because you wanted,
but someone thought it best for you
you too would change.

They came out of nowhere
telling us how to eat our food
how to build our homes
how to plant our crops.
Need I say more of what they did?
All is new—the old ways are nothing.
  they are changing
  be not too hard.

I talk to them
they turn their heads.
Do not be hurt—you have me
I live by the old ways
I will not change.

Tonight—my prayer plumes in hand
with the white shell things—
to the silent place I will go
(It is for you I go, please be there.)
Oh! Lady of the crescent moon
with the corn-silk hair—I love you
  they are changing
  be not too hard.

—Soge Track, 1969

MELLO RYE

Mello Rye, of Cherokee, Scottish and Irish descent, was born near the Cherokee part of the Indian Strip in Arkansas. At three years of age she was studying in the Bear Clan in the Cherokee tribe. The Bear Clan deals with the earth, healing, the Right Path.

From Red Fox of the Oglala Sioux, her last physical teacher, she learned how to use our racially mixed bloods as keys to connecting the world. She gives classes and takes groups on camping trips to learn Survival on Seven Planes. Her teachings are from the Sun Temple of the higher sciences. It is not sun worship, but the path of heading into the light, the source, personified by the sun's light, the Great Sun. Her group, **Mother's Garden**, channels energy for the Sciences of the Rings, for knowing what's coming ahead, for living with the cycles of the ages, for uniting spiritually no matter what our various religious taboos are.

Dedication in the Temple of the Sun goes in degrees. Mellow is a Sun Priestess. Holding a high Sun degree means to be alive to your people and to put all other things aside. Your main purpose in life is to carry the Light. Priests and priestesses of the Sun and Moon transcend tribal divisions and travel over North and South America, exchanging knowledge and uniting the people. They consider themselves part of other such knowledge spreaders the world over. Sun and Moon priestesses and priests do not enter into war.

It is the particular duty and trust of the Hopi people to preserve the Sciences of the Stars. The moon is seen as having to do with energies of the mind as it influences earth and the elemental fields of spirit entities. In February, 1974, it was noted that the constellation of the Turtle came over the United States again for the first time in 12,000 years. This constellation is called the Lyre in modern astronomy. It marks the dawn of a new age and a particular chance for humankind to sing with the singing stars, to wake up and come in tune with the rest of the universe.

Interview with Mello Rye
by Crystal Vision and Ebon Nether

Amid the raucous cries of outraged parrots, the barking of overly protective dogs and the purring of several contented cats, sat an elderly woman with twinkling eyes. Half Cherokee and half Scotch-Irish she talked casually of Magik and discussions with Isis, and walking on burning coals in Hawaii—"Well, it was not big thing. I was perfectly safe between the other two auras." This casual manner comes from a lifetime involvement with spritituality. And to hear Isis quoted in Mello's Arkansas twang is a treat indeed. Just to know this woman is a unique experience.

WHAT DOES IT MEAN THAT YOU ARE A SUN PRIESTESS?

It means that you know where you're going. You are pleased with where you're going. You are completely satisfied with yourself. You know why you're living, what you're supposed to do. When you came here, where you've been in the past. When you're gonna pass over and when you're coming back and what you're gonna do in your next lifetime. You as a Sun Person are involved in carrying the light of the sun which is only a symbol of the great light. It means your total involvement is to carry that light and shine that light wherever you may be, regardless of what circumstances you may come into. You find that the physical world really doesn't make much influence on you. You learn that you live in chemicals but you're supposed to know enough to handle it.

WHAT IS MAGIK?

Science. Science all the way. Listen to the phonetic sound of magik—ma. . .gik. That means that the lower science of the earth is going into action. There are different degrees of magik. The laws of the application of the sciences are studied and they are applied to produce a certain condition and effect.

ARE THERE GUIDELINES YOU CAN OFFER THOSE WHO ARE INTERESTED IN MAGIK?

Don't forget that magik is very heavy where the law of freedom is the first law. So you've got to remember this law of freedom in every plane of existence, in all associations with people, or all other life. On any of the planes, freedom is the first law. And if you remember the law of freedom you're not going to try to manipulate anybody else, or power structure anyone else 'cause the person who becomes knowledgeable under that law, they're applicable under that law. If you decide to use it wrongly then you're the first one who's gonna have their freedom chained up.

HOW DO WE AS WOMEN CONNECT WITH THE EARTH AND THE MOON?

The earth is only the mother of your chemical body. The body evolves from the

392

earth, from the plants, from the animals, it's a constant cycle. But it only shapes itself by the mind. And Diana or any of the other moon mothers is the mother of the mind. The earth gave us this flesh we live in. The fire that is in us is the sun, our mind is the moon.

DO YOU THINK DRASTIC CHANGE IS GOING TO COME ABOUT ON EARTH?

I don't think it's slow. I think it's very rapid and we're right in the middle of it, I just think enough people don't get involved and they don't wander around enough to see it. Any time that you see disturbances building up within a nation you'd better believe the changes came first. In the light I mean. Don't forget the light doesn't always bring what the world thinks of as peace. It's here now and it's very rapid and the need is very great that more and more people bring themselves together to form what I, when speaking to the native peoples, call campfires.

WHAT HAS BEEN YOUR INVOLVEMENT WITH THE GODDESS ISIS?

I have followed Isis from the white side of my blood to many, many continents and nations. And I have been fortunate to reach back and gather some of that material. I've followed Isis through Africa, I've followed Isis through Egypt, I've followed Isis through South America and now back to North America to help bring back the old knowledge and pool it into one pool. They are the wisdoms of the ancient people that have been scattered. Now is the time to bring them together. My next trip through the physical world will be back to Africa again because Isis will be returning to the people there in my next reincarnation. To us of the ancient people the word Isis means SHE and we know She has been born many times but came through in initiations when the time came that the person had developed their understanding enough that She came to dwell absolutely in their bodies and direct the action.

HOW DO YOU SEE WOMEN AT THIS TIME OF EVOLVEMENT?

Well, I see women now coming out and being the major factor in the structure of building a new world. We have to have a new world. We have to have new positions, new systems to work with, new tools to work with, actually new elements and new chemicals, and I see women having to foot most of this on all planes. Women have a great deal of power and they can bring the world into a better condition and into a better understanding. And they can stop wars. They can stop wars right now!

DO YOU THINK THAT THERE WILL BE ONE LEADER EMERGING?

I think that a number of people will emerge as leaders because I see the women coming up and they are in many frames of mind yet. It's like looking at a field of flowers and there are some here of one color, some here of another, some here of another; some are annuals, some produce their own seed and come up. They are different and they are growing in different fields and I see leaders coming up in all these different fields. Now they will have to get together eventually. I see that you will make some mistakes in some of the leaders that you are trying to put into politics.

DO YOU SEE ANY IMPORTANCE IN THE GEOGRAPHICAL LOCATION OF OREGON FOR WOMEN?
Isis came in a long time ago when we was rebuilding the ancient encyclopedias and so on and she kept on this Oregon trip. I kept asking Her, "Well, what is up there?" And She said the main thing up there is a cave with a piece of jade that was used at the time when they used to put personalities into temple altar pieces about 30,000 years ago.

DO YOU HAVE ANY ADVICE FOR WOMEN WHO ARE SEEKING THEIR SPIRITUAL ROOTS?
Well yes. I would but it's so old that I don't know. One of the oldest advices I can give and the truest is to know yourself first. And then look at the rest of the world. Because you're gonna see the rest of the world in the visions of your own eyes, and when you find things you don't like in other people believe me you've got them. So if you can, learn to know yourself and don't care what the rest of the world thinks. You can change yourself but don't let nobody else tell you how to change yourself. And remember that you are the I AM.

Mello can be reached at the following address: Mello Rye, Mother's Garden, P.O. Box 2265, El Cajon, California.

Moon Dance Ritual

This is a moon dance ritual. It originated from the ancient Dinaans, or people of Diana, or those we call today Native Americans. Because it is a request to the spirits for power, before beginning the ritual everyone should verbally decide what the energy being built is to be used for.

When we determine to do a Ritual, we knowingly become the instrument that joins and brings together all the Planes of Heavens and Earth, even the Nadors, those Planes directly beneath us. We are the conductors for all the energies we would invoke to our Plane of existence.

Our feet touch Mother Earth with reverence. Our mind knows and instructs our feet of the true feel that each time we step to touch the Earth it is to kiss with love our Mother Earth, the giver and supplier of our chemical bodies. Then soon we feel the earth respond and reach to us with a loving embrace.

We become like the tuning fork, the lightning rod allowing free flowing of energies. The flame in us rises to reach our hands, and we raise our hands high, turning the palms of our hands and inner tips of our fingers to the four Directions. We touch the Earth and reach to the Sky, in that all over embrace of Love and light. So in elemental action we direction the flowing of Love between Those and us—until we become a Blazing-Burning Rod of energy. We Send, Receive, Turn and Return again and again this Blazing Fire of Love from Earth through us, up into all the Planes and Dimensions, returning then again and again into the Earth Plane, through and with Her many children—US.

After several circling dances in this state of mind, then we are really ready to share love and to communicate with HER.

photos by a Rainbow Warrior of the Sun

Build fire, join in circle, clasp hands. Move to the right seven times chanting:

AH-WA-DEA-HA! (call to EARTHSPIRITS)
LEADER: I declare this circle to be closed and the world's reality excluded!
ALL: (three times) GODDESS OF A THOUSAND NAMES, ATTEND US!
   (Pause for short meditation)
LEADER: I invite the SKY SPIRITS to dance with me! (arms raised)
ALL: (three times) GODDESS OF A THOUSAND NAMES, ATTEND US!
LEADER: I invite the EARTH SPIRITS to dance with me! (arms lowered)
ALL: (three times) GODDESS OF A THOUSAND NAMES, ATTEND US!
LEADER: SEE us FRIENDLY SPIRITS!
ALL: (three times) GODDESS OF A THOUSAND NAMES, ATTEND US!
LEADER: HEAR us FRIENDLY SPIRITS!
ALL: (three times) GODDESS OF A THOUSAND NAMES, ATTEND US!
LEADER: Wimmin, the ANCIENT ONES come in power!
ALL: We SEE them come in power to/for (instant request) . . .
LEADER: Wimmin, they come among us in power!
ALL: We SEE them come in power (to/for . . .). . .
LEADER: Wimmin, they are HERE in power!
ALL: We SEE THEY ARE HERE IN POWER (to/for. . .). . .
(WITH MUCH FEELING!) ALL: The SKY SPIRITS love me!
                               The EARTH SPIRITS love me!
                               ALL LIFE loves me!
                               And I love me!
(At this time do an invocation for needs, healing or a statement to GODDESS, or drink pine tea, etc . . .)
CIRCLING TO THE LEFT, CHANT:
ALL: LOVING SPIRITS COME SING IN OUR SONG!
   LOVING SPIRITS COME DANCE IN OUR DANCE!
   LOVING SPIRITS COME SHINE IN OUR LIGHT!
   LOVING SPIRITS COME FLOW IN OUR THOUGHTS!
   LOVING SPIRITS COME LAUGH IN OUR JOY!
   LOVING SPIRITS COME BURN IN OUR FIRE!
   LOVING SPIRITS COME GLOW IN OUR SPLENDOR!
   THE CIRCLE IS NOW OPEN.
(Holding hands, or hands raised high with palms toward each other, we chant:)
It is done in togetherness—
It is finished in togetherness—
For we have said it in togetherness—
AND IT IS SO!

Because of this placing of Positive Action in the hands of the instruments, we in the Sun Degree do not open and close circles in the verbal way of the Moon Degrees, but in absolute togetherness, at the end of the ritual, in the most important part, we affirm and chant that we have said it in togetherness, And IT IS SO!

totem for bringing down the moon

VISIONS

Monique Wittig

Monique Wittig is a French writer who has created beautiful visionary literature out of her experience of women's culture. These excerpts are from two of her books, LES GUERILLERES and LESBIAN BODY, both available in English.[30]

On the hillside the women do round dances in the evening. Often and often I look at them without daring to approach. I know them all by their names from having studied them in the library books. I list their attributes, I consider their bearing, I am not sorry that their severity should have remained attached to the books since they are here before m/e so totally devoid of it. M/y heart beats at times when I see you among them m/y best beloved m/y unnameable one you whom I desire from the bottom of m/y stomach shall never die. I watch you holding the hand of Artemis laced in leather over her bare breasts then that of Aphrodite, the black goddess with the flat belly. There is also the triple Persephone, there is sunheaded Ishtar, there is Albina eldest of the Danaids, there is Epone the great horsewoman, there is Leucippa whose mare runs in the meadow below white and shining, there is dark Isis, there is red Hecate, there are Pomona and Flora holding each other by the hand, there is Andromeda of the fleet foot, there is blonde Cybele, there is Io with the white cow, there are Niobe and Latone intertwined, there is Sappho of the violet breasts, there is Gurinno the swift runner, there is Ceres with the corn in her hair, there is white Leucothea, there is moon-headed Rhamnusis, you all dance, you all beat the ground with the soles of your feet with increasing force. None seems fatigued, while Minerva the daughter of Zeyna blows her flute and Attis beloved of Sappho beats the tom-tom. If amongst all of them you are the only one to perspire it bedecks you m/y unique one, their complaisant fingers touch you, then you shine with many fires, rays leave your body descending to the ground, hammered for the nth time. I am troubled to see

398

you at your ease among the women eyes shining loins twisted by spasms your pelvis thrust forward in the rhythm of the dance. Amicably you share the sacred mushroom, each one bites the edge of the cap, no one asks to become bigger or smaller. At a sign from blessed Aphrodite all around you exchange their colours. Leucothea becomes the black one, Demeter the white, Isis the fair one, Io the red, Artemis the green, Sappho the golden, Persephone the violet, the transformations spread from one to the other, the rainbow of the prism passes across their faces while you unchanging in the chestnut colour of your hair you start to cry out while I regard you in your great ecstasy though deprived of the sacred mushroom awaiting you in the laurels with their hidden flower and you come near m/e at one moment or another.

o   o   o

There are there Elsa Brauer Julie Brunele Odile Roques Evelyn Sabir. They stand before the great gathering of women. Elsa Brauer strikes the cymbals one against the other when she stops speaking, while Julie Brunele Odile Roques Evelyn Sabir accompany her with long rolls on their drums. Elsa Brauer says something like, There was a time when you were not a slave, remember that. You walked alone, full of laughter, you bathed bare-bellied. You say you have lost all recollection of it, remember. The wild roses flower in the woods. Your hand is torn on the bushes gathering the mulberries and strawberries you refresh yourself with. You run to catch the young hares that you flay with stones from the rocks to cut them up and eat all hot and bleeding. You know how to avoid meeting a bear on the track. You know the winter fear when you hear the wolves gathering. But you can remain seated for hours in the tree-tops to await morning. You say there are no words to describe this time, you say it does not exist. But remember. Make an effort to remember. Or, failing that, invent.

o   o   o

The golden fleece is one of the designations that have been given to the hairs that cover the pubis. As for the quests for the golden fleece to which certain ancient myths allude, the women say they know little of these. They say that the horseshoe which is a representation of the vulva has long been considered a lucky charm. They say that the most ancient figures depicting the vulva resemble horsehoes. They say that in fact it is in such a shape that they are represented on the walls of palaeolithic grottos.

The women say that the feminaries give pride of place to the symbols of the circle, the circumference, the ring, the O, the zero, the sphere. They say that this series of symbols has provided them with a guideline to decipher a collection of legends they have found in the library and which they have called the cycle of the Grail. These are to do with the quests to recover the Grail undertaken by a number of personages. They say it is impossible to mistake the symbolism of the Round Table that dominated their meetings. They say that, at the period when the texts were compiled, the quests for the Grail were singular unique attempts to describe the zero the circle the ring the spherical cup containing the blood. They say that, to judge by what they know about their subsequent history, the quests for the Grail were not successful, that they remained of the nature of a legend.

○   ○   ○

The women say, unhappy one, men have expelled you from the world of symbols and yet they have given you names, they have called you slave, you unhappy slave. Masters, they have exercised their rights as masters . . . The women say, the language you speak poisons your glottis tongue palate lips. They say, the language you speak is made up of words that are killing you. They say, the language you speak is made up of signs that rightly speaking designate what men have appropriated. Whatever they have not laid hands on, whatever they have not pounced on like many-eyed birds of prey, does not appear in the language you speak. This is apparent precisely in the intervals that your masters have not been able to fill with their words of proprietors and possessors, this can be found in the gaps, in all that which is not a continuation of their discourse, in the zero, the O, the perfect circle that you invent to imprison them and to overthrow them.

○   ○   ○

They speak together of the threat they have constituted towards authority, they tell how they were burned on pyres to prevent them from assembling in future. They were able to command tempests, to sink fleets, to destroy armies. They have been mistresses of poisons, of the winds, of the will. They were able to exercise their powers at will and to transform all kinds of persons into mere animals, geese pigs birds turtles. They have ruled over life and death. Their conjoint power has menaced hierarchies systems of government authorities. Their knowledge has competed successfully with the official knowledge to which they had no access, it has challenged it, found it wanting, threatened it, made it appear inefficacious. No police were powerful enough to track them down, no paid informer so opportunist, no torture so brutal, no army so overwhelming as to attack them one by one and destroy them. Then they chant the famous song that begins, Despite all the evils they wished to crush me with/I remain as steady as the three-legged cauldron.

o o o

The women say that they perceive their bodies in their entirety. They say that they do not favour any of its parts on the grounds that it was formerly a forbidden object. They say that they do not want to become prisoners of their own ideology. They say that they did not garner and develop the symbols that were necessary to them at an earlier period to demonstrate their strength. For example they do not compare the vulvas to the sun moon stars. They do not say that the vulvas are like black suns in the shining night.

The women say that it may be that the feminaries have fulfilled their function. They say they have no means of knowing. They say that thoroughly indoctrinated as they are with ancient texts no longer to hand, these seem to them outdated. All they can do to avoid being encumbered with useless knowledge is to heap them up in the squares and set fire to them. That would be an excuse for celebrations.

"ALL ABOARD FOR THE MOON!"

REFERENCES

BOOKS AND CHARTS

Almanacs and Calendars

MOON SIGN BOOK, Box 3383-AC, St. Paul, Minn. 55165— $2.95 (New yearly).

THE DAILY PLANET ALMANAC, Pacific High School, John Muir Press, 1976.

I CHING TAOIST BOOK OF DAYS, 1976, Year of the Dragon, Ballantine.

SISTER HEATHENSPINSTER'S ALMANAC AND LUNATION CALENDAR, Michelle Brody, Box 111, Marquette, Iowa 52158 ($2.00).

PAGAN-CRAFT CALENDAR, Aidan Kelly, Hierophant Wordsmiths, 468 Hanover Street, Oakland, Ca 94606.

Magazines and Journals

WOMANSPIRIT QUARTERLY, Box 263, Wolf Creek, Oregon 97497 ($2.00 single issue; $6.00 per year).

QUEST FEMINIST QUARTERLY, 1909 Que St., N.W., Washington, D.C. 20009 ($7.00 per year).

Photos, Records, Etc.

ASTRONOMICAL PHOTOGRAPHS CATALOG, Lick Observatory, Univ. of California, Santa Cruz, Santa Cruz, Ca. 95064.

PUBLIC AFFAIRS OFFICER, Johnson Space Center, NASA, Houston, Texas (for moon photos).

MOON CIRCLES, Kay Gardner (songs and beautiful music), Olivia Records, Box 70237, Los Angeles, Ca. 90070.

DER MOND, Carl Orff, Phillips Records.

Moon Maps

I found some good maps on the moon available through the mail. The most informative came from the National Geographic Society Headquarters, 17th and M Streets, N.W.; Washington, D.C. 20036. It has a map of the near and far sides as well as more diagrams and explanations. It is about 2½' high by 3½' long. It is about $2.00. It is only available to individuals, not for resale.

Rand McNally & Co., 39 South La Salle Street, Chicago, Illinois 60603, prints a beautiful 4½' square color map of the moon's near side. It is about $4.00.

The Department of the Interior U.S. Geological Survey has prepared a geologic colored map of the near side of the moon. It is published by the U.S. Geological Survey, Washington, D.C. 20242.

Meredith Corp. makes a Globe of the Moon with a diameter of about 7".

Science

MOON: MAN'S GREATEST ADVENTURE; Davis Thomas, ed.; Abrams Books.

BODY TIME, Gay Gaer Luce, Pantheon.

THE FIELDS OF LIFE, Dr. Harold S. Burr, Ballantine, 1972.

COSMIC CLOCKS, Michel Gauquelin, Regnery, 1967.

HEALTH AND LIGHT, John Ott, Devin-Adair Co., Conn.

CELESTIAL OBJECTS FOR COMMON TELESCOPES, T. Webb, Dover, Vol. I, 1962.

FIELD GUIDE TO THE STARS AND PLANETS, Menzel, Houghton Mifflin, 1964.

Mythology, Anthropology and Politics

THE PHILOSOPHY OF CAMPASSION: THE RETURN OF THE GODDESS: Esme Wynne-Tyson, Vincent Stuart, 1962.

TOWARD A RECOGNITION OF ANDROGYNY, Carolyn Heilbrun, Harper Colophon, 1973.

ECSTATIC RELIGION, I. Lewis, Pelican, 1971.

RITES AND SYMBOLS OF INITIATION, Mircea Eliade, Harper Torchbooks.

THE WHITE GODDESS, Robert Graves, Noonday, 1973.

SEASONAL OCCULT RITUALS, William Gray, Aquarian Press, 1970.

WOMAN'S MYSTERIES, M. Esther Harding, Putnam, 1971.

MYTH, RELIGION AND MOTHER RIGHT, J. J. Bachofen, Bollingen Books, 1973.

DICTIONARY OF SYMBOLS, J. E. Cirlot, Philosophical Library, 1962.

SEVEN ARROWS, H. Storm, Ballantine, 1972.

THE FEMINIST BOOK OF LIGHTS AND SHADOWS, Z. Budapest, The Feminist Wicca, 442 Lincoln Blvd. Venice, Ca. 90291.

MEXICO MYSTIQUE: THE COMING WORLD OF CONSCIOUSNESS, Frank Waters, Swallow Press, cloth.

THE ANCIENT BLACK CHRISTIANS, Julian Richardson Associates, 540 McAllister Street, San Francisco, Ca. 94102 ($1.00).

L'ENIGME DES VIERGES NOIRES, Jaques Huynen, Laffont Publications, France.

BENEATH THE MOON AND UNDER THE SUN, Tony Shearer, Sun Books, $12.50.

THE ROOTS OF CIVILIZATION, Alexander Marshack, McGraw Hill, 1972.

MOTHERS AND AMAZONS, Helen Diner, Julian Press, 1965.

INTRODUCTION TO ENGELS: THE ORIGIN OF THE FAMILY, PRIVATE PROPERTY AND THE STATE; Eleanor Leacock, International Publishers, 1972, N.Y.

THE SECOND SEX, Simone de Beauvoir, Bantam, 1961.

THE DIALECTIC OF SEX, Shulamith Firestone, Bantam.

PRISONERS OF LIBERATION, Allyn and Adele Rickett, Anchor-Doubleday, 1973.

THE FEAR OF WOMEN, Wolfgang Lederer, Harvest Books, 1968.

CELTIC DRUIDS, Godfrey Higgins, England, 1827.

THE MOTHERS, Robert Briffault, George Allen & Unwin, 1959.

THE DAWN OF ASTRONOMY, A study of the Temple Worship and Mythology of the Ancient Egyptians; J. Norman Lockyer M.I.T. Press 1964, (First publ 1894).

THE HEBREW GODDESS, Raphael Patai, Ktav Pub. Co., 1967.

PUBERTY RITES AND THE ENVIOUS MALE, B. Bettelheim, Collier Books, 1962.

WITCHES, MIDWIVES AND NURSES; Ehrenreich and English, Feminist Press, 1973.

FEMINISM AS THERAPY, Mander and Rush, Random House/Bookworks, 1974.

THE GRAIL LEGEND, Emma Jung and Marie-Louise Von Franz, Putnam, 1970.

THE GREAT MOTHER, Erich Neumann, Pantheon, 1955.

THE GOLDEN BOUGH, Frazer, Macmillan.

Children's Books
THE MOON IN FACT AND FANCY, Alfred Slote, World Publishers, 1967.

FULL MOONS: INDIAN LEGENDS OF THE SEASONS, Lillian Budd, Rand McNally.

MOON OF THREE RINGS, Andre Norton, Viking.

CALENDAR MOON, Natalia Belting; Holt, Rinehart, Winston.

THE MOON JUMPERS, Janice Udry, Harper, 1959.

GOODNIGHT MOON; Margaret Brown, Harper and Row, 1947.

THE MOONSTONE, Wilkie Collins, Doubleday, 1946.

MOON MOUSE, Adelaide Holl, Pinwheel Books, 1973.

WAIT TILL THE MOON IS FULL, Margaret W. Brown, Harper Brothers, 1948.

SKYWORLD WOMAN: LE MUJER DEL MUNDO-CIELO, Rohmer & Anchondo, Children's Book Press, 1975; a bi-lingual Spanish-English goddess story.

Art and Literature
THROUGH THE FLOWER, Judy Chicago.

DRACULA, Bram Stoker, Signet.

LES GUERILLERES, Monique Wittig, Avon-Bard, 1973.

"OF MIST AND GRASS, AND SAND"; Story by Vonda McIntyre, in WOMEN OF WONDER, Vintage, 1975.

GEORGIA O'KEEFFE, Goodrich and Bry, Whitney Museum, N.Y., 1970.

SYMBOLS, SIGNS AND SIGNETS; Lehner, Dover, 1950.

THE MASTER OF MARY OF BURGUNDY, A BOOK OF HOURS; George Braziller Books, N.Y., 1970.

LEONOR FINI, La Guilde du Livre, Switzerland, text by Jelenski.

NOTES

1. WOMAN'S MYSTERIES, by M. Ester Harding, copyright © 1973 by The C. G. Jung Foundation for Analytical Psychology. Reprinted by permission of G. P. Putnam's Sons.

2, 3. FATHERS AND MOTHERS, "The Moon and Matriarchal Consciousness," by Erich Neumann, ed. P. Berry, Spring Publications, Fach 190, Zürich 8024, Switzerland.

4. KNOWING WOMAN, by Irene C. de Castillejo, copyright © 1973 by The C. G. Jung Foundation for Analytical Psychology. Reprinted by permission of G. P. Putnam's Sons.

5, 6. FATHERS AND MOTHERS, see note 2.

7. THE WHITE GODDESS, by Robert Graves, copyright © 1948 by International Authors N.V., copyright renewed 1976 by Robert Graves. Reprinted by permission of Farrar, Straus & Giroux, Inc.

8. WOMAN'S MYSTERIES, see note 1.

9. HOLLERING SUN, by Nancy Wood, copyright © 1972 by Nancy Wood. Reprinted by permission of Simon & Schuster, Inc., Children's Book Division.

10. CUTTING THROUGH SPIRITUAL MATERIALISM, by Chögyam Trungpa, copyright © 1973 by Chögyam Trungpa. Reprinted by permission of Shambhala Publications, Inc., 2045 Francisco Street, Berkeley, California 94709.

11. THE MOTHERS, by Briffault, published by George Allen & Unwin Ltd.

12. THE WHITE GODDESS, see note 7.

13. OCEANIC MYTHOLOGY, by Roslyn poignant, 1967 from The Hamlyn Group Picture Library.

14. RITES & SYMBOLS OF INITIATION, by Mircea Eliade, Harper & Row Publishers, Inc.

15. SEVEN ARROWS, by Hyemeyohsts Storm, copyright © 1972 by Hyemeyohsts Storm. Reprinted by permission of Harper & Row, Publishers, Inc.

16, 17. WOMAN'S MYSTERIES, see note 1.

18. TO THE LIGHTHOUSE, by Virginia Woolf, by permission of Harcourt Brace Jovanovich, Inc., Author's Literary Estate and The Hogarth Press Ltd.

19. THE WHITE GODDESS, see note 7.

20. LUNACEPTION, "Doing It," by Louise Lacey, copyright © 1974 by Louise Lacey. Reprinted by permission of Candida Donadio & Associates, Inc.

21. THE MAGIC FLUTE, by Stephen Spender, text copyright © 1966 by Stephen Spender, illustration copyright © 1966 by Beni Montresor. Reprinted by permission of G. P. Putnam's Sons.

22. From LOS NINOS ABANDONADOS, a film made by Danny Lyon in Columbia, South America, distributed by Serious Business, 1609 Jaynes St., Berkeley, Ca. 94703.

23. From FEMINIST BOOK OF REVIEW OF LIGHTS AND SHADOWS, by Shanti, Winter Solstice 1975, Woman Spirit Quarterly, Box 263, Wolf Creek, Oregon 97497. $6/year.

24. JUNG AND THE STORY OF OUR TIME, by Laurens Van Der Post, copyright © 1975 by Laurens Van Der Post. Reprinted by permission of Pantheon Books, a division of Random House, Inc., and Hogarth Press.

25. Riddle, Davis & Weaver, "Women and Spirituality," copyright © 1975 by QUEST: A FEMINIST QUARTERLY, INC., P. O. Box 8843, Washington, D. C. 20003. Reprinted from Vol. I No. 4.

26. LES GUERILLERES, by Monique Wittig, copyright © 1969 by Les Editions de Minuit. Reprinted by permission of Viking Pequin, Inc. and Peter Owen.

27. BEYOND GOD THE FATHER, by Mary Daly, copyright © 1973 by Mary Daly. Reprinted by permission of Beacon Press, Publishers.

28. Noel Phyllis Brikby and Leslie Kames Weisman, reprint from an article in Quest Quarterly, Summer 1975, which is available through Quest Quarterly, and represents a portion of a book in progress.

29. THE AMERICAN INDIAN SPEAKS, ed. by John R. Milton, University of South Dakota Press, 1969.

30. LESBIAN BODY, by Monique Wittig, translated from the French by David Le Vay, copyright © 1975 by Peter Owen, William Morrow and Company, Inc. Originally published in French under the title Le Corps Lesbien by Les Editions De Minuit, copyright © 1973 by Les Editions de Minuit. Reprinted by permission of Viking Pequin, Inc. and Georges Borchardt Inc.

30. LES GUERILLERES, by Monique Wittig, copyright © 1969 by Les Editions de Minuit. Reprinted by permission of Viking Pequin, Inc. and Georges Borchardt Inc.

Why did the moon go to the bank?

To change its quarters.

ILLUSTRATION CREDITS

o   o   o

SPECIAL THANKS TO:

Researchers: MAGGY ANTHONY, KIYOMI OTA, VERONICA STEVENS.

Manuscript Typing: LISA CASSIDY, BARBARA CORSO, JULIA DICKENSON, JOAN WENDELL. Proofreading: ELAINE CERNOFF.

Critical Manuscript help from: ELIZABETH OVERTON COLTON, MARION FAY, FREUDE. Editorial help: ANICA VESEL MANDER.

ASPECTS OF THE MOON: GODDESS DIRECTORY

Aah, moon deity, Egypt
Aegea, the Great, Greek
Agrotera, Fertility Goddess, Rome
Akua-ba, fertility, Africa
Al-Ilat, Semitic
Allatu, Queen of the Underworld
Althea
Al-Uzza, Arabic
Amazon, Armenia
Anahita the High, Persia
Anath, of Love, Canaanite
Andraste, the Druid Queen, Britain
Anna, of Britain
Annis
Amtea
Aphaea
Aphrodite, of Love, Greek
Ardvi-Sura-Anahita, of Persia
Arianhod, of Britain
Artemis, Hunt, Unchaste Love, Childbirth, the
    Many Breasted, Greek
Asherath, the Goddess of the Sea, whom Jezebel
    brought to Samaria
Ashtoreth, Semitic
Assinboin, Who Was Not And Gave Off Own
    Light, Native American
Astarte, the Womb, of the Two Horns, Greek
    Territories, Israel
Ataensic, of the Waters, Huron (North America)
Atargatis of the Sea, Greek
Athara, Mermaid of Ascalon
Athena, the Wise, the All-Dewy One, Greek
Atl, Mother Water, Aztec
Atropos, the Old One
Ay, of the Beautiful Face, Turkey

Belili
Binah, Great Sea or Goddess of Primordial, Her-
    brew
Blodenwedd, Moon of Britain
Brigentis, of the White Hills, Celtic
Brigid, the Triune Goddess of Poetry, Healing,
    Smithcraft, Great Goddess of Irish Celts, of
    Scotland
Brigit, the White Swan, Bride of the Golden Hair,
    Mother of the King of Glory
Britomartis, Mountain Mother, Creton
Brizo, the Enchantress of the Sea, Aegean

Cabar, the Great, the Saracen, the Turk
Calliope, the Beautiful Face, Greece
Callisto, the She-Bear
Candras, Moon of India
Cardea
Ceres, Wheat, Greek
Cerridwen, The Nine-fold Muse, Mother with
    Cauldron, Welsch Celtic, of Britain
Chandra the Protector, India
Changing Woman, First Goddess, Navajo
Chang-O, the Fairy Queen of China
Circe, the Enchantress, Greek
Citali, the Moon of the Aztecs
Coronis, the Raven
Cybele, Goddess of Wild Animals, Crete
Cynthia, of the Moon

Danu, of Britain
Daphne, of the Laurel, Greek
Daphoine, the Bloody One
Deborah, Hebrew
Dede, of Turkey
Delia
Demeter, the Barley Mother, the Harvest, Greek
Derketo, the Mermaid of Ascalon, Greek
Diana, Goddess of the Hunt, Opener of the
    Womb, of the Earth, Roman
Diktynna, of the Caves, Cretan
The Divine
Diviana
Doris, Moon Queen of the Dorians

Ea, thou that was before the earth was formed
Elythia of the Caves, Crete
Enodia, Moon Goddess of Thessaly
Epona, the Mare Goddess, Britain and Ireland
Erate, the Beloved One, Greece Erato, the Oak
    Queen
Erato, the Oak Queen
Etoine
Evan, Moon, Ireland
Europa, Cow Goddess of Crete
Eurynome, the Mermaid of Arcadia

Fleachta of Meath, Moon Queen of Ireland
Freya, War, Fields, Love, Scandinavia
Frigg, Scandinavia

Gaus, Giver of Ambrosia Milk, Mother Cow, India

Ge, the Source

Goda, the Bona Dea

Goddess of Incantation

Hathor, Mother, Egyptian

Haumea, Earth Mother, Hawaii

Heartha, Fire

Hecate, the Faerie, the Queen of Elfin, Dark Moon, Greek

Hel, of Death, Earth Mother, Northern Europe

Held

Helen, Greece

Helen-Denritus, pre-Greek territories

Helen-Selene, of Greece

Heng-Ugo

Hera, Rome

Herodiana, (heroine) of Greece

Hilde, of the Milky Way, Northern Europe

Hina, She-Who-Makes-White-Cloth, Hawaii

Holda, Earth Mother, Northern Europe

Holy Ghost, Dove of Wisdom

Hur

Iemanja, Chief Goddess, Goddess of the Sea, Sea and Moon, from the Brazilian Umbanda cult

Ina, She-Who-Makes-White-Cloth, Hervey Islands

Inanna, Goddess of Heaven & Rebirth, Sumeria

Indus, of India

Io, White Moon Cow of the Mycenaeans

Irini, Lady of Victory

Ishtar, Sexual Love, Babylonia

Isis, or Moisture, First of the Muses, Great Goddess, Horned Crescent, Egypt

Ixchel, White Lady of the Mayans

Jotma, India

Juno, Roman

Juno-Lutecia, the Roman Light

Kali-Durga, Dark Goddess, India

Khnesu, Bird God of the Moon, Egypt

Khons, Moon Deity of Egypt

Kilili, she who Leans out of the Darkness

Kuan Yin, Protectress Of Children, Buddhist Goddess of Mercy

Kubaba, pre-Indo-European Moon Goddess in what is now Greece

Kuu, the Moon, Finland

Kybebe, pre-Indo-European Moon Goddess in what is now Greece

Laphria, Aetolia

Latona

Leucippe, the White Mare, the White Horse, Mare-headed Mother, the Cruel Night Mare

Levannah, The Moon

Lilith, the Dark Moon, the Original Woman, Hebrew

St. Luan, of the Night, Ireland

Lucine, the Moon of Italy

Lugad, the Moon of Ireland

Lugidus, of Ireland

Luna, of Heaven, (Rome and France)

Lunus, of Ireland

Ma'at, Justice and Wisdom, Egypt

Magna Mater, Roman

Mah, Moon God, Persia

Mair, the Mother of Christ

Maja, the All-Mother, Vedic-Hindu

Manat

Marina, Patroness of Lovers and Poets

Mariamme, the Sea Lamb

Marion, The Maid of England

Ma-Tsu-P'o, Taoist Queen of Heaven, China

Mary, of England

Mawu, the Supreme Being, Africa

May Bride, England

The Measurer

Melusine

Mene

Merry, England

Mersekert

Mert

Min, the New Moon, Egypt

Moling, Ireland

Molua, of Ireland

Mona, the Teutonic Moon

Moon of the United States

Morgana, Lady of the Lake, Britain

Great Mother

Muldava, the Moon Doe of Lapland

Myesyats, Moon, Serbia

Myrrh, of the Sea

Myrrhine

Myrtea

Nana, the Tripart Moon of Assyria

Net, of Egypt

Neith, the Cow, the First Birthgiver, The Mother who bore the Son, who gave birth before birth was, Egypt

Ninda

Nipai-Gicux

Nisene

Notre Dame, Our Lady Moon, France
Nkosuano, the Moon Egg of China
Nuah, Moon God, Babylonia
Nut, Goddess of the Cosmos, Egypt

Olwen
Ops, Diana of Rome
O'Shion, Moon of the Gypsies
Ostara, the Saxon
Otsukisama, the Royal, Japan
Oupis, The Queen, Fair Faced, The Light Bearer, Greek

Panagia-Arkoudiotissa, the Bear Mother
Parashakti, the Trimurti Mother, India
Pasiphae, She Who Shines for All, Pygmy Moon Goddess, of Crete, Africa
Pe, Moon Mother of Fertility, African Pygmy
Pele, fire and the underworld, Hawaii
Persephone, Queen of the Night, Goddess of Spring, Greek
Phoebe, Moonlight, Greek
Phosphoros, The Light Bearer, a title of Hecate, Greek
Proserpine, Queen of the Underworld, Roman
Prothiria
Ptah of Multitudinous Forms, Egypt

Qadesh, Lady of Heaven, Egypt
Queen Marie, of Heaven and Love

Rhea, The Great Mother, of Crete
Rhiannon, of Britain
Rigantona, the Great Queen
Rimmon, the Image, Ireland

Samhain, of the Winter Fires, Irish Druid
Sarasvati, of the Healing Waters, India

Selk
Serq
Shaddai-El Chai, Hebrew
Sharrant-Shame, Queen of Heaven, Babylonia
Shing Moo. Our Lady of the Moon, Perfect Intelligence, China
Sin, Moon of the Sabians, Lord of Babylonia
Siva, of India
Soma, Somas, Drink of the Gods, India
Sophia, Mary Wisdom, Divine Wisdom, Greek Orthodox

Tabor, the Golden Calf
Tanit, Moon Wife, Phoenician
Tecuciztecatl, the Aztec Moon
Tiamat, the World Mother of Mesopatamia
Thammuz, Shepherd of the Stars, Hebrew
Thoth, Moon Deity of Egypt
Triformis, Greece
Trivia, Goddess of the Crossroads and Night Travel, Goddess of Enchantment, Greek
Our Lady of Turquoise, Early Semitic

Unkatahe, Goddess Against Disease, Northern Native American
Urikituu, the Green One
Urania, the Heavenly One

Vach, from the Ocean, Himalayas
Vesta, of Rome
Virago
The Virgin

White Shell Woman
White Goddess, of Poetry, the Muse, Britain

Zerynthia, the Dark Moon, Western Turkey
Zu-en, Wisdom, Sumeria

So let us remain altogether young and trembling right into old age, and let us try to fancy that we are merely starting out in life right up to the very eve of death . . . I am an optimist in spite of everything that has torn me to shreds, its perhaps my only quality.

George Sand

o   o   o

In a high wind the leaves fall from the trees. They go on to gather them in bread baskets. Some, scarcely touched, rot. They are scattered in the fields in the woods. In the baskets there are leaves of chestnut hornbeam maple clove guaiac copal oak mandarine willow copper-beech elm plane terebinth latania myrtle. Tebaire Jade scatters them in the room crying, Friends do not let your imagination deceive you. You compare yourselves privately to the fruits of the chestnut cloves mandarines green oranges but you are fruits only in appearance. Like the leaves you fly away at the slightest breeze, beautiful strong light subtle and prompt of understanding as you are. Beware of dispersal. Remain united like the characters in a book. Do not abandon the collectivity. The women are seated on the piles of leaves holding hands watching the clouds that pass outside.

—LES GUERILLERES,
Monique Wittig